S0-AGI-343

NOTHING
SHORT
OF
A
MIRACLE

PATRICIA TREECE

Our Sunday Visitor Publishing Division
Our Sunday Visitor, Inc.
Huntington, Indiana 46750

Four individuals in this book at this date have not been beatified or canonized. While there is every sign that their Causes, now under way, will be successful, I wish to declare my wholehearted intention to speak only provisionally of heroic sanctity and not anticipate the eventual judgment of the Church in any individual's regard.

First issued in 1988 by Doubleday, a division of Bantam Doubleday Dell Publishing Group, Inc., 666 Fifth Ave., New York, NY 10103.

Copyright © 1988, 1994 by Patricia Treece

All rights reserved. With the exception of short excerpts for critical reviews, no part of this book may be reproduced in any manner whatsoever without permission in writing from the publisher. Write:
Our Sunday Visitor Publishing Division
Our Sunday Visitor, Inc.
200 Noll Plaza
Huntington, Indiana 46750

International Standard Book Number: 0-87973-741-7
Library of Congress Catalog Card Number: 93-87105

Cover design by Rebecca J. Heaston

PRINTED IN THE UNITED STATES OF AMERICA

This book is for

JESUS

Even your greatest saints
only mirror you dimly.
Jesus, may we love you as
they do.
And may you gather us all,
writer and readers, into your
healing and life-giving arms.

Contents

PROLOGUE

"Nothing Short of a Miracle
Can Help This Kid"

March 14, 1921

Yawning openly on this gray afternoon, a young nurse makes a last round of her newborn charges in New York City's Columbus Hospital Extension on 163rd Street. In the final moments of an unusually busy shift, the weary nurse's thoughts are already far from babies as she bends over the whimpering Smith infant at whose midday birth she assisted two hours earlier.

Instantly wide awake, Mae Redmond gasps, "Oh God! Oh God!" for infant Smith's face is like charred wood, cheeks and lips blackened and burnt. Pus exudes from both tiny nostrils. Worst, where eyes should be are only two grotesque edemic swellings.

Horrified, Mae must struggle not to pass out as her mind grasps for how this can be. No one has handled the newborn after his normal delivery since she herself weighed and measured him and put in the eyedrops prescribed by law.

The drops! Suddenly her panic lunges in a definite direction. She staggers across the nursery and picks up the bottle of 1 percent silver nitrate solution used in the newborn's eyes. What she reads on the label makes her shriek hysterically again and again, "Doctor! Oh God! Get a doctor!"

Into infant Peter Smith's eyes, the rushed nurse has deftly dropped, carefully pulling back each lid to get it all in, not 1 percent silver nitrate solution, but 50 percent silver nitrate solution. Even 5 percent to 25 percent solution is used only on unwanted human tissue—tumors, for instance—because it eats away flesh as effectively as electric cauterizing tools. Fifty percent solution will gradually bore a hole in a solid piece of wood. And it has already been at work on the soft human tissue of infant Peter's eyes for two hours.

Dr. John G. Grimley is the first physician to hear the nurse's shrill cries. Looking at the badly burnt face and the bottle label, the suddenly ashen-faced doctor can only shake his head helplessly. A few minutes later he is reporting to an anguished Mother Teresa Bacigalupo, Superior of the Missionary Sisters of the Sacred Heart who own and run Columbus Hospital, that the nurse has accidentally destroyed a newborn's sight.

Desperately, the deadly bottle in hand, Mae meanwhile runs to find Dr. Paul W. Casson. But Casson cannot help the baby either. In fact the second doctor to see the infant will later recall that the sight of the tiny charred face and the 50 percent label knocks him speechless and breathless—at a loss for what to do. It is obvious to his experienced eye that the deadly solution has penetrated every layer of facial skin. And by now in those eye sockets there can be nothing left to treat. All Casson can do is put in a call that Dr. Michael J. Horan, who delivered Margaret Smith of a "perfect son" less than three hours ago, should return immediately to the hospital.

As he is telephoning, Mother Bacigalupo scurries anxiously into the nursery, interrupting him to plead he do something to save the baby's sight. Casson can only explain no human remedy can restore destroyed tissue. "Nothing short of a miracle," he ends, "can help this kid."

Her whole body bowed with sorrow, the nun says resolutely in Italian-accented English, "Then we will pray."

"God! Do!" the doctor urges, his face as stricken as her own.

When Dr. Horan arrives, Casson meets him in the hall and tries to break it gently, saying only that "a slightly stronger solution of silver nitrate" has been used for the Smith infant's eyes.

Dr. Horan exclaims at once, *"Anything* stronger than 1 percent solution and that's a blind baby." A minute later as he bends over the crib, the eyes which are now beginning to exude pus like the nose are so swollen he cannot open them.

Horan sends for an eye specialist and waits, a nervous wreck, Casson notes. Three doctors have already seen the baby and, except for ordering cold compresses to reduce inflammation, they can do nothing for him.

The eye specialist Dr. Kearney's expertise merely confirms the other men's medical knowledge of the properties of nitrate.

Barely born, *if* Peter Smith lives he will be totally blind. He will also be terribly disfigured, since, when a burn goes through all the layers of skin, the body cannot repair itself with new skin, but only with scar tissue.

That afternoon and evening as the spiritual daughters of Frances Cabrini, foundress of the hospital and their order, go off duty, they gather one by one in the chapel. All the long night they remain there begging Mother Cabrini, dead only three years, to obtain from the bountiful heart of Jesus the healing of the Smiths' whimpering infant.

At nine o'clock the next morning, when Kearney and Horan arrive at the nursery, to their astonishment they find baby Peter's eyelids much less swollen and pussy. Gently the eye specialist opens the eyelids, his stomach tightening as he prepares to see the ravages on the delicate eye tissue of the deadly acid.

Instead, looking back at him with the vague, slightly unfocused gaze of the one-day-old are two perfect eyes.

Dr. Kearney and Dr. Horan are staggered, as are Casson and Grimley when they arrive. Mae, who shudders to recall how she held back the baby's eyelids to make sure the drops went in, can only sob with delirious gratitude.

Amid the smiles and backslappings someone points out something else inexplicable: the horribly charred skin is healing to smooth infant satin, instead of blistering and contracting.

But no smiles are so broad as the nuns'. They knew Mother Cabrini's sanctity personally. Now that she proved it they exult. Her prayers have obtained this "impossible" cure from the Lord.

In 1938 Mother Cabrini is beatified by the Catholic Church, one of the miracles cited as signs from God in favor of this step being the healing of Peter Smith. Seventeen years old, he attends the ceremonies in St. Peter's, Rome, where onlookers notice his striking and expressive eyes that need no glasses and his smooth-skinned face. Only those who know to look carefully for them make out the two tiny scars which mark where deadly nitrate solution once burned a furrow down his cheeks.

Today sixty-six-year-old Father Peter Smith, longtime pastor of Immaculate Conception Church in Edinburg, Texas, grins and says his case certainly proves "the age of miracles has not passed."

INTRODUCTION

Friends in High Places

This book is about cures like Peter Smith's. Cures which are given members of our human family not by medical skill, but by God. Further, this book is about physical healings given by God in answer to the prayer of saints. Cures will include those in which a living saint turns to God in prayer as well as cures in which, at the time of the healing, the saint prays with the perfected prayer power of those who see God face-to-face.

In filling this gap in the literature of Christian healing, it is my intent to show our human family's "wholest" people, the saints, not only as God's frequent instruments of healing, but as fully real people who need to *receive* God's healing as well. To avoid a deadly repetitiousness in doing this, I vary the emphasis and depth of my inquiry, probing one saint's own remarkable cure at more length, another's spirituality of healing to greater depth, and still another's life journey in somewhat more detail. To make the humanness of saints more accessible, I have favored those who lived, worked, and vacationed in North American areas the reader may well know personally. Finally, for immediacy, the reports of the well-authenticated healings that make up the bulk of this book are from the mid-nineteenth century to the present, the most recent occurring in 1987. And, the sampling of saints I present are nineteenth- and twentieth-century figures, the sole possible exception being America's first native-born saint, Elizabeth Ann Seton.*

God loves us, so however unworthy any of us feel, we can go directly to him in prayer for our own healing. Great cures have occurred this simply. I think of a clergyman with a heart so bad he had to rest all week if he gave one Sunday sermon. Told he was about to die by his doctor, he asked God for a new heart to use in the Lord's service. A few days later he celebrated his new life in God by climbing a mountain. Still, the very fact that people who pray in all faiths pray for others' healing, not just their own, and when ill, ask friends, relatives, clergy, and prayer partners to pray for them, reveals that it is natural to human spirituality to participate, as receiver and giver, in intercessory prayer.

God sent Jesus, his only begotten son, to redeem humanity. Among his works was prayer for the sick, who were healed. The Redeemer's healings still continue. The late writer Catherine Marshall, to mention someone whose integrity is unquestioned, had a vision of Jesus which began her healing from tuberculosis. But the Lord has never reserved healing for himself. During his earthly ministry, he sent out seventy-two apostles to heal, not through their own holiness but empowered by his. And this continues, nonsaints down the ages praying for healing in the name of Jesus and God responding with miracles. Thus anyone, not just the holy, can practice intercessory prayer for healing.

But it is also a natural gesture in human spirituality to turn to the holiest members of our human family when one needs someone to pray for—that is, to intercede for—oneself or others. In Christianity, once Jesus ascended, people turned as humanity still does to those closest to the Lord—who predicted at the Last Supper they would do his works, and even greater wonders.

In the New Testament book of Acts, for instance, is the ac-

* The period of her spiritual maturity and works is the first quarter of the nineteenth century, but she was born in 1774.

count of Peter saying to a man crippled from birth who was begging in his usual place at one of the doors to the Jerusalem Temple, "I have neither silver nor gold, but what I have I give you. In the name of Jesus Christ the Nazarean, walk!" Instantly the man was healed.

Of the astonished crowd that gathered Peter asked, "Why does this surprise you? Why do you stare at us† as if we had made this man walk by some power or holiness of our own?" Then he explained that God healed to glorify the name of Jesus, in which the petition was made. Peter wanted it clear, as does every saint, that Jesus is the only God-man. He alone is the Redeemer-intercessor who pleads for us, as Paul figuratively puts it in Romans, at the right hand of the Father. All Christian intercession, from your prayer today for a family member to St. Peter's cure of the lame beggar two thousand years ago, travels "through" Christ whether his name is mentioned explicitly or not.

The crowd, however, knew instinctively that God also cured because of Peter's holiness. This holiness Peter, measuring himself against the purity and perfection of Jesus, could emphatically deny—and did. Still the people who sought him out to intercede for their healing believed God listened with special attention when the converted fisherman prayed. They believed this for a very good reason: his prayers were answered by cures. Acts also tells of some individuals who tried to work miracles in the name of Jesus and failed.‡

Scripture uses phrases like "the miracles he worked" (Acts 8:6) of the apostle Philip, or "he healed him" (Acts 28:8) of Paul. Today people speak of the "healings of" modern "miracle workers." Such phrases can obscure reality.

A miracle by definition is always *God's* wondrous work, the man or woman who prays being only a humble petitioner.

A good example of the saint as healer in this regard is Anto-

† Typically of a saint, he acts as if his companion is involved in the cure.
‡ See Acts 19:13–16.

nio Claret (1807–70), at one time missionary bishop of Cuba. Working during one period in Catalonia, Spain, Claret found himself in a situation similar to that of many areas today. Opposing civil war factions kept seizing the town of Viladrau. By the time the place had changed hands with enormous carnage thirteen times, the medical men had all fled. Claret says in his *Autobiography,* "Thus I had to become not only the spiritual but also the bodily physician of the people. . . ."

While he consulted medical books and dispensed simple advice, the canonized saint, founder of the Claretians, also admits:

> During my stay in Viladrau all the sick of the town, as well as those who were brought there from other places, were cured. As word of this spread, in whatever town I went to, people would bring me a large number of sick persons suffering from all kinds of illness. There were so many sick and so many different illnesses, and I was so busy hearing confessions, that I didn't have time for prescribing physical remedies. I told the people, instead, that I would commend them to God, and in the meantime I would make the sign of the Cross over them, saying, *"Super aegros manus imponent et bene habebunt."**

Regarding results, the saint says only, "After I did this, they said that they were cured." Actually physicians testified to remarkable events such as the sudden cure of "a horrible wound in the side, exposing several ribs."

The saint's explanation for the cures is typical of the holy.

> I am of the opinion that these people were cured through the faith and trust with which they came, and that Our Lord rewarded their faith with both bodily and spiritual health, for I would also exhort them to make a good confession of their sins, and they did. Furthermore, I be-

---

* "They lay hands upon the sick and the sick get well" (quoting Scripture).

lieve that the Lord did all this not because of any merits of mine—I don't have any—but to show the importance of the Word of God that I was preaching. . . . Our Lord God was calling their attention to His Word by means of these bodily healings. And indeed people came in droves, listened fervently to the Word of God, and made general confessions in their own towns, or even in others, because often it was impossible to hear the confessions of the many who wanted to confess.

My God, how good you are! You use the very weaknesses of the body to cure those of the soul. You make use of this miserable sinner to heal both bodies and souls. . . . Yes, Lord, health was yours and you were giving it.

While it is true that a cure is always God's gift, down the ages miraculous healings are especially associated with those we call saints; and in a sense the holy ones have no choice. When a Peter or Antonio Claret (who began as a manufacturer) is converted, jettisons everything that stands in the way and runs after God with every ounce of life in him, he becomes so empty of ego he is an open conduit for healing; for Jesus promised that he, the Father, and the Holy Spirit would dwell in those who love God with a whole heart and live out that love by treating each individual as the child of God he is. As Claret said, where God is, there is healing.

Equally true, if contradictory, I could say the saint does not get more answers to prayer because he or she is holier than you or I. She gets more answers because she is more open to, believes more in, God's goodness. This lively faith or trust permits miracles. And it opens the one praying to God even further so that she, too, becomes herself a miracle, i.e., a marvelous work, a saint.

All saints are healers. By the very definition of mental health, which is the ability to give and receive love, the holy are the most psychologically whole members of our human race and exert a magnetic pull on people of good will.

"Everyone just loved to be with him."

"We all wanted to be near her."

Studying the lives of nineteenth- and twentieth-century saints for this and other books, I heard such phrases repeatedly from those who knew saints. Why? Because in spite of human foibles, even occasional blunders, the holy exude a love that calms, that comforts, that gives new energy and life—in short, that heals. Consider this statement about one nineteenth-century saint by another. Youth worker St. John Bosco (1815–88) says of his mentor, the educator of priests and apostle to condemned prisoners St. Joseph Cafasso (1811–60): "A single word, a look, a smile, a gesture, his very presence was enough to dispel depression, drive away temptations, and produce good resolutions." Or again: "A certain priest [likely Bosco himself] . . . was often so exhausted as to be hardly able to breathe, but . . . if he happened to meet Don† Cafasso he immediately felt courage reviving in his heart and strength in his body . . ."

I think, too, of the English psychiatrist who has told how he sent troubled patient after patient to a British spinster named Caryll Houselander (1901–54) in the 1940s and '50s. This holy woman, the doctor claimed, "loved back to life" both neurotics and full psychotics.

If statements like these on saints seem a lot to swallow, let me note that as I wrote this Introduction a physician sampled a group's white blood counts before and after showing a documentary film on Mother Teresa of Calcutta. The white counts, an indicator of the body's resistance to infection, showed positive changes from just viewing Mother Teresa via TV.

Children feel the magnetism of these Holy Spirit-filled people too: the late Father Alfonso Volonte of Corpus Christi Church

† *Don* is the Italian title for priests, similar to the English "Father."

in Port Chester, New York, has told‡ how, even when St. John Bosco was old and unwell, the sight of him at one of the schools for poor boys he founded would cause "a free-for-all to get near him." One of Father Alfonso's most precious memories even in great old age was the day, as one of those youngsters, he actually managed to grasp the hand of the saint, who smiled "as only Don Bosco could smile" and let his free hand rest on the young Alfonso's head while saying a few treasured words to the boy.

Many of the holy, including Don Bosco, are sought out specifically for physical healing. Of this particular group of saints it is said they have the gift of healing, a phrase which reminds that, if all saints are healers in one form or another, God still gives—even to saints—his specific gifts as he wills.

Except in a limited portion of Protestantism that insists there have been no miracles since the opening days of Christianity, all Christians agree that holy people who "come in the name of the Lord" to pray for the sick, with or without laying on of hands, continue the tradition begun when Saints Peter and Paul healed to glorify Jesus' name. When the healer-saint dies and people still ask his prayers, the fact that cures continue, sometimes by the hundreds or thousands, shows that death does not end prayer power.

I believe the cures of saints, living or dead, carry other messages for our human family as well. Through the wondrous cures, God seems to say we come to our fullest development as human beings, as the saints did, when we need and serve, not just God in a one-on-one relationship that lets the world go by, but each other in and for him. The desire to be spiritually self-sufficient, to never ask another's prayer, is a form of pride as surely as the individual who only prays for self is an egotist. Moreover even genuine wonder-workers fall from grace with a thud when they begin appropriating to self the credit for cures

‡ Reported in *Father Alfonso* by Peter M. Rinaldi. For complete references cited, see Bibliographical and Other Sources, p. 219ff..

that belongs to God. With these reflections, let us consider again the healing of Peter Smith.

When the doctor encouraged a nun to pray for the infant, he humbly acknowledged his medical skill could not do everything. When the nun got other nuns to join her in prayer, she acknowledged she was not all-powerful as an intercessor. And when the whole group praying their hearts out still humbly turned to the holiest person they knew, their dead leader St. Frances Cabrini, they, too, admitted their need. Frances Cabrini, no longer knowing God's goodness by faith or even human experience but face to face, must have turned even more trustingly to God. While only the baby received a physical cure, all who prayed were graced, not least by protection from pride in "the miracle my prayers worked."

By answering prayer in which the living join hands with the dead as intercessors, God reminds us of the reality of eternal life and reveals how thin is the veil between this life and the next. Far from gone beyond our reach, the holy in death, as in life, are at God's disposal as instruments of His grace. That great intercessor Bl. André Bessette (1845–1937) told worried friends not long before he died, "What I can do for you now is nothing to what I'll be able to do for you when I'm in heaven." St. Thérèse Martin planned to "go on working for souls until the end of time." Evidence abounds that holy people are doing just that.

Christians know that, even though his human life span was cut off two thousand years ago, it is still possible to become intimate friends with Jesus. It is also possible, many know by experience, to become close friends with the holy dead. Sometimes the friendship is initiated by the saint, who returns to this world for a moment to carry out some design of God's. Dead St. John Bosco has returned on a number of occasions to heal people, including a dying young woman of twenty-three who saw him clearly in 1918, thirty years after his death. She described his curly hair and engaging smile faithfully although she had

never seen a picture of the dead saint until *after* her instantaneous cure from immobilizing chronic polyarthritis, with numerous deadly complications, including colitis, hemorrhages,
and urinary inability. Dead Bl. Frances Schervier came to
Brooklyn, New York, a few years ago and cured a man of terminal cancer. The man did not even know his wife had been
asking the dead Franciscan nun's prayers until he told his
spouse that "this lady" had appeared to him, and was shown a
picture of the saint. Padre Pio is making similar visits, including
one in 1984 to seventeen-year-old high school student Paul
Walsh, a Ridley Park, Pennsylvania, accident victim healed of
serious injuries. These returns of the holy acting as God's messengers are, in fact, numerous. But I treat the subject in a separate book, as I do healings in which a saint's relics play a major
role. I do this because so lost is any general wholesome understanding in Christianity, including Catholicism, of these ways of
God that they need careful handling and thorough explanation
not to be confused with very unwholesome phenomena.

   Friendship with a dead saint is even more often—undoubtedly nudged by the Holy Spirit—initiated by the living. Father
Solanus Casey, the recent Irish-American healer-saint, began a
friendship with Thérèse Martin about a decade before her canonization as St. Thérèse of Lisieux after reading her autobiography. "Wonder-worker" Bl. André Bessette turned to his great
friend St. Joseph, the foster father of Jesus. Many of us nonsaints could tell of our friendships with dead saints, whether
people who were friends or relatives or individuals known, like
the beatified and canonized saints, only in God. I think of Angela Boudreaux (pp. 156–57) of Gretna, Louisiana, and her
family's special relationship with Father Francis Xavier Seelos,
who died in 1867. The possibility of friendship with the saints
in heaven, as with Jesus, means we Christians are never without
another human being to pray for our healing, however isolated
we may be from other believers. Not only that but we may be
sure when we appeal to a saint for prayer, that we indeed have

a friend in high places, one who rests, like the apostle John, against the very heart of Jesus.

But all this business of my asking my friend to pray for me and she praying to St. Frances Cabrini that Frances will pray— well, it's cumbersome to the point of ludicrousness and down-right inefficient, say critics.

Undoubtedly.

But wasn't Jesus' sending out the seventy-two to heal ineffi-cient and unnecessary? Jesus healed the centurion's servant from afar. Certainly the Redeemer had the power to see every ill in Palestine and heal everyone that was cured by the seventy-two with a lot less fuss. All we can say is efficiency does not seem his highest priority. Apparently he preferred to have sev-enty-two disciples learn to give God's healing and he wanted even more people to learn to receive God's healing through their fellow, flawed, inadequate human beings. In the case of his saints, God certainly does not need them either to work miracles; but anyone studying the lives of the holy can only conclude that it seems to be God's good pleasure to give his greatest miracles to the world through their hands.

How he gives miracles of healing through his saints is ex-plained by saying the saint intercedes for others, as Scripture (1 Timothy 2:1)* requests. But to see a saint's prayer as persuad-ing God to override his will is to misunderstand: the essence of sanctity is to will precisely what—and only what—God wills. The best we can do is admit that the precise mechanics of God's use of his most developed human creatures to carry his healing gifts is one more mystery of his grace.

Some people fear that any honor given saints somehow takes away glory from God. This book offers irrefutable evidence, I believe, that, however you or I feel about honoring saints, God honors them by the miracles he works in answer to requests for their prayers. If there are no visible miracles occurring through

---

* "I desire"—(the words are Paul's)—"therefore, first of all, that supplications, prayers, intercessions, and thanksgivings be made for all men."

the prayer of a saint during her lifetime, where there is true holiness, miracle cures regularly take place following the saint's death.

All in heaven are saints. The Church honors them yearly on the Feast of All Saints. But alone the saint who is officially titled "Blessed" or "Saint" is held up to Catholics, and all interested people, as "a living page from the gospel," that is, a Christlike person at the apex of human development, one whose union with God gives prodigious prayer power. While certainly not implying any worthiness to be worshipped—that would be blasphemy and utterly condemned by the Church—being officially designated "Blessed" or "Saint" (beatified or canonized, respectively) entitles the individual to veneration, that is, *honor* as a spiritual giant.

Obviously such judgments require the ultimate in human prudence. A supernatural institution as well as a flawed, human one, the Church reserves the final word to God. Let me explain.

To avoid error in proclaiming that anyone is a saint, the earthly Church spends years going over every facet of the individual's life. What is looked for is not inhuman perfection—as this book will show even these heroes of our human family retain individual crotchets and little failings. In fact, it can be argued that, without these, holy individuals would lose their humility and dependence on God's mercy. What must be found for sainthood is not just ordinary human goodness, but *heroic* virtues, such as Don Bosco secretly providing a home for a down-on-his-luck man who had tried to assassinate him, because Christ says to love your enemies. Not always so dramatic, this bottomless love for and in God may take seemingly insignificant form, such as Thérèse Martin's many small—but by no means easy—acts of love, like choosing to spend time with another Carmelite nun usually shunned because she drove everyone nuts. In healers like Brother André Bessette or Father Solanus, heroic charity is seen in complete self-giving, often around the clock, year after year, to others' healing and growth.

To gather evidence of virtue, testimonies under oath are taken in the principal places the person lived. No quick scrutiny, these filled thirty thousand pages on a saint like Don Bosco, who lived to age seventy-two. In addition the words (including written) and deeds of the individual, are carefully examined. A wild youth such as that of St. Augustine or St. Francis of Assisi means nothing if followed by true holiness.

Many Causes, as these investigations of sanctity are termed, fail. If one withstands all inquiry, a decree of heroic virtue is proclaimed, and the individual is formally titled "Venerable." From here to beatification, the whole Process works on the confident assumption God will pick up the Cause if he wants it to continue. How does he sign which people he wants held up to the world as model Christians and intercessors of his healing? His signal fires consist of healings like that of Peter Smith, cures explicable only in reference to God. These must occur, as Peter's did, in direct response to people's prayers for the saint's intercession. The whole process can be summed up: no miracles, no beatification. After beatification, no new miracles, no canonization.

Over the often long years of a Cause, the sheer bulk of prayer-answers forms a compelling testimony on behalf of an individual's sanctity. But it is the presence of major cures meeting seven criteria set down by Pope Benedict XIV† for an authentic Church-named miracle that makes a saint eligible for beatification and later canonization.

The seven criteria are:

1. The disease must be serious and impossible (or at least very difficult) to cure by human means.
2. The disease must not be in a stage at which it is liable to disappear shortly by itself.
3. Either no medical treatment must have been given or it

† Then Cardinal Lambertini.

must be certain that the treatment given has no reference to the cure.

4. The cure must be instantaneous.
5. The cure must be complete.
6. The cure must be permanent.
7. The cure must not be preceded by any crisis of a sort which would make it possible the cure was wholly or partially natural.

The task of weighing any proposed case against the criteria is done not by theologians or Church officials from the Congregation for the Causes of Saints, but by eminent medical men whose expertise on the disease in question, not their religious conviction—or lack thereof—is the important point. The physicians who treated the cured individual will be asked to testify before a courtlike tribunal. Other medical men, with no personal emotional involvement in the case, make the decisions. If a healing, however stupendous, does not meet all seven criteria, the Church, *while not denying that it may be, even at times undoubtedly is, supernatural in origin,* withholds the formal title "miracle" to avoid the slightest taint of promoting spurious miracles.

In another book, I have given an example of a rejected cure in the case of Gerard Baillie, a child whose blindness from atrophy of his optic nerves and both retinas was instantaneously healed at Lourdes through the intercession of the Blessed Virgin Mary. Gerard sees in spite of physiologically being "unable to see since the atrophy remains." While this is a miracle to doctors as well as to us ordinary observers, the cure was rejected as a *formal* miracle because technically the disease (bilateral chorioretinitis and double optic atrophy) still exists.

In this book, then, whenever I refer to a cure as accepted for a saint's beatification or canonization miracles, you will know this healing has met the seven rigorous criteria of the Church under the most searching medical inquiry. I also freely use the word "miracle" in well-authenticated cures like Gerard's that are merely humanly impossible.

Body, mind, and soul are a unity, so that every illness has its emotional, intellectual, and spiritual factors. Likewise, healing can begin in the human person's soul, emotions, or intellect, not just in the body. Thoughtful readers may wonder if even healings meeting the seven criteria or at least lesser cures received after appeal to a living or dead saint's prayers are not examples of the placebo effect. An individual expects to be cured through a given saint, an intellectual conviction that generates positive emotions such as hope and confidence, in turn stimulating the body's physical systems so that healing ensues with nothing supernatural involved. Undoubtedly this is a good description of some so-called lesser cures; if belief in a saint's help can succeed where medicine couldn't, this is nothing to look down on: it reflects how important it is that in healing, the whole person, soul included, be treated and it points out how much greater are the resources for facing life's hazards of those who have a living faith.

Nevertheless, while there are plenty of cures in this book that could be cited as evidence that the sometimes derisively labeled psychosomatic dimension may be operative in wonderful ways, there are many others—take Peter Smith's, for example—where such a rationale would be ludicrous.

If one-day-old Peter Smith was influenced by anything "human," the most logical factor to cite would be the healing prayer he received. Researchers with scientific, not theological, credentials, in places like Georgia's Agnes Scott College in Atlanta, UCLA, and London's Institute for Psychobiological Research have used skin response meters, blood tests, blood pressure meters, and electroencephalographs to see if anything that can be measured scientifically happens to someone receiving healing prayer.

Just as the physicist knows invisible particles are there because of what they do, these researchers—men of medicine and science, many non-Christians—have found that healing prayer is a real force or energy even if invisible, *because it changes things.* Besides causing seeds to sprout faster and increasing plants' rates of growth over that of plants that are not prayed for, healing prayer for human beings has numerous positive effects as measured by blood cell count, skin temperature, blood pressure—even brain waves.

Further, healing prayer can achieve this result across hundreds of miles when the individual praying has sufficient gifts. This prayer energy that someone praying for healing projects, we Christians believe is both "natural," since anyone of good will, including non-Christians, can "do it," and "supernatural," since, whatever the belief system, anyone of good will praying for healing we believe, taps into or opens the door for the healing power of the Holy Spirit.

Many of us Christians are familiar with studies like those with nurses at New York University which show individuals who merely have a healing *intent* without reference to prayer or God benefit others *if* they themselves are in good health, not tired, and not depressed. Other, less well-known studies, such as those by the C. Maxwell Cade research group in England, show that certain individuals have strong innate healing gifts— again, as long as the individual remains well, rested, and without mental distress. Such gifts seem as hereditary as other, often-termed psychic, abilities. Further, there is some evidence these natural powers can be increased to a degree by the practice of meditational exercises and techniques which increase psychological integration, compassion, and empathy for others.

However, the book you are beginning, I believe, shows quite convincingly that prayer energy—at least on the level generated by saints—goes much farther than the energy of well-intentioned individuals or even the real healing gifts of empathetic psychic healers. As mentioned, all these people are limited by the need to themselves be in excellent shape. If in distress, fatigued, or ill, studies indicate, they may actually slightly worsen the condition of the individual they are, in good faith, attempting to help.

Prayer for healing, on the other hand, has helped others even if the one praying is herself sick or tired. In fact in the Catholic tradition, our very bodily weaknesses, whether from fatigue, old age, or illness, can be "offered up" as a prayer with power to benefit others—including carrying physical healing.‡ While it is a complex topic beyond the scope of the present book, because it requires very thorough discussion of the difference between those authentically called and those suffering religious neurosis and other forms of delusion, there is even a rare vocation in the Christian community in which certain individuals are called to heal others by suffering redemptively in union with Christ. Pertinent here is that all the saints profiled in this work to the end of their days grew in power to transmit God's healing; there was no decline with either old age or chronic illnesses. Saints, in fact, have even healed on their deathbed, like housewife/healer Bl. Anna Maria Taigi (d. 1837), who, after weeks of illness had exhausted her, still cured her confessor half an hour before she died.

This power in states of powerlessness underlines God's role, especially in a cure like Peter Smith's, where something like eye tissue is not just healed but literally remade.

At least fifty individuals have been canonized to date whose lives passed in the brief era to which I limit this book. And this says nothing of those canonized in this period who lived earlier. Nor does it mention those beatified nor those named Venerable. Cures are associated with all these* except some Venerables.

In 1980 the first American Indian saint, Kateri Tekakwitha, was beatified in St. Peter's. Present for the imposing ceremony

‡ See my leaflet on the subject "Even Disabled, the Christian Is Never Useless."
* Although in the case of martyrs Causes do not require such signs, voluntarily laying down one's life as a Christian witness being considered wondrous sign enough, cures are found here too. For a recent example, see Albert Groeneveld's short book *A Heart on Fire* on Dutch World War II martyr Bl. Titus Brandsma.

was eleven-year-old Peter McCauley of Phoenix, Arizona. At the age of four Peter had been partially deaf in both ears when a visiting Jesuit suggested to his family they pray that Venerable Kateri ask God to heal the boy. On the last day of a novena for this intention, Peter McCauley was instantaneously healed. God touched him through a woman dead almost three hundred years. That's right: Bl. Kateri Tekakwitha died in 1680.

I use this cure to stress that, even with its many healings, the book in your hands is the tiniest sampling of the miracles going on all around us through the intercession of God's saints. No single volume could contain all the healing miracles attributed to *just twentieth-century* saints.

And from the apostolic era to the present, hundreds of saints exist. While healings in relation to a saint may gradually peter out as newer saints take the place of older ones in public consciousness, this is not always true. A small number of saints who actually walked with Jesus—consider St. Jude, St. Joseph, and the Virgin Mary as the most prominent—have ongoing reputations as channels of the Lord's healing in untold numbers of cases. Some saints have centuries-long associations with cure of particular conditions or types of illness, such as St. Blaise with throat difficulties. Shrines of canonized saints like John Neumann regularly receive reports of healings even when these are no longer "necessary" as signs favoring a Cause. To these still-active "old saints" add that the Congregation for the Causes of Saints has over one thousand cases under investigation as I write (fifty of these Americans). In addition, there are Causes still in the preliminary or local stages, which precede a case's being officially opened by Rome.

To say that God is healing at all times and among his ways are abundant healings through his saints, then, is a statement absolutely free of even the slightest exaggeration.

What all this means when a healing is needed for self or others is that the intercession of the saints is a huge available channel for healing, in addition to the many others such as

XXX   INTRODUCTION

every one of the sacraments,† regular "soaking prayer"‡ by friends, relatives, or others, attendance at special healing services or masses, laying on of hands by those who care for one or those with healing charisms, and one's own personal relationships with Jesus, the Holy Spirit, and God Our Father.

The Church requires only two to four authenticated healings for a beatification—and that number again before canonization* —because of the time and expense of investigating a healing to meet Lambertini's dicta, especially that the cure be permanent. In actual fact, many cures may take place during a Cause, with just the greatest of these sent to Rome as indications that God is signaling his desire to have this individual officially honored by the Church. In the case of St. Jean Marie Vianney, better known as the Curé d'Ars, after the death of this great nineteenth-century miracle-worker, from many claimed cures only thirty were sent to Rome. But each of these was of a caliber to potentially qualify as an official Beatification miracle. Twenty-four extraordinary cures from the nine years since his death were selected out of many others and sent to Rome in 1966 on behalf of Fr. Solanus Casey of Detroit; while in the case of André Bessette forty cures from the fourteen-year period ending in 1958 were sent to Rome from almost eight hundred im-

† My files include such cases as the woman whose broken bone refused to heal for months—until, without thinking of her health, she went to confession. To her surprise, the leg healed immediately. She conjectures something else in her had to be healed before the leg could mend. Other cases include a dying boy given baptism, confirmation, first confession, and first communion all in one day. His terminal cancer condition immediately changed and he recovered.

‡ Popularized in *The Power to Heal* by Francis MacNutt, who attributes it to Methodist clergyman Tommy Tyson, this term refers to regularly, (daily or weekly) repeated prayer of some minutes to an hour for healing.

* The requirements vary with such particulars as whether the proposed saints lived so recently that testimonies to their virtues are firsthand, whether they have been handed down, and so on. Moreover, as explained on page xxviii, martyrs' Causes do not require further signs such as healing, while the Pope may decide to waive the requirement for a given miracle to hasten the process. Otherwise, to be certain a healing is permanent (one of the seven criteria) it may be necessary in some diseases to wait until the cured individual dies.

portant enough to be studied by Canadian medical men during that time.

Some people think you must be a certain kind of person to receive a miracle. Actually miracles go to every kind of person, from nuns living quiet, pious lives to an alcoholic healed of terminal cirrhosis of the liver and pneumonia while in his death coma, a cure accepted for the beatification of Bl. Clelia Barbieri (1847–70). They go to babies like Peter Smith too young for faith and to individuals "too old to hope for a cure" like Anna Maccolini, whose cure at age seventy-eight was accepted as a canonization miracle for St. John Bosco. They go to the devout and those who must say like another man cured by Don Bosco, "How can I pray? I have no faith. In fact, I don't believe in God." While they are primarily received by Catholics, that is simply because few non-Catholics turn to the saints. Where a miracle was besought through the intercession of American St. Elizabeth Ann Seton for a Protestant, the Protestant received a cure so extraordinary† it was accepted as the saint's canonization miracle. During his lifetime, Father Solanus Casey was associated with the cures of many non-Catholics, including a Jewish child desperately ill with spinal meningitis and one or two rabbis. So whoever you are, there is no reason to disqualify yourself from asking the saints for help.

True saints instinctively use techniques that focus attention in healings away from themselves and toward other possible carriers of God's grace. Praising the Lord for the cure, they may refer, as instrumental, to a dead saint's prayers; the spiritual power of one of the sacraments, such as a good confession; the good works and/or faith of the recipient (see p. xvi); the power of the Mass; or the prayers of a support group. What they will deny absolutely is that they or even their prayers caused the cure. And this is sincere. The authentically holy always see themselves like Don Bosco, who, complimented on his immense

† Detailed in my forthcoming book on healings involving relics.

achievements, could only murmur embarrassedly, "It is all the work of His hands" or shrug off praise with a sincere "Me? I always needed everybody's help!"

Saints with true healing gifts also often hide—whether this is instinctive or deliberate I can't say—behind the use of sacramentals. For instance, after Jesus appeared to homemaker Bl. Anna Maria Taigi and told her she would have the power to heal in one hand, she always cited the gospel admonition to anoint the ill with oil. The ball of oil-soaked cotton in her hand diverted attention effectively. Other saints use holy water, or a crucifix. The most humorous—yes, saints can be very funny—cover-up is probably Bl. André Bessette's. This French Canadian beatus at times adopted such a brusque, downright cranky attitude when working some of his more remarkable cures that the nervous recipient was only too ready to agree that, whatever did it, it couldn't be any sanctity of André's.

Once enrolled as saints, individuals are no longer confined to the areas and eras in which they lived; when all those who testified to their virtues and sheer human goodness are long gone, the saints are still not forgotten. Through the Church, they belong to the world and to all ages.

This means they also belong to you.

But it is possible you will read this book and still feel no inclination to ask a saint's intercession. Let me summarize a letter by St. Maximilian Kolbe responding to someone who wondered if he should mimic Kolbe in seeking the prayers of the Virgin Mary. Kolbe assured the questioner that everyone must pray with complete freedom in such matters.

One person, the saint said, will be drawn to take all requests to the Holy Spirit, another to Jesus, a third to God the Father. A fourth, I might add—like newly beatified Carmelite Elizabeth of the Trinity (1880–1906)—delights in addressing all three at once as the Trinity. Another individual may often ask one of

God's saints, as Kolbe did Mary, to pray for him or her. There is no "best" way.

Most of us, in fact, pray now one way, now another. If this book merely reminds readers that saints are as ready to pray for us as our other friends, it has accomplished its purpose.

AUTHOR'S NOTE

Those who feel inspired to find a living saint for healing prayer will want to keep in mind that healer and saint are not always synonymous. Most healers are compassionate people without being saints. And there are some morally dissolute people who are "healers," like the individual described in Francis MacNutt's book *Healing*, who used to get out of his drunken stupor just long enough to conduct healing services. Individuals who at one point may have had potential for sanctity may fall victim to pride in "my ministry" and become clogged channels of grace. Worse, some flamboyant so-called miracle-workers are like the late Jim Jones of Guyana-massacre notoriety. Jones's "Christian healing services" were planted with phony ill and fake cripples by the "holy minister," then "miraculously" healed. This type of "saint" is at best a huckster after your money, at worst an evil person who destroys anyone falling under his spell.

❧ 1 ❧

Just a Red-Blooded American Male— and Miracle Worker

Dearborn, Michigan, 1940

Sixteen-month-old Elizabeth Fanning lies listlessly in her mother's arms. Anxiously, drawn-faced Mrs. Fanning coaxes her child to take even a spoonful of the liver soup recommended by doctors. But although Elizabeth's swollen belly and twiglike limbs make her look like a starvation victim, the lethargic baby has no interest in food of any kind. Little Betsy, as her parents call her, has a fatal disease: the blood cancer known as leukemia.

What makes her case especially tragic is that the illness may be the result of new medical technology. Born in August 1938, Elizabeth appeared normal. But, three or four days later, a thick, red growth appeared on her cheek, while a red birthmark marred the child's neck. To stop the growth and prevent the spread of the unsightly birthmark, a series of radium treatments were given. The cheek growth disappeared and the birthmark's spread was halted. But after this "success" the child simply stopped growing normally. She seemed lifeless. Even her hair drooped, and grew no more.

A specialist's deadly diagnosis was only confirmed by a trip to Minnesota's renowned Mayo Clinic. The spleen should be removed, all doctors consulted agree, but the Mayo physicians in Rochester warn that the baby is already too weak to live through such an operation.

2

The rich nutrition of liver soup may buy a little time, but the doctors all warn Mrs. Fanning there can be but one outcome to childhood leukemia.* The mother must prepare herself that she may simply find the child dead in her crib at any time. So sure is Elizabeth's death that her doctors in Dearborn waive any further fees.

Then Mrs. Fanning's aunt, who belongs to a spiritual group affiliated with St. Bonaventure's Franciscan Capuchin monastery in Detroit, suggests little Betsy be taken to a lively, seventy-year-old priest there called Father Solanus Casey.

"He's a saint and he heals people all the time," Mr. and Mrs. Fanning are told. With no earthly possibility for their dying daughter's recovery, the Fannings drive to Detroit. They carry the child, who at a year and a half cannot walk, up to the door of St. Bonaventure's.

The Franciscan who greets them so warmly wears the Capuchin brown robe, its pointed hood thrown back on his skinny shoulders. In spite of his untrimmed white beard, the old priest has the shining face of a happy child, his blue eyes as innocent as their baby's.

As he listens to their personal tragedy, Father Solanus's face radiates loving compassion. In spite of the many other sufferers waiting to speak with him, the Fannings sense that he is totally —and peacefully—at their disposal. The only thing, he assures them, that can stop the power of God at work in our lives is our own doubt and fear. He urges the parents to concrete acts that will foster their confidence in God's goodness. Let them try to overcome their sadness and anxiety, which "frustrates God's merciful designs." He even recommends they thank God *now* for what he will do in the future, *whatever that may be.* This kind of confidence in God "puts him on the spot," he explains with a grin. He tells them of some healings he has witnessed, cases just as "hopeless" as their daughter's. The Fannings enroll

---

* Happily, no longer the case.

Betsy in the Capuchin Order's Seraphic Mass Association† with a donation to the missions. Each also makes a personal promise to God of a spiritual nature. (Samples: an infrequent Protestant churchgoer commits to "go every Sunday"; a Catholic who goes to communion weekly commits to go twice weekly; spiritual reading is promised, in one case from the Bible, in another from the work of a saint.)

Now, in his unusually high-pitched yet whisper-soft voice (the leftover, it is believed, of childhood diphtheria, which killed two of his sisters), Father Solanus talks to listless Elizabeth for a few minutes. Then he says matter-of-factly, "You're going to be all right, Elizabeth." Ignoring her skeletal appendages and distended stomach, he hands her a piece of candy as if the child *he* sees is well.

Elizabeth Fanning has been leukemic almost her entire short life. She has never done the things babies do, any more than she has ever attained the rosy looks of normal babyhood. But as her parents begin the drive home to Dearborn, Elizabeth has a new alertness. For the first time in her life, she watches everything with interest. She smiles. She sits up.

Her parents are startled, almost shocked, but are so happy at the sudden, inexplicable change that they stop at a restaurant "to celebrate." Mrs. Fanning says:

> The place was crowded—and Betsy—who only an hour before had been lying in my arms as limp as a rag doll—immediately became the "life of the party." She waved to the people about us, jumping up and down. She was full of life.

Soon she was walking. In the late 1960s, when Betsy's mother was interviewed by James Patrick Derum for his book on Father Solanus *The Porter of Saint Bonaventure's,* Mrs. Fanning recalled:

† At present called Capuchin Mission Association.

When I brought her back to the doctors, they were incredulous. She looked so different—healthy, lively, and her once wispy, lifeless hair was now curly.

"That's not Betsy!" they exclaimed.

But it was. While childhood leukemia remained a fatal disease for many years after 1940, little Betsy Fanning simply didn't have it any more after visiting Father Solanus Casey.

"You'll be all right," the Capuchin priest had said simply. Betsy was no isolated instance of his prophecy proving correct. For half a century, Father Solanus's gift of healing was so great that, beginning in November 1923, when he was stationed at Our Lady Queen of Angels Monastery in Harlem, his superiors asked him to keep a notebook of prayer requests and answers. Always obedient, he tried. But "the holy priest," as people referred to him even in his first priestly assignment at Sacred Heart Monastery in Yonkers, New York, in 1904, had so many demands for prayers, it proved impossible to record them all, even in his eighteen- or nineteen-hour days. This became clear after his death, when scores of people were interviewed regarding physical cures and other favors they said they received after Father Solanus enrolled them in the Seraphic Mass Association, the organization that combined mutual prayer support, including prayers and remembrances at mass by all the Capuchins, with aid to the missions. Even the six thousand notes from just his twenty-one years at St. Bonaventure's must be only a fraction of the Detroit total, since only a few of the cures interviewers found in that city had been recorded.

About one in ten of these notes has a follow-up entry. Many of the healed either never took the trouble to come back and report or Fr. Solanus never got around to entering their statements. Known cures, whether logged or not, include everything from cancer to heart disease, from deafness to diabetes, from polio to bone disease, from broken backs to infertility. A few samples from the log which include a follow-up are given pretty much verbatim but without addresses:

March 8, 1925—Mrs. Stella Sherwin, 47, from McKeesport, Pa., suffering from gall stones when, on Feb. 10, her daughter, living in Detroit, enrolled her in S.M.A. and sent her the certificate. The time of her cure corresponded with that of the issuance of the certificate.

July 26, 1926—Russell Jay, 17, . . . 49 inches tall is enrolled . . . (non-Catholic). Asks Fr. Solanus to "make me grow."

Jan. 2, 1927—Today Russell Jay reported he grew 4½ inches—1st change in 12 years—Now developing normally.

Oct. 12, 1931—Mrs. Mary E. Reynolds, 59, of Clinton, Ont. 17 years with epileptic seizures. Enrolled about July 25th. Has not had a shadow of an attack since. Deo Gr.‡

Dec. 9, 1932—Doraine Innes, 8, of Montreal. At 4 had meningitis of brain—then paralysis and curvature of spine and cross-eyed. Enrolled in 1930. Since day of enrollment has been able to walk without crutches.

August 8, 1935—Floyd McSweyn, now 24, of Merrill, Mich. In May 1933, fell 18 feet to cement floor, received to all reckoning fatal skull fracture. His mother tells us today that Fr.* assured her "the boy will be better inside of five hours." [He was] blind and dumb and totally paralyzed at

‡ This Latin phrase for "Thanks be to God" is found over and over in the ledger.

* In his detachment he writes of himself in the third person as having made this prediction. Because of the altered brain states associated with sanctity, he may actually have been unaware that he said such things.

time mother phoned. . . . Completely and permanently recovered—save hearing in one ear.

Dec. 29, 1937—John Charles Kulbacki, 6, blind since 3 weeks old; was enrolled in S.M.A. 6 weeks ago. On Xmas Day when at "Crib" here in Church, was almost frightened as he exclaimed—pointing to the lighted "crib": "Look, Mama." Deo Gr.

Nov. 19, 1938—Thanks—Marlene, 6, was inward bleeder [note: hemophiliac] before she came. . . . A year ago was prayed for and enrolled—had 5 hemorrhages day before—has never bled since. Deo Gr.

Oct. 27, 1943—Patrick McCarthy, 44, . . . lip cancer. Threatened starvation. Nov. 9 Dr. Wm. Koch . . . hardly able to speak from emotion at the wonderful improvement [in McCarthy]. . . .

Jan. 7, 1945, Robert Hamilton, 44, enrolled last Wed. expecting brain tumor operation on Friday. Drs. who had X-rayed his head were astounded at finding no tumor.

Modesty wouldn't have prevented recording any cures.

"If people were cured before his very eyes," according to a Capuchin quoted by Derum, Fr. Solanus's eyes "would fill with tears, and he would seem utterly amazed at the power of the Mass. . . . [in his mind] their cure had no connection with him. . . ."

Few dreamed that the thousands of physical cures, changes of heart, and other graces God gave through Fr. Solanus Casey, like a great tree from a tiny seed, had all grown from one act of blind trust in God made by the young Casey as a seminarian.

Born in Prescott, Wisconsin, on November 25, 1870, Bernard Casey, Jr., as Solanus was christened, was the sixth of sixteen handsome, sturdy, well-liked children born to Irish immigrants. His mother's brother a Wisconsin priest, his father's brother a Boston judge, the Caseys were an intelligent family of prosperous farmers. They raised their large brood in an atmosphere combining care and firm discipline with Irish folk songs, daily family prayer, and spiritual reading, and good American and Irish literature read aloud by the father on cozy family evenings.

If Barney grew up caring and well balanced, he felt it was because he had an idyllic childhood, whether as part of the baseball team made up of nine Casey brothers or reveling in the beautiful Wisconsin fields and waterways. At eighteen, after two years of a happy relationship, he proposed marriage to a girl a year younger whose mother promptly sent the intended bride away to boarding school. He kept dating, but his main energy seems to have veered away from marriage. After diverse jobs, including prison guard (typically he made friends with various prisoners), the devout young man made up his mind he was called to serve God as a priest. At twenty-six he entered the local diocesan seminary but failed there, because it was run by Germans in German and Latin. As they showed him the door, the seminary heads encouraged Barney to enter a religious order instead. Making a novena for guidance, he heard an unforgettable voice direct, "Go to Detroit," and found himself in a Capuchin seminary where the courses were again taught in German and Latin.

Because of his spirituality, the Capuchins were not about to let him go—in fact, one superior predicted even then that Casey would be an American Curé d'Ars—but neither did they want a priest who hadn't mastered all the theological nuances taught in their academic courses. Solanus, as they had renamed him, was asked in 1901 to sign a statement, the crucial segment of which translates from German as:

... Since I do not know whether as a result of my meager talents and defective studies I am fit to assume the many-sided duties and serious responsibilities of the priesthood, I hereby declare that I do not want to become a priest if my legitimate superiors consider me unqualified. ...

Had pride or self-will reared its head, Solanus's whole future ministry would have been aborted. As it was, however hurt and baffled the intelligent and hardworking young man may have felt—something he never discussed—he made a heroic act of trust in God, who, he believed with all his heart, had brought him to this German immigrant-founded institution.

He signed.

To his great joy, he was ordained in 1904, but to his humiliation he was made a priest simplex, that is, a priest who could say mass, but "doesn't know enough" to hear confessions or preach. Again, enormous temptation to despair, to anger, to self-pity, to depression, to every kind of negative response. Instead Solanus, in his thirty-fourth year, made the response of a person at least close to holiness: he accepted what would be a lifelong humiliation and prayed week after week, month after month, until he could actually thank God for apparently making him so ineffectual a priest that his superiors were hard put to find anything for him to do except manage the altar boys and answer the door as a porter.

A fellow Capuchin who knew him has remarked that it was through his ever more spiritualized and finally joy-filled response to this humiliation that Solanus Casey became holy. As the years passed, it also became clear that the apparent blight on Solanus's life of being a simplex priest was actually part of God's wonderful design, for it was through the Capuchin's assignments as porter in New York, Detroit, and Indiana that God carried out the immense ministry he entrusted to the man judged "too dumb"† to be a full priest.

† Crosby estimates his actual I.Q. at 135.

If his whole ministry grew out of Casey's heroic surrender to God's designs, the young Capuchin was not born a saint, but a red-blooded American with normal human feelings and weaknesses. He had a rebel streak and tendencies to independence and individualism that had to be sublimated to living in community. Capuchin Michael H. Crosby, in his study *Thank God Ahead of Time: The Life and Spirituality of Solanus Casey,* also notes that throughout his life the emotional Casey would "battle with feelings that could easily get expressed in anger, intolerance and excessive concern over little things." A kind of perfectionism had to be softened to keep him from excessive rigidity or anxious scrupulosity. An impulsive person who tended to act first, think later, with his idealism, emotionalism, and perfectionism, he had a tendency when young to criticize others, if only to himself. Yet, as is so often the case with this type of personality, he himself was sensitive to criticism and liked compliments.

Since he was always a well-liked, well-adjusted, "people" person, one can see that these human frailties were not extreme; still they had to be worked through—a matter of years, not one or two good resolutions—for Solanus to find that union with God and charity toward all from which miracles spring. Single-minded and perseveringly in love with God, Solanus grew ever more aware that, however "together" or even holy he appeared to others, he had his own imperfections and needed neverending healing himself.

It was this knowledge of himself as one who needs conversion that gave Solanus compassion for others. His awareness of his human status as a sinner kept him safely anchored in humility, while his experience of God's grace in his weakness continually deepened his trust in God so that by his later years Solanus was "uniquely unshaken by doubt, anxiety, or fear," says Crosby.

Similarly Father Solanus's innate compassion for the ill was reinforced by his own physical sufferings. Already back in the Milwaukee diocesan seminary, he suffered from chronic quinsy, that is, abscesses of the tonsils and surrounding area, which not only made him feverish much of the time but caused pain and swelling in his throat so that each word became a strained croak.

In his early thirties he was in great anxiety over trouble with his eyes. He found healing when he took action against his fear of losing his sight by trying to be thankful to God and positive that whatever was occurring would be to his benefit if he let God work. Next he says:

I had completely lost the hearing in my left ear and the same condition was rapidly threatening the other side.

Returning from an ear specialist with a throbbing earache after a very painful treatment, with the prospect of becoming deaf, he decided he needed someone else to pray for him. He turned to a woman he had never met but whom he felt he could count on as a friend in heaven after reading her biography. He made her, he says, "a mental proposition": she should pray for his healing and he would reread her book. The healing through Thérèse Martin, today canonized as St. Thérèse of Lisieux, increased in Solanus the absolute trust in God Thérèse recommended. So did a brush with death around 1920, when he survived gangrene. By 1940, when he was seventy, a chronic health problem was ulcerated eczema or psoriasis on his legs which caused open, oozing sores and hospitalized him periodically. Spiritually, his health was so good, however, that he was believed, by the majority of those who knew him, to be a saint.

Because of this psychic-spiritual wholeness, the skin problems, which would later advance to skin cancer and a streptococcus skin infection causing terrible itching and pain, did not preoccupy him. Even intense pain did not turn him inward: instead it increased his empathy for others in pain. But, by age seventy-six, while he desired to go on until he "died in his tracks" with his service to people of every creed, color, or condition, his superiors decided to officially retire him as the only way to prolong his life.

Still, even at eighty, between bouts with his skin diseases, his energy was astounding. Unless sick, he always ran up the monastery stairs to his room on the second floor. He played tennis and volleyball with young men and, if he fell, leapt up like a youngster and went on playing. If there weren't any games going on, the skinny octogenarian went jogging "to keep in trim."

Saints abound in paradox, and Solanus's care for exercise and healthful diet is part of a paradoxical attitude toward his health: he wanted to keep fit, but even when he was very sick or in great pain "the thought of saving himself" by not making himself available to people who bombarded him by phone, letter, or in person "would never have entered his head," because, more than he wanted anything else, he wanted to give himself to God through service to suffering humanity.

More and more, even in illness, he said from his depths, "How wonderful are all God's designs for those who have confidence." In 1949, hospitalized with legs like "raw meat," blood circulation loss was feared. Doctors stood by to amputate both legs, while every three minutes a nurse checked the seventy-nine-year-old's circulation. Fr. Blase Gitzen, interviewed by fellow Capuchin Michael H. Crosby for Crosby's biography of the holy American, recalls that Solanus's condition was so serious that his hospitalization was kept secret to spare him the people who followed him everywhere. Still, when Fr. Blase visited Solanus in a Fort Wayne, Indiana, hospital:

To my utter surprise, despite a big DO NOT DISTURB sign on the door, I found fifteen people in the room. . . . Some had come from as far away as Detroit. How they found him, I'll never know. But here he was, propped up in bed, with a white canopy over his legs, amiably chatting with his visitors. And sure enough, every three minutes, a disapproving nurse came in to check the pulse in his legs.

His attitude toward his illness was one of such lack of concern, that I was curious whether he knew how seriously ill he had been and brought up the subject on the way home from the hospital. Yes, he knew that his legs might have to be amputated, but he had the attitude: "If they came off, it was alright; if not, that was alright, too." He showed absolutely no shock, surprise, worry or upset. . . .

He later remarked he felt his soul profited greatly from the month he spent in the hospital. His attitude was the same during his next hospitalization, in 1950—he cooperated fully with his doctors but left the outcome unworriedly to God.

When Solanus was young he had prayed for his own healing. In these later years he seems to have experienced in his physical sufferings another way he could give himself to what he called "my two great loves, the poor and the sick." That was to make of his sufferings a kind of prayer in union with Jesus in the form of reparatory suffering along the lines of Paul's "I make up in my own body what is lacking in the sufferings of Christ" (Col. 1:24). Offering his illness, he sought healing for others but only self-giving in every possible form for himself. Thus he could say to a spiritual son who visited him during his last hospitalization and asked "Where do you hurt?"

"My whole body hurts. Thanks be to God. Thanks be to God." Then he explained, "I'm offering my sufferings that all might be one. Oh if I could only live to see the conversion of the whole world!"

There was no self-glorifying in such remarks. Solanus, who had as a young man liked to hear himself praised, was long past caring what anyone but God thought of him. Even years earlier he had seen clearly that God graciously lets those who seek to serve him participate in his divine activity; for that one can be grateful; to be proud would be silly. To a fellow porter, Br. Leo, he wrote, "How can we ever be grateful as we ought to be for such a vocation!"

At the same time he did not believe he had a glamor job. Listening to people's troubles of every kind for nine or ten hours a day, he once admitted to Br. Leo, could be unbearably monotonous. But even when the complaints against life and their fellow man were "petty, selfish, and drearily like those voiced by scores" of others, those he received for Christ's sake felt only love radiating from this priest who, with gentleness and compassion toward their weakness, tried to move them just a bit closer to God and their fellow man.

No inhuman ascetic, when he could he catnapped, even sliding to the floor to curl up under his desk. It also helped to get away and play his violin—however badly—to Jesus in the empty chapel.

Humor was another outlet. It twinkled in his reply to the young fellow who came in griping that Fr. Solanus blessed his car and on the way home it was totaled. "Ah, and look at you. Not a scratch!"

To whoever came—and he had callers of every kind—Solanus could humbly admit he did not have all the answers to the mysteries of illness and other suffering.

"I don't understand why children have to suffer," he said simply.

But he was willing to share the things he felt he did know. Above all, he told his callers, "God cares for you; only fear and distrust on your part can thwart his good designs." Let petitioners do something generous for God, within their own faith tradition, certain that this always calls forth a loving response from God. Above all, let each individual express confidence in God by "thanking him ahead of time" for whatever he is going to do for you. This was not slot-machine religion: the thanks did not guarantee the outcome of your choosing but was a statement of confidence that whatever God did would be "healing," *even if* a particular condition is going to be the means of passing over to the next life. In this vein, when Solanus's prophetic gift let him know someone would die, he still seemed able to "heal," in the sense of achieving a wonderful change in the person's outlook on death.

Paradoxically, while Solanus took no credit for healings or graces, to help those who came to him, as well as out of his love affair with God, the American Capuchin was a mighty prayer. Besides his many regular hours of prayer with the community, he loved to slip into the chapel whenever he had a break. There he would beseech God for his petitioners, full of joy and confidence in God's loving response. At times, other Franciscans would find him lost in prayer before the tabernacle in the middle of the night. And because he was human, sometimes they found him on the floor there fast asleep.

Father Solanus also fasted to obtain graces for the sick. One man, who was to drive him someplace one day, recalls another Capuchin telling him behind Solanus's back that the old priest was weak from fasting for someone. Would the driver swing by his home en route and his wife have a meal ready? "Out of politeness, he'll eat." The ruse worked, for Solanus was never one to let anyone know of his fasts any more than he ever talked of those long middle-of-the-night prayers.

In 1957, just a few months away from his eighty-seventh birthday, new, very painful skin eruptions were diagnosed as severe erysipelas. From the Greek for "red skin," this is an acute streptococcus-caused disease of both the skin and the subcutaneous tissue.

Hospitalized, he was rapt in God much of the time, nurses noted, in spite of the fiery red scales which erupted all over his body. His face shining, he would muse "the love of God is *everything*." Yet, in the way of authentic mystics, he remained down-to-earth and good-humored.

"How 'bout a blessing, Father?" a young nun asked breezily.

"Sure, I'll take one," he teased, knowing she wanted his. Yet when she mourned aloud at having to cause pain in his poor raw hands by removing an intravenous needle, he comforted: "Don't feel bad. Think of Our Lord's hands."

Needles, tubes, and everything else, like the excruciating disease sucking his life away, he used as just another offering to God. To a spiritual son he confided, "I looked on my whole life as giving, and I want to give until there is nothing left of me to give."

His friend says:

●━◆◆━●

I looked at him there on his deathbed, clothed only in a little hospital gown, a rosary in one hand and a little relic in the other, and felt like crying out, "My God, there is scarcely anything left of him to give."‡

●━◆◆━●

But the friend was wrong. As the next chapter shows, even in this final illness Father Solanus was a giver, while after death freshly uncovered healings from his lifetime would merge with new cures to testify that the dead saint's ministry was far from over.

‡ This testimony by Fr. Gerald Walker, O.F.M. Cap. dated April 14, 1980, found in Fr. Marion Roessler's "Written Reports Concerning Fr. Solanus Casey," is quoted in *Thank God Ahead of Time.*

⚜ 2 ⚜

The Best-Loved Man in Detroit

Detroit, Michigan, 1957

Thirty-eight-year-old Gladys Feighan is overjoyed, on a visit to St. John (sic) Hospital from her home in Utica, to learn that Fr. Solanus Casey, "the best-loved man in Detroit," is a patient there. It has been a dream of hers for years to get to Fr. Solanus, revered by so many as a living saint; but for some time his Capuchin Franciscan superiors at St. Bonaventure's monastery have made it hard for anyone to see the ailing eighty-six-year-old priest. Before that, when he was "retired" to a Capuchin house in Huntington, Indiana, she had actually prepared to make a trip there, but both her physician and her pastor advised against travel because of her pregnancy.

Terrified to lose another baby, she had listened to them. And lost another child, she reflects sorrowfully.

Mrs. Feighan is a sufferer from the Rh blood factor.* Like most women with this problem, her first pregnancy was normal. But since her first child, she has had one miscarriage and two babies born dead.

An acquaintance with a similar history made that trip to Indiana and has three more living children to show for it.

Now Gladys sees the brown-hooded robe of a Capuchin in the corridor. Running after it, she begs the brother who is look-

* Today rarely a problem, due to medical advances.

ing out for Fr. Solanus if she can please see the ill man "for just a few minutes."

Br. Gabriel can make no promises. Frail old Fr. Solanus has been brought in by ambulance, very sick with a skin infection, maybe dying. And people have no consideration. A woman who asked to see him for a minute stayed over half an hour. . . .

The more Brother talks, the lower Gladys's face falls. But in the end, he says he'll go ask.

What he doesn't tell Mrs. Feighan is that to ask is an empty formality with Fr. Solanus: in his fifty-three years as a Capuchin priest, he has never said no to seeing anyone, whether it was the middle of the night, the middle of his meal, or the 150th person of a day. The man has absolutely no instinct for self-preservation. Because of his great devotion to his vow of obedience, he accepts the restrictions placed on him by superiors who know the mobs coming, phoning, and writing for his prayers day after day, year after year, have taken the last drops of the holy old friar's strength. But he has been heard to groan to himself, "Oh, why must they keep me from seeing the people?" To give himself to God by giving himself to others until there is nothing left is the one desire of his Christlike heart.

Soon Gladys is in his room. Let her tell it as she related the experience for the book *The Porter of Saint Bonaventure's:*

When I entered . . . Father Solanus was sitting at a little table. He welcomed me, asking me to sit down.

"What is your name?" he asked.

"Mrs. Feighan."

"No—your given name?"

"Gladys."

"What, Gladys, do you want from God?"

"I want a baby. Another baby."

"A baby! For a woman to want a baby—how blessed. To hold God's own creation in your own hands."

I told him about my Rh factor; that I was well toward

my middle thirties; that I feared it wouldn't be long before I might be too old to bear children.

"I do so want another child," I told him. "Perhaps I am selfish."

"No," he answered me, "you are not selfish. For a woman to want children is normal and blessed. Motherhood entails so many responsibilities—bringing up a child as it should be brought up is doing God's work. One doesn't always meet women who want children."

[Gladys expressed concern about her children who had died before they could be baptized.]

"That's not for you to concern yourself about," he answered. "Just have confidence in our dear Lord's infinite love."

Father Solanus's mind seemed above earthly things. He was ecstatic—so much so that I could hardly ask him a question. After answering my first few questions, he did nearly all the talking. His words to me were of God's infinite love for us, and of how we should place all our confidence in that divine, all-embracing love. As he spoke, he was trembling with emotion. Finally he said, "Kneel down, and I will bless you, and your husband and all your family."

The other Capuchin was there, and a Sister of St. Joseph [who was] one of the hospital sisters, and they knelt too.

Then he said to me, "You will have another child, Gladys. Your Blessed Mother will give you another child. You must believe this with all your heart and soul. You must believe this so strongly that before your baby is born you will get down on your knees and thank the Blessed Mother [for her intercession]. Because once you ask her, and thank her, there's nothing she can do but go to her own Son and ask Him to grant your prayer that you have a baby."

Tears were in his eyes.

When I reached home, I was shaken for a couple of days but uplifted. I felt confident, happy.

Not long after, on July 31, 1957, the mystic Franciscan, conscious to the last, died peacefully. He was buried in the small Franciscan graveyard next to St. Bonaventure's.† There, several years later, Gladys came with her children. She had become pregnant in 1962. Her doctors feared another dead child. But she was jubilant and confident. That confidence was rewarded —with twins.

Thank God Ahead of Time quotes another mother with a similar tale. Bernadette Nowak also had borne one child, then lost three due to the Rh factor. When she became pregnant in December 1956, she wrote Fr. Solanus, who replied urging her to name the child right away after two of God's saints and enroll in the Capuchins' mass association. He would certainly pray for her "good intention." When he died, the following summer, the pregnant Mrs. Nowak was one of thousands who filed past his coffin. When she approached the casket, the baby, who had been very still for days, suddenly began to leap inside her. Her whole dress moved, to her embarrassment.

Anthony Joseph was born not long after with the cord wrapped twice around his neck and with a knot in it. But Mrs. Nowak wasn't worried. She had felt Father Solanus's comforting presence throughout the fast and easy delivery. And indeed her son was fine.

Others had similar tales of graces received. The mother of Capuchin missionary Bishop Cuthbert Gumbinger told her son in 1959 that she attributed her recovery from a heart attack to the intercession of Solanus. Bishop Gumbinger was no doubter: Father Solanus had appeared to him in a dream and immediately afterward obtained several things the missionary needed.

† In 1987 the body was exhumed (a required step in the process toward canonization, to protect from theft or veneration of the wrong remains) and reburied in the north transept of St. Bonaventure's Monastery Church.

Gladys Redfern was another grateful individual. In 1964, three examinations and X rays showing a tumor in her breast, she entered Highland Park General Hospital in Detroit May 22 for surgery the following morning. In her prayers she was asking Father Solanus's intercession that the lump might prove benign. That night the doctor stopped by her room and made his last examination before the operation. The lump was gone.

Besides the new cures, people talked of healings from Father Solanus's lifetime, many newly surfaced. A few samples:

Six-week-old Cynthia Evison was not expected to live through the night in March 1954 when her mother telephoned Father Solanus. As she sobbed out the doctor's verdict that the baby's wildly erratic heart would not make it through the night, Fr. Solanus insisted, "You'll bring your baby home from the hospital in a few days. I'll go down to the chapel right now and pray for her."

The next morning, when the doctor bent over Cynthia to examine her, he gave such a cry that a nurse, thinking the baby was dead, rushed to his side. But it was joy, not dismay, that prompted the physician. Little Cynthia's heart was beating normally. Mrs. Evison, after Father Solanus's death, could point to a child who was "the picture of health."

Cynthia's was not the only cure received by a distraught mother over the phone. One day the priest received a telephone call that baby Kathleen Ann Wolfe was close to death from early celiac disease, a condition in which an infant or young child, unable to digest fats, suffers malnutrition and such life-threatening symptoms as chronic diarrhea. Could the baby, Mrs. Wolfe asked, be brought cross country to receive Solanus's blessing?

"Now, now," the priest consoled, "that's not necessary." He had the sorrowful mother kneel by the phone holding the infant while he blessed them. Then he advised Mrs. Wolfe to use the money it would have cost her to travel to "do something for a poor family."

Kathleen Ann recovered.

Because of his special love for the poor, Father Solanus loved to help out at the Capuchins' soup kitchen whenever his callers gave him a free hour. Capuchin author Michael H. Crosby reports the two following incidents: Ray McDonough was a soup kitchen volunteer whose daughter Rita gave birth to a little girl with a clubfoot. Ray asked Father Solanus to visit the baby. The Franciscan did. Holding the little foot in one hand, he blessed it in the name of the Trinity. On the next viewing, the same doctor who had pointed out the clubfoot to the mother scratched his head and said that the foot was perfect. The baby, Carol, is now a mother herself and has never had any foot trouble.

Arthur Rutledge, who worked for the fire department, was another soup kitchen volunteer. He was being rolled into the operating room in a Detroit hospital one day when Father Solanus happened by.

"Hey, Art, what's up?"

Art explained he had a tumor.

"Where is it?"

"In my abdomen—my stomach."

Solanus put his hand on the area.

"Have the doctors give you a last check before they operate," he said a minute later before continuing down the hall.

Art did. The tumor was no more.

When he was "retired" to Indiana, Father Solanus also gave a helping hand to Father Elmer Stoffel, with whom he helped care for the Capuchins' beehives. One day around 1950 Father Elmer was stung by several bees. When Solanus saw his confrere on the ground rolling in pain, he immediately blessed him. Elmer at that time was blind to Solanus's holiness and, in fact, disliked him so much that he sent many a barbed comment the healer's way. Yet, to his chagrin, he had to admit that the second he was blessed, the pain vanished.

William King of Detroit, the son of a Protestant clergyman, had serious eye trouble. His Catholic boss at the Grand Trunk Railway suggested he see Father Solanus. King demurred until his doctor said one of his eyes would have to be removed to try to save the sight in the other one. So dim was his vision at this time that his wife had to lead him into the porter's office. Father Solanus urged the couple, since they wanted a favor from God, to do something for him in return. He suggested they begin attending their Protestant church every Sunday instead of just whenever they felt like it. King's eyes were cured.

So were many other sick or weak eyes—like those of John J. Regan of the Detroit *News*. In 1929 hot casting lead blew up in his face. When Mrs. Regan got to Harper Hospital, she saw her husband's chart and the diagnosis "permanently blinded." She passed out. Coming to, she rushed to Father Solanus, who promised her John would see. Back she ran to the physician who had just operated on her husband. He assured her gravely that was impossible: the best her husband could hope for would be to tell light from dark. Two weeks later, when John Regan's eyes were unbandaged and he said, "I see you," to the physician, the man declared it a miracle. Regan's vision tested excellent.

As the 1940s opened, real estate man Luke Leonard saw himself as "an alcoholic bum." Living in a seedy hotel, he decided one day he was getting nowhere "tapering off." Without any hope of success, he mustered the courage to quit cold turkey.

At once he plunged into the nightmare of delirium tremens, hallucinating monsters and trembling uncontrollably. Walking the streets hour after hour, he bought a soft drink, only to find he shook too badly to get it to his mouth unaided.

Low-voiced Father Solanus usually saw everyone in one room, but he took Leonard behind closed doors and let him pour out his fear, self-loathing, and near despair. Two or three times another friar peered in, saying, "Father Solanus, others are waiting, some from out of town."

"Ask them to wait a little longer," and the white-bearded priest went on listening.

Finally Leonard ran down. Father Solanus leaned toward him. "When did you get over your sickness?"

"You mean my drunk, Father?" Leonard replied, doubly astounded. In that era alcoholism was not considered an illness, nor could anyone consider Luke Leonard free of addiction. Then Father Solanus laughed, a laugh Leonard says was "gentle and encouraging."

A few minutes later the drinker was back on the street, but now he felt, he says, "strengthened and with a free, elevated spirit."

He never took another drink.

Another individual who gained new inner strength from the saintly Capuchin was Mildred Boyea of Dearborn, Michigan. In the manner of some overbearing obstetricians of a blessedly dying school, hers informed her angrily near the end of her first pregnancy that she had eclampsia, also called toxemia of pregnancy, which causes high blood pressure, convulsions, coma—and death. He figured to lose the child, he told her as if this were somehow her fault, and would be lucky not to lose her, too. In an emotional tailspin, the young wife ordered straight to bed went instead to Father Solanus, who promised his prayers.

"Have faith."

"I haven't got that kind of faith," she answered honestly.

"You must," he insisted. Then he told her she would have "a beautiful baby" and she herself would be "all right."

That night, unexpectedly, she gave birth without the predicted tragedy. The old doctor groused, "I've heard about the guardian angels you damn Catholics have hanging over you, but you had more than angels last night." Mrs. Boyea agreed; next to her guardian angel, she believed, stood a praying saint.

In 1957, when Father Solanus was on his deathbed, a hospital cleaning woman approached the younger of his two priest brothers, Monsignor Edward Casey. She wanted to know how Father Solanus was.

"Pretty well."

"I'm praying for him," the woman said fervently. "I owe him so much." Then she told Monsignor Casey about the accident that threw scalding water into her face. The worst pain of her terrible burns had been that people found the sight of her repulsive because of her disfigurement. By the time she went to see Father Solanus at St. Bonaventure's, she never left her home without hiding under a heavy veil. The old priest did not blanch when she lifted it. Instead, blessing her, he compassionately placed his hand on the very grotesqueness that others shunned. "After that," the charwoman confided, "it almost entirely disappeared."

After Father Solanus's death, some of his lay friends got the Capuchins' permission to form the Father Solanus Guild. To them, Father Solanus's life is a model for followers of Christ. To make that life known and promote his Cause, they collect both his writings, mainly letters, and testimonies about him from those he converted, counseled, and/or healed. They accept prayer requests for his intercession. And their quarterly publication gives spiritual inspiration through Father Solanus's words as well as a place to report new healings and favors.

Early in 1966, reports of twenty-four of the more important cures were sent to Rome as one of many formal steps in favor of opening his Cause, which was permitted in June 1982. A sampling from cures reported to the Guild in the 1980s offer their testimony that Father Solanus after death is still as compassionate and willing to bring others' needs to God as he was when he gently greeted the troubled and sick in places like New York and Detroit.

From Illinois a woman reports:

When I was five months pregnant, I was hospitalized for an undiagnosed illness. For two to three weeks I had bouts of fever with extremely elevated heart rates. When no cure could be found, my aunt enrolled me in the Father Solanus Guild *without my knowing it.*‡ The fever suddenly broke that very same day and did not return.

The letter goes on to tell how the baby she bore that year was healed from the undeveloped-lungs syndrome that claims so many infant lives.

One of many heart cures is the son who has had a heart attack five years earlier and now suffers cardiac arrest. His mother begs Father Solanus's prayers. Twenty-four days later, the son is back at work. Best, tests show no damage to the heart.

A woman who has twenty-four inches of intestine removed credits Solanus's intercession that nothing is malignant.

A person disabled for over twenty years but able to function independently becomes ashamed to go out because of drooling from a shaking mouth/chin. To the doctor's surprise, a month's persistent prayers for Father Solanus's intercession and the unsightly symptom vanishes.

A husband sends his thanks. His wife had been in a Connecticut hospital where extensive tests reviewed by three doctors revealed lymphoma tumors in the kidney and pelvis. The young man added his wife to those seeking the dead Capuchin's intercessory prayers. Exploratory surgery found no malignancy—and no tumors. The letter ends, "I honestly think that Fr. Solanus's intercession resulted in a clean bill of health."

A woman has been diabetic since childhood. This type of diabetes,* requiring daily insulin and constant monitoring of the blood, is a chronically life-threatening disease with a host of potentially fatal complications. For such an individual to try to

‡ Italics this writer's.

* Called juvenile, as opposed to adult-onset diabetes. The latter is often so mild it can be controlled by diet alone.

bear a child is extremely risky. Determined to do so, this wife has only short-term miscarriages and the heartbreak of a full-term stillborn child to show for her risks. Yet she tries again. Her mother writes the Guild that even spending six months of the "difficult pregnancy" in the hospital, her daughter still must let the baby be taken prematurely by Caesarean.

The grandmother can see through a window the nurses and doctors surrounding the newborn, who, she says, "appeared lifeless."

"Is the baby's condition critical?" she begs a scurrying nurse, only to be put off with insensitive remarks that imply: What can you expect in such a situation? Thinking of the previous still-birth, the grandmother agonizes, "Oh, please, God, not again! Father Solanus, please pray for her." Even when she is told to go home, on the way she repeats, "Please, God; Father Solanus, please pray for her."

She admits she has no idea, for at the time she knows little of him and nothing of his special concern for mothers and babies, why she feels led to ask Father Solanus's prayers. Today, how-ever, she is sure Solanus's request to God is the main reason for her "miracle" granddaughter, who survived a good deal of time in intensive care and is neither, as had been predicted, retarded nor diabetic.

From New England, the grateful parent of a fifteen-year-old boy writes in 1987:

———•———

My son, age 15, was diagnosed as having lymphoma [can-cer of the lymph-node system]. Two biopsies were done. The surgeon told us that he was quite sure the biopsies would be malignant and that we should not even consider that they would be benign. We were devastated, but we told the surgeon that we believed in miracles. We asked for the intercession of Father Solanus.

Praise be to God, the biopsies were benign and the sur-geon was amazed. My son had further testing with an oncologist and all was fine. I thank Fr. Solanus for his intercession and I praise the Holy Name of God. Fr. Solanus's intercession must be so powerful before the throne of God.

Amen.

❧ 3 ❧

"No Comparable Case in Medical Literature"

Catholic immigrants poured into America in the nineteenth century. Low on the economic and social totem poles, the newcomer's spiritual poverty was often greater: with no knowledge of English, in far too many cases the immigrant could not understand a sermon, be counseled in confession, or read a Catholic periodical. On his deathbed he had little hope for recognizable words of priestly comfort. To answer these needs, heroic priests and nuns left their homelands, many times never to see their families again.

An intelligent, quietly good-tempered young seminarian from Bohemia,* short, stocky, big-eyed John Neumann heard the call from God, he thought, to missionary life. The wrenching part was telling his supportive, pious family, who were already preparing new clothes for his first mass and happily contemplating his years of service in their little town.

Two brief anecdotes courtesy of Redemptorist Michael J. Curley's biography† of Neumann describe the parents who molded this sturdy lad.

An industrious small businessman with a tiny home factory of three or four employees where stockings were loomed, Philip Neumann once discovered a thief was quietly stealing from him. When he confronted the fellow in the act with witnesses,

---

* His father came from Bavaria, in today's West Germany; his mother was Czechoslovakian.

† *Bishop John Neumann C.SS.R.: Fourth Bishop of Philadelphia.*

instead of sending for the police, he asked, "How can you go on offending God like this?"

"I'm so poor," pleaded the thief.

"But if you'd only let me know, I'd *give* you what you need," Neumann declared. Then he made the witnesses promise to say nothing about the matter, added a bit more to his robber's take, and dismissed the man with a reminder that whenever he was in need he should come for Neumann's help.

Agnes Neumann, who cheerfully bribed whichever one of her six children was handy to attend daily mass with her, was known for her charitable tongue.

— • • • —

If by chance someone began to blacken the character of another, she would stop the trend of the conversation by saying "Oh, what use is this talk about another's sins? We, too, have our weaknesses, and God is so patient with us!"

— • • • —

Visitors who refused to take the hint were not invited again. The deep spirituality of such parents set young John free to be a missionary.

But even with his family's unselfishness, young Neumann was beset with bureaucratic difficulties when he actually tried to leave for America. Checks for many months both at home and from America grinding away at his idealism, the young linguist (he already had under his belt German, Czech, Greek, Italian, Spanish, Latin, French, and English) proved himself a true son of his parents when it came to doing God's will whatever the cost. When others backed out he made the trip alone, paying his own way. Worse, he was unordained, all ordinations having been postponed indefinitely in his home diocese, and no bishop had agreed to receive him for ordination in the United States. That strength of character and courageous reliance on God was typical of Neumann, who would become a saint by simply putting one foot in front of the other wherever God pointed the way, no matter what the obstacles.

Arrived in New York City in May 1836, the young man found all obstacles suddenly melted away: he was greeted with open arms for his knowledge of languages and ordained at the old St. Patrick's Cathedral on Mott Street within a month.

After serving his fellow immigrants in such places as upper New York State, Pittsburgh, and Baltimore, John Neumann was proposed as bishop of Philadelphia, a town which had burned a church, convent, and forty homes in anti-Catholic riots just eight years earlier.

Humble and self-effacing, Neumann, who had joined the Redemptorist religious congregation to find support for a deep interior life, appealed to everyone—his religious superiors, American bishops, even various houses of nuns to help him "escape" becoming a bishop. But when the Pope ordered him to accept the job, he quietly proved a real father to his people and an innovator: his was the first diocesan school system and the first diocesan Forty Hours Devotion to the Eucharist. He not only welcomed various other religious orders to his diocese but, at the Pope's urging, founded an order of sisters as well. A prodigious worker, in spite of economic depression and the prevailing prejudice against anything Catholic, he built and staffed schools, churches, convents, orphanages, and other charitable institutions. Above all, he was the good shepherd: children running to him for a shy smile and the candy ever present for them in his shabby coat pocket; the poor encouraged to count on his openhearted charity whatever his own financial worries; and the suffering sure of a supportive word. To offer those words, he taught himself new languages (it is said he could get by in eleven), at least well enough to meet the needs of his multilingual flock, whether Gaelic-speaking coal miners or the Italians for whom he founded the first national parish conducted all in their native tongue.

This workaholic (he made a vow never to waste time and kept it) was still an ardent lover of God who, besides his ongoing prayer life, tried to set aside a whole day each month to be alone with the Lord.

You understand the man's soul when you see him, smiling benignly, lost in the crowd at the dedication of one of the new churches, while his associates bask in glory, heading the ceremonies in the bishop's place up on the altar. No wonder wise people looked beyond Neumann's unprepossessing manner to whisper that their soft-spoken bishop was surely a saint. Still, if his prayers healed anyone during his lifetime, it is a well-kept secret. Indeed the only miracle recorded of his life is how one man could so totally pour himself out in love of God and service to the human family.

Worn out at only forty-eight, he collapsed on the street and died.

What he himself had judged a life that fell short in many ways, others saw differently. Mrs. Mary Allen, who had written her friend the archbishop of Baltimore her conviction of Neumann's sanctity, now wrote in another letter, "we miss our bishop very much; we go to his tomb to pray. . . ." From the day of the funeral, January 9, 1860, cures were attributed to the bishop's intercession, one of the first being that of a child who had never been able to stand.

Only four years after Neumann's death, Father Luhrmann, rector of St. Peter's Church in Philadelphia, where the bishop is buried, asked a mother superior for an additional sister to teach at his new primary school for boys.

Mother Caroline responded she had no sister to spare but Sister Anselma, who couldn't teach any longer because she was almost stone deaf.

Somehow priest and mother superior, faced with 120 to 140 little boys, conceived the idea that Neumann, who had begun so many schools, would intercede. They told poor Sister Anselma to take on the boys and that the bishop, who was such a promoter of Catholic education and friend of children, would help her.

The tomb of the bishop was just outside the school. On her way in each morning, Sister Anselma knelt at the grave and said three to five Our Fathers and Hail Marys, depending upon how close the hour to starting time, asking the good bishop to see her through. Then she marched into class.

After a while her boys were so well taught and managed that sixty little girls were added, bringing the class up to two hundred children at its maximum.

Those who went there and those who dropped in unanimously agree that "perfect order and tranquillity ruled in that school at all times." In fact the other teaching sisters referred to it as "a model school."

How was this possible?

Once the classroom door closed behind her, Sister Anselma could hear as well as any pupil. She fielded questions, heard recitations, and had no trouble catching little Mary whispering to Billy Murphy in the last row.

Once the tired schoolmistress locked the schoolroom door at day's end, however, anyone who wanted to talk to her had to scream. She was once more deaf. Apparently she had taken the injunction a bit too literally: instead of asking Bishop Neumann's prayers for healing her ears, she had asked only to be able to teach. And that was exactly what she got.

On October 25, 1891, an Episcopalian friend visited Mary Catherine Monroe, a widow whose malignant uterine tumors were inoperable. At that time, the emaciated former schoolteacher was so feeble she could scarcely walk across her boardinghouse room. Only fifty years old, the Catholic convert was completely occupied in preparations for a happy death.

The visitor knew her deep spirituality and had come to ask a favor.

"My sister in New York is dying," she explained. "I've heard miracles can be obtained by praying at your Bishop Neumann's tomb. I want to go there and pray, but I don't know how one acts in a Catholic place. Won't you, please, come with me?"

Mary Catherine had to smile. A dying woman like herself would never be able to make it to the basement tomb in St. Peter's, she explained, in spite of her complete willingness to pray for her visitor's sister.

Mrs. Clayton, the visitor, was not quite as oblivious to her friend's condition as she seemed. At once, she reported she had already arranged for three other women to join them. For Mary Catherine's pointers on Catholic tomb etiquette—and one imagines her presence there in prayer—the healthy foursome would simply carry the devout convert wherever necessary.

"How can I refuse?"

Hauled in, however ungracefully, to the bishop's tomb, Mary Catherine led the four stalwart Protestants in fervent prayer for Mrs. Clayton's dying sister. She never dreamed, she explained later, of being so presumptuous as to pray for herself. Doctors had said she must die and she had simply accepted the verdict as God's will.

So she was shocked when a gentle voice which she alone heard instructed, "Now pray for yourself." In response, the cancer victim said the briefest possible prayer. Immediately a "strange thrill" passed through her body and she thought she was dying. Then she knew she was, in fact, healed.

The figure of skin and bones who had so laboriously been lugged down the basement steps now zipped up those stairs, walked back to her boardinghouse refusing every offer of a ride or assistance, and charged up the three flights to her room. She was vibrantly healthy from that day until she died, a decade later, still cancer-free.

As for Mrs. Clayton's dying sister, she got off her deathbed too—and lived another five years.

Another cure whose details were collected by Father Joseph Wissel, the postulator of Neumann's cause, was that of Mrs.

Sarah McKeough of the Manayunk section of Philadelphia. Mrs. McKeough had tumors in her breast. Two surgeries had not helped. With a new operation scheduled, she made a novena, each day praying at the bishop's tomb.

The final day of the novena was the day for surgery. In fact she went straight from St. Peter's to the surgeon's. Putting her to sleep with ether, Dr. Gross, the surgeon, was using her case as part of his course on surgery. A number of medical students watched as he marked the very visible protuberance of the tumor site with a pencil. He would cut on the lines he had just drawn. Making a few remarks to the class, he turned and picked up his scalpel, then bent to make the incision. He stopped, because the little mound of malignant flesh was gone. Palpating and probing to no avail, the suddenly flustered professor-surgeon muttered, "Is it possible I could have been deceived [in thinking there was a tumor here]?"

But the class had seen the mound. Their professor was no hallucinator: in the seconds it takes a man who has done this hundreds of times to select his scalpel from the tray of ready instruments, a tumor had withered, died, and vanished without a trace.

Interestingly enough, the patient soon woke up, said, "Don't touch me—I'm cured," leapt up, and went home.

The flabbergasted physician wrote her two or three weeks later, requesting she come in for an examination. He found nothing. When she explained about her novena and how the tumor had disappeared on its last day after she completed her final prayer for Bishop Neumann's intercession, he could only say, "Well, Mrs. McKeough, that may be, but I don't believe it."

To give one last example of the flood of cures that many saw as God's way of pushing the Cause of his good servant John, there is the case of Sister Carlotta, who was born Margaret Murphy. A strong and healthy young woman of twenty-one when she entered the Order of St. Joseph, a year later she began to experience pains in her left side. After five years of this misery, an operation removed diseased ovaries. Sister returned to teaching, but the surgeon had left some wire by mistake inside her, and this caused a new problem. A second surgery to correct this physician error led to a worse one: a ligament of her leg was cut beyond repair. Now the young nun could not walk, even on crutches. A third operation botched things even more.

A fighter, Sister Carlotta made eight novenas and, after the last, was partially cured, only to slip on a stair six months later. The bad fall that resulted landed her in a wheelchair.

In August 1898, when she made her perpetual vows, the officiating bishop recommended a novena to Bishop Neumann. He urged that her whole religious community make it with her and promised he would join them in prayer for the nine days. Her relatives also petitioned the holy bishop, making a daily visit to say the novena prayers at his tomb.

On the ninth day, Sister Carlotta went to communion as helpless as ever, rolling up to receive the Eucharist in her wheelchair. Immediately upon swallowing the host, a strange feeling coursed through her body. She jumped out of the wheelchair and walked to a pew. She was cured.

The next day, when the community doctor dropped by to see Sister Carlotta, the mother superior greeted him.

"Before you go see the dear child," she said, "tell me in confidence just what you think about her case."

Gravely, the physician volunteered his medical analysis that Sister Carlotta could not live much longer.

"I see. Thank you, Doctor." Mother looked very thoughtful. Then she summoned Sister Carlotta.

The doctor could only stammer that he had never been more surprised in his life and that this was a true miracle.

Along with the more important testimonies under oath to the bishop's heroic practice of charity, faith, hope, and other virtues, cures like these were eventually presented to Rome as signs from God in favor of John Neumann's holiness. Three were selected, after rigorous inquiry, as the official beatification and canonization miracles.

The earliest of the trio took place in Sassuolo, a town near Milan in northern Italy in May of 1923. Attending a Catholic boarding school there, the Institute of St. Joseph, Eva Benassi was only eleven when she began having headaches and abdominal pain and seemed drowsy much of the time. Dr. Louis Barbante treated her, but she only got worse. Eventually a diagnosis was made. The poor child had acute diffused tubercular peritonitis. By the time this was understood, she was beyond medical help. In the advanced state of the disease now, Eva became weaker and weaker. On a Monday a priest prepared her for death, because the doctor had told her father that his daughter would most likely not live through the coming night.

Sister Elizabeth Romoli, a teacher at St. Joseph's Institute, visited Eva between eight and nine that evening. The nun explained how her own father recovered from an illness through the intercession of Bishop Neumann. Praying for the saint's intercession, Sister Elizabeth touched the young girl's swollen stomach with a picture of the bishop. She also inspired the Benassi family to join her and other nuns in seeking Neumann's intercession. Sometime during what should have been the night of her death, Eva was completely healed.

Examined by the physician who thought he would be writing out her death certificate that morning, Eva Benassi was in excellent health. After a long investigation of the cure, nine physicians appointed by the Sacred Congregation of Rites agreed that Eva had indeed suffered acute diffused peritonitis. Her healing, they proclaimed, was instantaneous, perfectly complete, medically inexplicable, and permanent.

In the final examination of her case, which took place in December 1960, thirty-seven years after her cure, Eva, forty-eight years old and the mother of two children, still enjoyed perfect health.

The second healing that went through the rigorous investigatory process to be named an official miracle was that of J. Kent Lenahan, Jr., of Villanova, Pennsylvania.

On the evening of July 8, 1949, Lenahan, a frisky nineteen-year-old, was standing on the running board of a moving car. When the driver suddenly lost control, the swerving vehicle crushed the young man against a utility pole.

Taken to Bryn Mawr Hospital, Lenahan's injuries gave no hope for recovery: besides minor things like his broken collarbone, his skull was crushed, a fractured rib thrust through one lung, an eye hung over his cheekbone, and he was bleeding copiously from his mouth, nose, and ears. His temperature was 107, his pulse 160. The best news, considering the pain of such injuries, was that he was comatose.

Physicians informed his parents that there was no possibility of recovery. Medical treatment was abandoned. But Kent's mother refused to abandon hope. Although she'd been warned it was just a matter of hours until her son's death, she raced out to the Dominican nuns of Camden, who began a novena to then Venerable John Neumann; she and her husband also went themselves to the saint's shrine and prayed. Then they took a piece of Neumann's cassock belonging to one of their neighbors to the hospital. Praying fervently, they touched the bit of cloth to Kent. Just after all those prayers, their dying son's temperature dropped inexplicably from 107 to 100 degrees.

Five weeks later the "hopeless" youth left the hospital—walking without aid.

A few years later, working as a band leader and music teacher, Lenahan was asked about his healing. His explanation: "They couldn't explain what happened, so I guess it was the Man upstairs."

Before the canonization, the Church also accepted as a true miracle the healing of Michael Flanigan.

Michael was five years old when he fell down the stairs, injuring his right leg, which remained swollen over the right tibia and caused him pain in the following months. Walking only with a limp, that October (1962) he entered Misericordia Hospital in Philadelphia for treatment. While doctors suspected cancer, the biopsy revealed no malignancy. Dr. C. Jules Rominger treated Michael with antibiotics and immobilization in a long leg cast. He went home somewhat better, but in January 1963 the leg began to swell and to be tender and painful. From February 7 to March 9, he was again hospitalized, the diagnosis still osteomyelitis of the right tibia. Home again, in June the entire leg was swollen, tender, and a strange bluish red, sending him once again to Misericordia. This time, following further X rays and biopsy, the news was grim: Michael had Ewing's sarcoma, a lethal bone cancer which is hopeless once spread beyond the initial area. In Michael's case, the disease had metastasized and was in both lungs and his jaw, as well as the tibia.

Told their son had no chance of recovery, the Flanigans, like so many parents before them, took Michael to Bishop Neumann's shrine in St. Peter's. This was in the early fall of 1963.

After several visits by the West Philadelphia family and many prayers, by October all cancer had vanished from the child's jaws and lungs. By Christmas that year, when Michael should have been dead or dying, according to every known medical history of metastasized Ewing's sarcoma, there was no trace of the deadly disease anywhere in his body. Nor would the cancer ever return.

Investigators naturally asked what role might the medical treatment Michael received have played in his cure. He was treated with both radiation and with chemotherapy, using Vincristine, a derivative of the periwinkle plant, *Vinca rosea*. The radiation initially reduced but did not destroy the tumor masses. Chemotherapy, given between August and October, resulted in a healthy decline in the white blood count and a marked regression of the lung nodules but had to be discontinued on October 2 because of severe side effects.

The lung nodules began to grow again and were radiated again, whereupon they regressed. Expectation would have been that eventually the tumor growth would have outstripped the body's ability to take radiation, which itself is fatal beyond a point, and/or chemotherapy, which also poisons the body. Death would then ensue.

Michael's physician, Dr. Rominger, wrote me regarding his patient's recovery from metastasized Ewing's sarcoma: "There is NO comparable case to this [one] in world medical literature." In other words, others in the same stage of the disease, given the same treatment, simply did not recover.

Another physician, a member of the panel of medical doctors investigating the cure, stated Michael's chance of survival after treatment "was practically zero."‡ Today the same doctor, emphatic that he has no belief in miracles, insists treatment must somehow have saved the boy. Still the investigatory panel, including this cancer specialist, found at the time that, in spite of medical treatment, the healing of Michael Flanigan could be termed "miraculous" with complete propriety.

The Flanigan youngster's near-lethal bout with cancer was the end of any medical problems. Still even those cured by miracles do not live forever. Like his friend in heaven for whom Flanigan, as an adult, told an interviewer he "felt an almost personal closeness," Michael Flanigan, the married father of two, died young of a sudden, massive heart attack.

‡ The outlook for Ewing's sarcoma patients is brighter in 1987.

❦ 4 ❧

Miracles in Philadelphia

When John Neumann became the first male American citizen to be canonized, on June 19, 1977, for the members of his Redemptorist Order who staff the shrine where the saint is buried in Philadelphia, his new status meant not only rejoicing, but a sigh of relief. No longer would they have to run down medical attestations and watch changes of address for individuals claiming that the dead bishop's intercession had gained them a miracle. But if the tedium of investigating cures for qualification as official miracles was over, the cures were not.

Ten years later the regular bulletins published by the prayer center often contain stories or letters from those whose gratitude prompts them to contact the shrine to detail cures the recipients attribute to St. John Neumann's intercession. Furthermore the priests who work at the center are often approached by visitors who enthusiastically report healings for which they are now making a thank-you "visit." Father Charles Fehrenbach, for instance, shared with me from his personal log of cures a number of extraordinary cases. Like the logbook kept by Father Solanus Casey, these are often abbreviated accounts, but they make it clear that a lot of people in the United States believe St. John Neumann's prayers triggered healing of everything from simple deafness to advanced cancer.

Setting aside the cures I was told about in which the relics of the saint kept at the shrine play a major role, this brief chapter

will give the reader some idea of the variety and magnitude of
the healings still being reported to the Philadelphia shrine.

The quoted material that follows is taken either from Father
Fehrenbach's log, from shrine bulletins, or from letters reporting cures. In most cases either I or someone from the shrine has
condensed the account, since my purpose here is to suggest
something of the scope of the saint's after-death apostolate as a
bearer of God's healing, not to give as many details as possible
of individual healings. Because of this I have also kept identifi-
cation sketchy, using only first names or none.

After prayers for St. John's intercession, a child underwater
more than three minutes and thought drowned is completely
well without any sign of brain damage.

An eighty-year-old widow of Nashua, New Hampshire,
writes her thanks. She explains, "I've had arthritis about twelve
years and was contemplating having an artificial hip put in."
Regularly asking the saint's prayers, she reports, ". . . after six
months I was walking as straight as could be, without the help
of a cane and no more pain."

An Episcopalian priest, aide to General John Collins (a Redemptorist priest serving as Chief of Chaplains for the U.S. Air
Force) visits the shrine to pray for his wife, who has just been
diagnosed as having multiple sclerosis. At the time of the visit,
she is suffering intensely and has no control of some organs.
Within a week after the husband prays at the shrine asking God
for relief for his wife, she returns to the hospital. There further
tests suddenly discover she does not have MS, but a tumor on
the spine. Removing it restores her to perfect health. Doctors
say that had one more week elapsed, she would have been crippled for life.

Also grateful are the parents of premature Joseph Francis.
The two pounds, two ounces baby had a massive cerebral hemorrhage at birth. A shunt to the stomach was done, but then
spinal meningitis was discovered. Because it was thought the

child would not live, the shunt was removed. Two weeks later, as he still lived, a second shunt was done. At this time the prognosis for the baby's future was epilepsy or cerebral palsy. Following two seizures from the spinal meningitis, it was believed the baby's phenobarbital medication would be necessary for life. At the age of a year, he is doing fine *sans* phenobarbital, a fact his parents attribute to the saint's intercession.

Pictured in the spring 1986 bulletin is another little boy. Before birth his spleen had pushed its way through a hole in his diaphragm, preventing proper lung functioning. The grandmother holding "normal, healthy" young Scott Daniel credits the saint's intercession with successful surgery. Of course Neumann would no doubt counter that a good grandmother's prayers equal any saint's.

A man from Villas, New Jersey, where miracle recipient Michael Flanigan lives at that time, writes about his wife's amazing cure from psoriasis. After a week of treatment during which the saint has been asked for his prayers, the woman's doctor exclaims, "I feel like God." Other dermatologists, called in to see the wonderful results, say, "Miracle!"

From New York comes a healing that shows how often the intercession of a saint is but part of the overall picture in a healing. I quote the condensed account directly from a 1981 bulletin:

[The individual], 18 years old, was baptized, confirmed, anointed and enrolled in the scapular on July 6. Next day he made his First Communion. That same night, started novena to Mary and St. John Neumann. Prayer was that if he was not cured of the terminal cancer he had, God would give him the grace to suffer willingly and accept His will. . . .

Next morning the pain was completely gone; he ate and drank for first time in months without becoming sick, and the lump on his hip was gone. Every day since then he has been riding his bike, hiking, jogging, and no signs of the cancer have returned. The doctors don't know what to make of it!

A woman comes to the shrine in April 1985 from her home in Blackwood, New Jersey. In his log, Father Fehrenbach, as usual, carefully notes her full name, address, and phone number, then jots just the highlights of the healing. In this case, highlights are enough to leave the reader with complete understanding of why Annette is grateful to God and St. John Neumann. Just a month earlier, in March, she has been diagnosed as stage-four lymphoma. Stage four is about as bad as the deadly lymphoma can get. The bedridden cancer victim turns to God and asks the saint's help. Without any medical aid, a disease, which might easily in stage four be fatal even *after* aggressive treatment by radiation and chemotherapy, simply disappears. Father's note ends as do so many: "Doctors cannot explain the cure."

A twenty-three-year-old man has severe hepatitis. Bedridden for eight months, he loses thirty pounds and has signs of early cirrhosis of the liver. He will need a liver transplant. After two months of prayer asking St. John's intercession, his jaundice is gone, he has gained back twenty pounds, elevated liver enzymes count is returning to normal, and his surprised doctor exclaims, "You probably won't need that liver transplant!"

A fourteen-year-old boy is in Children's Hospital with a malignant tumor on the back of his neck. Doctors believe the cancer has spread through his entire body.

"Am I going to die? I'm afraid," the child cries as they prepare him for further exploratory surgery. Father Fehrenbach, contacted by the parents the day the boy enters the hospital, has those at the shrine praying. The priest also puts a small relic in the mail to the hospital. Two days later the envelope is returned. The boy is no longer hospitalized. Shortly thereafter his grandmother visits the shrine to give thanks and tell the story. The last presurgery tests showed a very changed picture. No longer any signs of malignancy anywhere, astounded doctors simply sent the boy home.

A senior citizen testifies:

•—••—•

Five years ago I thought I was doomed to a life of darkness because of retinal hemorrhages in both eyes. I could not see an object placed right before me. I had exhausted medical attempts in Philadelphia, Pittsburgh, and elsewhere. . . .

•—••—•

After asking Neumann's prayer help, she says:

•—••—•

I am enjoying my golden years abundantly, reading, attending travelogues with my husband and, with his help, taking care of the housework and gardening. With a heart full of gratitude, I am faithfully devoted to St. John Neumann.

•—••—•

From New York City comes a letter brief enough to print in full:

•—••—•

Last March 28, 1979, my husband Dr. M.Z. of Cebu, Philippines, got sick of liver cirrhosis. He was continually being treated for ascites [fluid accumulation in the abdomen] until July 4, 1980, when he was confined in a hospital. His abdomen became more and more enlarged but he was skin and bones, weighing 128 pounds. He started gaining weight and his waist reduced from 97 cms. to 79 cms. He has no more fluid in his abdomen and the doctor thinks that recovery was due to the miraculous intervention of beloved St. John Neumann.

How did it happen? Well, last May the relatives of my husband and I made a pilgrimage to the Shrine in Philadelphia, purposely to request the miraculous healing of my husband. Praise the Lord! We had our miracle!

•—••—•

Another individual, who writes from Brooklyn, New York, gives a first-person account:

On Saturday, April 8, 1986, I first noticed a large lump on my neck, two or three fingers' breadth from the collarbone. It was surprisingly big and ugly. Doctor suspected malignancy. Even if benign, it would be extremely difficult to remove because of its depth. On Monday, April 14, I went to Philadelphia by train and visited the Shrine of St. John Neumann. I spent several hours in the church . . . hoping that the lump would go away then and there. But it didn't.

I felt more than halfway certain the cancer would prove fatal and I spent my time praying more for a good death than for a cure. I had an appointment with the doctor at 2:00 the following afternoon. Crossing the street in front of his office a moment before 2 o'clock, I prayed again for the saint's intercession. . . .

When I opened my shirt, the doctor said, "The tumor has disappeared!"

Another individual writes in gratitude that a friend's brain tumor, removed after prayer for the saint's intercession, has left "no impairments. She is perfectly well again."

While complete cures are frequent, other people are grateful for partial cures or improvements. For instance, someone from Maryland reports: "Eighteen years ago I had surgery of the intestine . . . because I suffered from fistula, abscess and a long-standing inflammatory process. The surgery left me with diarrhea every day of my life and a difficult and stressful problem of control. Since my visits to the Shrine, I have improved considerably and I want to express my gratitude. . . ."

A child who is only twenty-one months old has serious diabetes. In a coma for ten days and with the very lethal complication of intracranial pressure, he is not expected to live. If he does, say physicians, he will be unable to walk and otherwise without "any quality of life."

On the feast day of St. John Neumann, the parents visit the shrine on their way to the intensive care unit where the toddler lies unconscious. After their prayers that the saint—who was always so kind to children—will intercede with God, they go on to the hospital. There they find the dying child awake and out of his coma.

In 1986, when he is eight years old, his mother reports that "he is almost completely recovered," although he still has "some diabetes and some signs of brain damage."

If a saint's shrine is a place where one is confronted by the fact that miracles take place all around us, a shrine is also a place where the mysteries of suffering and death are very much in view. At the Neumann shrine, as at every place where the saints are vehicles of God's healing, not everyone is healed. The Redemptorist fathers are extremely open about this fact and about the occasional case in which it seems there has been a permanent miraculous recovery and actually, after a period of restored health, the former condition returns and the individual dies.

In the 1980s a bulletin reported the case of a little boy who had seemed to be cured of cancer of the spine with paralysis that left doctors doubting that he would ever walk again, if he lived. Walking, running, playing, the child enjoyed several years of life, then died. Publishing this heartbreaking news, the fathers can only say truthfully, "God's ways are not our ways," and promise the family their continued prayers.

That those prayers may make a significant difference in dealing with the tragedy of losing a child I find unintentionally indicated in Father Fehrenbach's notes, where he scribbles to himself about the marvelous hope and faith he found in the parents of another tiny cancer victim who died.

Many people who contact the shrine are deliriously grateful

for changed diagnoses after asking St. John Neumann's prayers. Three samples:

•—••—•

My friend was in Kennedy Hospital for treatment of a brain tumor. Two CAT scans showed this and need of surgery. Before a final dye-injection test, we prayed to St. John Neumann. . . . The test showed no sign of any tumor.

•—••—•

In January [1981] I was diagnosed as having cancer of the bladder. I immediately began a novena to St. John Neumann. . . . Just before scheduled surgery, the diagnosis was changed to simple inflammation of the bladder. Some people say "mistaken diagnosis." I say "miracle!"

•—••—•

A mother of six called the shrine for prayers as she had cancer of the thyroid. Tests were being made to see how extensive the malignancy was. The following day she called the Redemptorists back. Doctors now said there was no sign of cancer or tumor—just an enlargement of the gland, which was treatable medically without any surgery. The lump had been the size of a lemon before simply vanishing. She credits St. John Neumann's intercession.

•—••—•

To close this brief sampling of God's works through the shrine to his saint John Neumann, is this testimony of a Philadelphia woman:

•—••—•

I feel obliged to report what, in my mind is an instantaneous miracle through the intercession of St. John Neumann on October 6, 1979. Calling on my parish priest, while waiting for him, I noticed a statue of St. John on the table. I picked it up, held it to my left ear and prayed, "St. John Neumann, please restore the hearing in this ear." I am a senior citizen and have been deaf in that ear since childhood because of a punctured eardrum. Until that moment I had never prayed for restoration of hearing, the doctor having told me the situation was hopeless.

[From the instant of this prayer she could hear but, wondering if it was imagination, she asked her parish priest, in whom she confided, to say nothing about it until she could see a doctor.]

This I did on October 16. The doctor examined my deaf ear thoroughly and advised me that while I still have a punctured eardrum I am now hearing through my conductive nervous system. I no longer have deafness in my left ear. I will be forever grateful to God and St. John Neumann.

5

Crazy About Jesus

"You have only two years to live," the doctor says solemnly to his thirty-nine-year-old patient.

The ethereal-looking little nun does not flinch. In her high clear voice she thanks him for his frankness. Fifteen minutes later, her small black bonnet once more covering the blond curls flattened by pulling them severely back from a middle part, Francesca Cabrini's diminutive figure in its long-sleeved, cape-shouldered black dress, a simple crucifix worn over her heart, heads down the streets of Rome to the convent of the Missionaries of the Sacred Heart.* If the sick woman looks as fragile as some delicate bird, her luminous blue eyes are nonetheless peaceful, her smile almost amused.

That afternoon in 1889, far from preparing for death, the young head of the order is deep in negotiations for leading her first missionary group to work among Italian emigrants in New York City, where the Americans will call her Mother—and one day Saint—Frances Xavier Cabrini.

"While I work I'm well; I get sick the minute I stop working," she will later laugh. If works of charity are the lamp she holds

---

* The term Sacred Heart is an attempt to emphasize in almost visual terms not Jesus' human vascular organ, but his immense love—both human and divine—for humankind in his "laying down his life" for our human family and in the tender concern he has, with the Father and the Spirit, for each of us as individuals. Honor to the Sacred Heart is in no way distinct from the whole Jesus; it is worship of him emphasizing the same aspects of his divinity and humanity exemplified by the older term "the Good Shepherd."

against the world's darkness—in the process somehow retarding her own physical disintegration—the oil for that lamp, as she says herself, is prayer. In the many hours of prayer a day she needs† to slake the spiritual hunger of her passion for Jesus lies some of the secret of how Francesca carries a work load that would daunt the healthiest individual. There also lies the key, no doubt, to her happy, even disposition when the doctor says she should be disposed to depression and mood swings with her ailments and sensitive temperament.

Mother Cabrini herself, with the sense of humor and simplicity that keynote her character, takes no medical prognosis as the last word. "I shall live as long as God wishes," she smiles, and leaves it at that. Others believe she is so holy that, in her being, spirit dominates and lends strength to her emotions and body. Doctor Morini, who gives her two years to live, says he cannot fathom how a woman in her physical condition sustains her level of activity, besides having such psychological stamina. Astounded, this nineteenth-century man of medicine comes to a profoundly holistic conclusion: "God helps His saints," he ventures, "and [He] plays with them."

In fact one can almost hear the divine laughter as God chooses a rag like Cabrini's body and sends it out to cross malarial tracts in Central America, to climb on muleback in the snow the immense mountains separating Chile from Argentina, and to trudge up endless stairs and down fearful alleys in the tenement sections of New York—all to bear his gifts to members of our human family.

And when some Goliath needs putting in place, the Lord sends the tiny, fragile nun as his David. With the temper she is born with purified of all malice in her recognition of her own need for God's forgiveness, she can stand toe-to-toe with the intimidating official who wants to stop an orphanage in New

† The exact number is impossible to estimate, as she did much of her personal praying at night when she was alone; in one crisis in Seattle near the end of her life, however, it is known she prayed fifteen hours straight.

Orleans and say evenly, but with a salutory hint of fire, as she looks up at his imposing height: "Try to destroy this work if you dare and you'll pay dearly for it." He withdraws his opposition.

Although she has not a dime and must beg for all her projects, God also uses the frail nun to confront backbiters like the society woman in Brazil who gets some straight talk from Cabrini right in front of her fashionable and wealthy friends. The woman changes. And another school is established. If, in the process of her work for him, Cabrini gets malaria atop her other ailments, what does it matter? She is dying anyway. However, when it seems she *will* die on the ship taking her on one of her thirty-seven missionary crossings of an ocean, she has only to say to Jesus: "If you will only let me finish my journey!"

"He, so benign, listened to me; and now I feel well and I've recovered my old energy," she writes her daughters. She is betraying no secret. The nuns who live with Cabrini know the ongoing miracle of her survival better than she. They say, ". . . We couldn't help noticing that although Mother was so frail in health, she always appeared strong and happy" when working for the family of God—even if this means going all day without food to get auction bargains for a new school for the poor or getting thoroughly drenched looking for a site for one of her charitable institutions. To give herself this way to the Sacred Heart of Jesus, the focus of her congregation and her spirituality, she will pay with exhaustion and fever—but only after the work is done, they remark. For all of us in search of health or desirous to maintain our health, saints like Mother Cabrini are a good reminder of what doctors have long observed: people with very precarious health, even terminal conditions, can often live inexplicably long, productive, and satisfying lives when they have something important enough to live for.

In the case of genuine mystics, like Francesca, there is even a further dimension, a kind of supranatural sustenance given to saints apparently to reveal that their very energy often comes not from ordinary sources, but from their divine lover and Lord.

As if to drive home this point, Francesca Cabrini is such a tiny eater that in no way can she be said to gain from her food adequate fuel for her undertakings. The spiritual source of her energy is also clear from her sleep patterns. She rises at four to begin praying, and who knows how far into each night she prays. In the early days, another nun shares her room but finds her bed moved elsewhere one day. Her error: when she awoke in the middle of the night and the room's darkness was flooded, *sans* lamp, with the Shekinah light of God's presence, she exclaimed to Mother Cabrini, "Do you see that?"

"It's nothing. Go back to sleep," Cabrini countered. But from then on she tries to be alone at night. However little she rests, she assures her daughters that her sleep is that of a child. Even awake, as the nun who serves as her traveling secretary observes, "No infant ever lay so safe in its mother's arms as Francesca Cabrini did in the Sacred Heart of Jesus." Today from books like Norman Cousins's *The Healing Heart* we have some understanding of what an antidote to illness a saint's level of belief in God's love and care is. "This trust in God," says the secretary, "was the secret of all her works." It is also, I suggest with her nuns and doctor, another part of the secret of her vitality and longevity.

When she is sixty, someone who works with her closely observes that Cabrini "enjoys perennial youth." In bouts, anyway. That winter to spring (1910–11) the malaria she has caught on missionary journeys, on top of her earlier conditions, keeps her in bed several months. Yet when she hears the Holy Spirit's call she is up and off. Her "last two years" God will stretch to almost three decades. Occasionally that will require a minor miracle.

Once, confined to bed and in a high fever, after seven days she has a dream or a vision of St. Joseph.

"I'm longing to receive Jesus in Holy Communion," she tells him. "If you could obtain for me to be free of this fever, for only an hour even, I could go."

The fever vanishes. She rushes downstairs and receives communion. An hour later the fever returns, but milder. It is the turning point. A few days later she is back at work.

Two years later she again collapses, in mid-March. Having made all the arrangements for her death, she lies calmly in what appear to be her final hours. Then, in the early hours of the next day, the feast of St. Joseph, there is an extraordinary change. She recovers.

A couple of years later, in 1915, on a train to Seattle, feverish with another malaria attack, she confides to her nun companion, "I didn't expect to make this trip again. But for some months the Lord has made me feel that He wants another project completed by me in Seattle. If He really wants it He will give me the strength. . . . It's true I'm not well, but I'd be worse if He didn't sustain me."

Sustain her he does—if at times barely—through a fury of persecution in Seattle, where even the bishop who invited her forbids her work. Eventually, after Cabrini has been wrung emotionally and physically to the last drop, Seattle gets a new hospital.

Not for nothing is Francesca Cabrini's lifelong motto: "I can do all things through Him who strengthens me." Her whole life is an encouragement that God really does choose the weak things of the world to do his mightiest works. Trained as a teacher but always longing to be a missionary, in her youth she is twice rejected by even a nonmissionary order, who explain, "Face it, Francesca. You're just not strong enough for a nun's life."

In 1880 a spiritual director who has held her back for seven years on a project of his choosing finally says, "You want to be a missionary. I don't know of any missionary orders for women, so found one yourself."‡ Just then her always shaky health col-

‡ Hers is not actually the first.

lapses; but she doesn't moan, "It's too late," just clings to her motto and says, "I'll look for a house."

Spiritually the thirty-year-old is ready. She has been formed during the preceding seven years, as all saints must be, by circumstances that either foster despair and cynicism or forge spiritual greatness. In her case she has carried the burden of straightening out a collapsing orphanage while working under the orders of the woman, probably certifiably insane, who is destroying it. From that debacle seven young women follow Cabrini as her first spiritual daughters.

By the time of her death in Chicago on December 22, 1917, sixty-seven institutions on three continents will be enlarging lives, rolling back the darkness of ignorance, poverty, illness, and prejudice. Among those her goodness touches are armies of street urchins and tenement dwellers in places like Newark, New Jersey, and New York City; disabled and working miners and their families in Scranton, Pennsylvania, and Denver, Colorado; Italian prisoners at Sing Sing and other penitentiaries; five thousand orphans in such cities as Los Angeles, New Orleans, New York, Denver, Seattle, Madrid, Paris, and London; upperclass boarding schools to influence those who can help Christianize their world in several Latin American countries; countless day schools in the Americas, Europe, and England; and one hundred thousand sick treated in the hospitals she founds in cities like Chicago, New York, and Seattle. Especially dear to her heart are the hostels for young women studying to be teachers that she establishes in her native Italy, knowing a teacher brought to God is an instrument that may touch hundreds, even thousands, of lives.

Along the way, she has also almost singlehandedly changed the image of Italians in the United States from despised "dagos" and "wops"—eleven of these "white niggers" are lynched just before her arrival in New Orleans—to people like any others with their own right to share in the American dream.

For the most part, God spares her the terrible burdens of

saints with the charism of healing, but occasionally he seems to use her in this way. A Mrs. de Luca knocks at the convent of a school founded by the saint in Rio de Janeiro. When the visitor learns Mother Cabrini is not in the country, she tells the nuns how she met the missionary on a ship crossing and confided her intense sorrow that after years of prayer she still has no children. Mother Cabrini ordered her to rejoice and have faith, "for you will have a son." Since Cabrini has that gift of many saints that often permits her to see the future, is this simply prophecy? Mrs. de Luca doesn't think so. She is accompanied by the son she insists "Mother Cabrini's prayers obtained for me from heaven."

Another incident is told under oath by Sister Maria Pastorelli for the Beatification Process. This Italian nun, at work in Rio, got smallpox and was nursed back to health by Mother Cabrini. Sometime later, Sister Maria, still teaching in Brazil, became ill with gastric troubles and headaches. Suddenly the sick nun seemed to see Mother Cabrini, who, in those days of slow, steamship travel, was definitely in Chicago. Sister Maria felt Mother Cabrini remove the wet compress from her forehead as she scolded the young nun affectionately, "Why are you lying here, my daughter? Get up and go about your duties."

A moment later, Sister Maria snapped out of the dream or vision. She found the cold compress inexplicably gone. More important, she was perfectly well.

While there is no need to make too much of the incident, it suggests that just as God sometimes sent his dead saints on healing errands to Francesca, he sent her while still alive— through a dream experience linked to ESP or the phenomenon known as bilocation—to carry his healing to Sister Maria.

On her many missionary journeys—most of them demanding sea travel of one whose near drowning as a child had left her with a lifelong fear of water—Mother Cabrini nourished her far-flung daughters with chatty, affectionate, and humor-studded letters. In these are mystical outbursts betraying her ardent love of God, like her passionate statement that the "whole world is too small for all" she longs "to do for Him." But it is not such words which made the world acclaim her a living saint, but her deeds—above all the radiant goodness which showed in her every act. The miracles during her lifetime—putting out a fire enveloping a building full of sleeping children with a great sign of the cross, or multiplying foodstuffs, money, even building supplies—were further signs.

After Mother Cabrini's death, from a burst blood vessel, God spoke in favor of holding her up before the world as a model follower of Jesus Christ by a number of inexplicable healings. One of the earliest that met all the Church's qualifications for an official miracle and was accepted for Mother Cabrini's beatification was the cure from blindness of Peter Smith, described in the Prologue to this book.

Here is the second official beatification miracle:

To the discomfiture of certain male biographers, Francesca Cabrini had a strong sentimental streak. Perhaps this was evidenced in the second beatification cure.

As a child, Francesca imagined the paper boats full of flowers she dropped into a river by her priest uncle's house were missionaries off to China.

Even as a child her longing to become a missionary was so intense that when someone teased, "Missionaries don't get any dessert, you know," Francesca promptly gave up all goodies, "to prepare myself." Yet if she had not been ordered to found her own group of missionaries by a priest who grasped something of her spiritual stature, Francesca Cabrini would probably never have reached her goal, since religious orders refused women with poor health like hers, who might prove merely a drain on their resources. With her mystic's view of reality, Francesca reacted strongly against this "sensible" outlook. She asked one order which had twice turned her down to refer their physical or personality rejects to her. If someone sincerely wanted to give herself to God, Mother Cabrini would work with her so she could succeed. "And I will *never,*" she promised her daughters, "send anyone away because of her health."

That open-door policy is probably the only way Italian Sister Delfina Grazioli got to be a Missionary Sister of the Sacred Heart. Anyone but Mother Cabrini would have rejected someone who had had a rotten digestive system even as a kid. After every meal, Delfina didn't just belch, her stomach cramped. Sometimes she vomited. But she got along well enough to even be sent out as a missionary to Seattle, where Mother Cabrini and her daughters had established another Columbus Hospital* and a big orphanage with its own school on Beacon Hill, overlooking Lake Washington.

About 1913—this is still during Mother Cabrini's lifetime—the disturbances in Sister Delfina's digestive organs became more acute; only twenty-four years old, during the next seven years, in addition to her overall digestive difficulties, she had all the pain of a serious gallbladder condition, which doctors eventually discovered was causing duodenal adhesions.

Let a physician who got to be on very familiar terms with Sister Delfina's interior describe what should have been the last four years of the young nun's life. Surgeon Milton D. Sturgis reported:†

●—◄●►—●

Sister Delfina was referred to me for an operation October 14, 1921, [after an X ray showing] adhesions [that is, scarred tissue which can create problems such as obstructing food's passage, etc.] around the pylorus, duodenum, gallbladder and colon. It was clear she had these adhesions because she had suffered previously from severe infection in these areas [the reader will want to remember, this is pre-antibiotic medicine].

* Today renamed for the saint.

† I occasionally expand his abbreviated medical phrases to clarify a medical term or otherwise make what he is saying more intelligible to us nonmedical readers. Generally I bracket my explanatory additions, but not always.

I removed the adhesions, as well as the gallbladder plus the appendix, which also was chronically inflamed.

[Sister Delfina] again came under my care when I operated on September 12, 1922, for obstruction in the area of the pylorus [that is, the outlet of the stomach to the small intestine]. I found extensive adhesions practically closing the pylorus radiating to the abdominal wall. This obstruction to the pylorus was so extensive it was thought advisible to do a gastro-enterostomy [a procedure in which a new opening from the stomach is created].

Following this operation she was for a time improved, but her symptoms then returned.

On the 22nd day of March, 1924, she was again operated on, at which time the opening from stomach to duodenum [small intestine] made in the second surgery was closed, while the upper four and a half inches of duodenum was removed.

. . . Her condition was not permanently improved, so again in February 1925 she was operated on by me for the fourth time for adhesions which produced an acute angulation of the duodenum with a physiological obstruction [that is, a blockage from a kinking of the intestine]. Again all the adhesions [that is, scarred tissue] were removed and I brought the upper part of the colon to where it belongs below the liver. As always her recovery from the surgery was without anything unusual but her general condition remained the same.

The general frailness of her physique, her lack of natural resistance and the unsatisfactory results attending the operation—[all made me] consider her case hopeless; and it seemed certain she would soon pass away. I remember that at that time I made such a statement to the authorities in the hospital.

The doctor who had referred Sister Delfina to the surgeon concurred with Dr. Sturgis that the case was "hopeless." When Delfina refused a proposed fifth surgery, this physician, Dr. Leede, did not push the idea, since no operation had made any real difference in her condition. Instead he advised she be sent to a house of rest in the country. This was done, but perhaps this stress-relieving move had been made too late: at any rate, it had no positive effect on Sister Delfina's digestive system.

Fevered, vomiting more and more frequently, and in severe pain, Delfina "declined rapidly." As her end neared, the bishop of Alaska took an interest in the dying young nun.

"Ask God for a miracle through the intercession of Mother Cabrini, your foundress," he advised. Delfina did, her religious community joining in. No improvement occurred all of November, and at the opening of December 1925, she hung between life and death. December 4, she asked to go to confession and receive the last sacraments to prepare herself for a good death. This was done on the fifth.

Invoking the intercession of their dearly loved foundress, the nuns—almost all of whom had personally known Mother Cabrini before her death this same month eight years earlier—and the orphans in their care began another round of prayers for Sister Delfina's healing; but even to her fellow nuns it seemed the most pressing prayers should be for "a happy death," because, as one later testified, "this outcome seemed inevitable."

Then, the night of December 13 to December 14, Sister Delfina had a dream. She was with her beloved Mother Cabrini, who was seated on a chair in the nuns' community room. A third nun, Sister Carmela, was there as well. With a luminous smile and happy laugh, Mother Cabrini pointed her finger at this nun and said to Delfina, "I'll send you with Mother Carmela."

Immediately Sister Delfina woke up. But behind it this numinous dream left no cure. Instead Delfina experienced more atrocious pain than ever, so much that she could no longer even talk, except for a word or two said so faintly that, to hear her, the listener had to put an ear to the dying woman's mouth.

In spite of all this suffering, Delfina had new hope, for Mother Carmela was in charge of the laundry, the garden, and the working men employed by the sisters. If Mother Cabrini said, "I'll send you with Mother Carmela," Sister Delfina reasoned this meant she was going to be capable of work. "It's certain I'm not going to die," she said to herself. "Mother Cabrini must be going to obtain my cure."

With these wishful or heroically hopeful thoughts, depending on one's point of view, she endured the intensified suffering which continued December 14, 15, and 16.

On the sixteenth the dying nun still had enough faith in the dream message to whisper to the community superior, "Mother, our Mother Foundress is fulfilling the Bishop of Alaska's request for a miracle."

The mother superior, a nun named Mother Tranquila, later testified, "Yet even as she said this to me her condition was so atrocious that she was writhing in agony. And her voice was so feeble, the words gasped with such difficulty that I paid no attention. She saw that I hadn't understood, so she made an effort and said another time, 'Our Mother Foundress is going to obtain the miracle that the bishop of Alaska has requested and cure me.'

"Hearing this from her and seeing that she was suffering immensely, I thought she was delirious and her death must be very near."

In her testimony, which I am translating from the Italian, the mother superior explains how she tried to be helpful to the young woman she believed delirious and in her death agony. First she prompted Sister Delfina to simply accept whatever God desired for her. Be indifferent to whether you're cured or about to die, she urged.

"Perhaps Jesus, your Divine Spouse, is near," she hinted.

In answer she says, "Sister gave me a marvelous, unusual smile."

It was all Delfina could manage.

In spite of her longing to tell her dream, she had choked out all the words she could. Now she could only abandon herself to her agony.

Meanwhile Mother Tranquila went to phone Mother Cabrini's daughters at the other Seattle establishments so they could all unite in prayers for Sister's death hour.

But she hung on.

Early the next morning a priest came to give her the blessing for the hour of death. Afterward, as usual, someone brought her a little cup of coffee solely for her to moisten her dry mouth. She had a little and did not vomit, as she usually did if she actually swallowed anything. The dreadful pain was also easing, even beginning to disappear bit by bit. Saying nothing of any of this, at ten o'clock that morning Delfina asked the infirmarian to bring her a little orange juice.

Once more alone, Delfina drank the juice. When it, too, was not vomited, she knew: the Mother Foundress had obtained her cure. But still she said nothing. At noon, as usual, they brought her weak tea. As always, it was not to drink, but to moisten her dehydrated mouth. Not only did this not come back when she drank it, but Sister Delfina was beginning to feel hungry. The pain was now entirely gone. In fact she no longer had any sense of illness.

Around three o'clock Mother Enrica, another nun, brought her a few sugared almonds, something she could suck to get a little saliva going in her dry mouth. To Mother Enrica's great surprise she found Sister Delfina sitting on the bed eating the grapes that were left by her bedside for the same purpose.

"What are you doing?" asked the startled nun.

"I'm eating grapes. I'm hungry." Then the hollow-eyed sister whose body had refused for so long to retain anything said, "Bring me something to eat. I'm cured."

Sugared almonds followed the grapes. Whatever they brought, she ate. That evening, she plowed her way through a full supper and felt strength begin to return to her emaciated body.

In her skeletal state, eating or not, she was ordered to stay in bed. But loudly proclaiming her miraculous cure, she begged the dead Francesca Cabrini to obtain for her the further grace to be out of bed on December 22, the date on which Cabrini had begun her heavenly life in 1917.

That grace, too, was granted.

December 22, Sister Delfina was in the chapel receiving communion. She continued to gain strength. And once well, she stayed well—better in fact than she had ever been.

Those most astonished by the recovery were the nun's physician and her surgeon.

Dr. Sturgis concludes his report quoted earlier by saying, "I can scarcely express my amazement at her final recovery and her restoration to normal health and activity." There is no doubt in his mind, he adds, that the cure was "miraculous in character and due to the spiritual means employed," not medical help.

Like Peter Smith, Sister Delfina Grazioli was at the ceremonies for Mother Cabrini's beatification. Until her death, at age seventy-seven, on November 25, 1967, the woman whose digestive system had been a mess even as a child remained a living symbol that Mother Cabrini wasn't kidding when she held out welcoming arms to would-be nuns with rotten health.

Following those 1938 ceremonies, healings through Francesca's intercession continued. In 1945, the year before Mother Cabrini's canonization, Theodore Maynard, a biographer assisted by the sisters, refers to a number of remarkable cures. A few of these include a child dying of peritonitis healed in Chicago; a young woman cured in 1938 of meningitis in Lodi, Italy, the affluent Lombard town where Mother Cabrini's family were solid citizens; a nun recovered inexplicably from heart problems in New York City; and a doctor classed by himself and his fellow physicians at Seattle's Columbus Hospital as "terminal" from an unnamed disease, who turned to Mother Cabrini and was healed.

When the Church settled on the cures that would undergo the rigid inquiry to meet canonization requirements, two healings from Cabrini's hometown were the winners. Both happened in Lodi in 1939, the year following Francesca's beatification.

Let me detail one of these as a final sample of the caliber of healings with which God continues to use weak, little Francesca Cabrini, the Mother Teresa of Calcutta of her day, to bless his world.

Paolo Pezzini had been kicked in the stomach by a horse as a youth. From that time he suffered from gallbladder trouble. His symptoms at times included severe pain accompanied by hemorrhages. A strong, rangy-looking man, by the time he was thirty-two he actually spent a lot of time sick in bed.

Employed as chauffeur to physician Dr. Giampiero Pedronini, Paolo was treated by his boss with various medications the doctor thought might help. Relief was always temporary, however. In fact his problem was getting increasingly acute as years passed, and on December 26, 1938, while he was driving Dr. Pedronini's car, he was suddenly stabbed by such ferocious pains that he lost control of the car, which swerved into a canal.

Somehow, in spite of his pain, Pezzini got out of the car without injury, just soaked to the skin. This seems to have started a cold which within six weeks had become double pneumonia, as diagnosed by Dr. Pedronini on February 13, 1939. From the fourteenth to the sixteenth, in spite of his employer's treatments, the chauffeur's condition worsened. Besides the chills, fever, and abdominal pain, he now showed signs of a poisoning of his whole system. On the seventeenth he suffered cardiac arrest.

Dr. Pedronini felt there was no more hope. The patient was given the last sacraments. On the nineteenth the kidneys failed, so Paolo "became convulsive and delirious, then passed into . . . unconsciousness and coma."

All treatment beyond making Paolo comfortable was suspended as useless.

Meanwhile the friends of the patient, along with Dr. Pedronini, who knew better than anyone that only a miracle could save Paolo Pezzini, were making a novena to Blessed Francesca Cabrini, asking for either a healing or that his period of suffering be shortened.

On the evening of February 20, the comatose man was surrounded by friends praying the rosary and invoking Mother Cabrini. Also present was Father Caesar Barzaghi, a Barnabite priest, who was reciting the Church's prayers for the dying.

Suddenly the man in the coma opened his eyes. He sat up in bed.

"What's going on?" He gaped at the priest in solemn stole holding the prayer book.

"Why are you all here?" he puzzled, looking at his friends. In the general awe and clamor of excited cries and explanations, someone ran to fetch Dr. Pedronini, who lived nearby.

He came in and immediately noticed Paolo had regained his natural color and his sight and was breathing freely with no sign of mucous-filled lungs. He was also moving with the ease of one who has no pain, indicating the uremia was gone. His mind was clear, if baffled to learn that he had just been on his deathbed moments before.

Asking the group to step outside for a minute, Dr. Pedronini gave his employee a thorough going-over. The lungs were clear. Kidneys were okay. Heart okay. To his astonishment, the doctor found there had been an instantaneous and perfect cure from the double pneumonia and every one of its deadly complications.

Still wanting to be prudent, the physician asked Paolo to remain in bed quietly for a few days. At the end of that period, he went over the chauffeur's body with a fine-tooth comb. The scrupulously careful examination only confirmed the complete healing. Paolo returned to work. He had no relapses.

More incredible still, as weeks and months passed, it became clear that in the second Paolo Pezzini was turned from a man in his last moments to a well one, he was also cured of his chronic gallbladder troubles. He simply never had another gallbladder attack.

This cure, instantaneous, perfect, and permanent, was seen by the Church's investigating medical commission as a very good sign that if Francesca Cabrini was crazy about God, if she literally couldn't do enough for him—it's safe to say the feeling was mutual.

❧ 6 ❧

"Who Said You're Going to Lose Your Sight?"

The apprentice machinist is handling a glowing red ball of molten lead. Suddenly it explodes in his face. From forehead to chin, from left ear to right, his flesh, kissed by the fiery metal, melts away. The horrified boss applies great gobs of Vaseline* and sends him home. The night is agony. The next morning, his face one great swollen blister, the condition of his eyes sends him rushing to an eye doctor. Grimacing in displeasure, the specialist orders dark glasses at all times and eight days in a dark room. Then he'll take another look.

Sitting in pain in the dark lasts one day. Young and impatient, unable to stand "being cooped up," as he later explains (I translate his French):

❧

I asked my fiancée to accompany me to the Oratory [literally: place of prayer; here referring to the Shrine of St. Joseph in Montreal]. Minus seventeen degrees outside or not, I resisted all efforts to dissuade me.

At the Oratory I asked Fr. Clément for Br. André.

"He's having lunch at the monastery." Without being discouraged, I [went down the hill and] rang the monastery bell. Father Deguire, who answered, recoiled at the sight of me. I asked to see Br. André. He wasn't available. I

* A much recommended treatment for burns to the middle of the twentieth century; today felt to do more harm than good, by cutting off air.

pleaded, argued and suddenly the good Brother himself came out into the hall inquiring what was going on.

"Brother André," I said, "you can see I'm too young to lose my sight; you can do something!"

He replied and I give you every word exactly as he said it: "Who said you're going to lose your sight? You have confidence in St. Joseph's intercession? Good! Go to the church, attend mass, go to communion in honor of St. Joseph, continue your [medical] remedies. Add to them a drop of oil of St. Joseph† and make the following invocation: St. Joseph, pray for us. All will go well. Good day now. Have confidence!"

I did exactly what he said. After mass, I went to eat a little something in a restaurant. Seeing me, the lady who ran the place was touched to tears.

That evening, my fiancée carried out applying the oil and invoking St. Joseph. The next morning, oh, wonder, lifted as if they were leaves of cellophane, the scarred, blistered flesh came off my face; the area [even] of the eyelids was completely healed—my appearance, in fact, was as perfect as one could desire: there was no sign of wound, healing flesh or scar; no pain. I went to work. And what a stupor [I caused] among my workmates!

The following Sunday, I returned to the Oratory to thank the good Brother André, who said, "Thank St. Joseph; continue to pray. Good day!" The most, well to me, comical thing was the lady at the restaurant, who kept asking me, "But are you really the gentleman who had his face so burnt last Sunday? I can't believe my eyes!" And she told the thing to everyone who would listen.

† From the votive lamp burning before St. Joseph's statue in the shrine. Such things have no intrinsic healing power.

Lucien Galarneau's testimony from the dossier of the beatification Cause, dated April 23, 1944, cites a number of witnesses to the 1925 cure.

But did eighty-year-old Brother André Bessette—who, after all, gave only sixty seconds of instructions and didn't even use the words "I'll pray for you," let alone lay hands on the injured man—have anything to do with the cure? It would seem unlikely. Until one looks at the life of the featherweight (only five feet, three inches and fragile-boned, he weighed less than many children) French-Canadian known universally as "the Wonder-Worker of Montreal."

For some twenty-eight years (beginning when he was almost sixty), Blessed André Bessette's typical day saw him open by 8 A.M. his little eight by ten "office" in the shrine to St. Joseph erected by grateful recipients of favors. Standing all day for six and a half hours or more, he received several hundred people (two hundred to four hundred was usual, seven hundred one of his heaviest days), at a rate of about forty an hour, thus most for only a minute or two. Ignoring the chronic pain in his own stomach, the frequent headaches and, in his late eighties and early nineties, heart problems that sometimes caused him to pass out and necessitated his being carried up the ninety-nine steps from monastery to shrine, he listened with bent head and lowered eyes to the world's troubles. Then, with a voice so permanently damaged he sometimes bled from the strain of hours of use, he whispered recommendations as banal as those received by the young burn victim.

"I came all this way and waited in line all these hours for *that!*" many thought; yet few left untouched, captured for God many times by what the old man was: a saint. Albert Cousineau, for one, has written‡ how as a ten-year-old boy with health problems he feared might prevent his becoming a priest, he came to Brother André expecting not only lengthy attention,

‡ In the booklet "Brother André. As I Knew Him."

but an instant miracle on his behalf. He got a few seconds' advice on prayer in a feeble, if affectionate, voice. Then "Next," and he found himself outside the door. Disappointed, the ten-year-old decided to hang around until the brother was completely free to attend properly to his important problem. But at day's end along came a very sick man who obviously had an appointment. Since Br. André never closed his office door, the boy had no problem eavesdropping as the Holy Cross brother consoled and prayed with a man suffering from terminal cancer of the jaw. Soon young Albert slipped away.

"I was bathed in a profound peace," the later bishop of Cap-Haïtien remembers, "my mind . . . at ease."

Occasionally Brother André laid hands on (children or men only) in a manner which often seems to have little relation to what we today know as the beneficial physical effects of loving touch.* While at times he rubbed vigorously an affected part such as an arm, leg, or neck either with the oil of St. Joseph or a medal of this saint to whom he recommended most of his cures, other times he simply passed his bare hand over the area without touching the individual. On one occasion even Fr. Clément, whose eyesight had been restored by André's prayers questioned, "Surely you don't think you are going to make his feet work by rubbing these boards?" It was a case of a man so badly injured that his feet seemed only attached to his body by a bit of skin. The man's suffering was so great that he had two wooden boxes constructed to protect each foot from the jostlings necessary to be carried through the crowds to Brother André. Now the saint was rubbing these boxes! He kept a number of ill men in his own little room so they would not have to come and go. Perhaps this case was one of those, for the account says the brother spent some of his time for three or four days rubbing prayerfully on the wood. Then he said, "Now we're going to

---

* See, for instance, *Therapeutic Touch* by Dolores Krieger, R.N. and professor of nursing.

take off these boxes and I believe your feet will be in fine shape." They were.

The oil, the medals—none of what he did in this line was necessary, he agreed when questioned. True, in some cases he might indicate the rubbing helped increase the circulation of the blood. And to one individual he said his hands produced the same effect as St. Joseph's oil—which is as close as he ever came to admitting he had the gift of healing. But, most commonly, he explained the value of the oil, the medals, or other tools of his trade as helping the sufferer to think about St. Joseph. From such thoughts and meditations, said André, "arises confidence in his intercession." That people found it healing just to receive André's attention or even be near him would never have entered that tired old head.

Unlike nonsaint healers, who usually spend their time (up to an hour) with a client, eyes closed, concentrating on the treatment or prayer, most of Blessed André's interviews passed, on his part, in questioning† if the health seeker's relationship with God was what it should be. To his Holy Cross superior, the same Albert Cousineau who had once feared he could never become a priest, Brother André confided that if his visitors were on good terms with God, he began by advising such things as daily communion ("God can refuse us hardly anything when he is in our hearts," he liked to say).

That he also advised prayer for the intercession of St. Joseph is well known. Less understood is how the saint saw St. Joseph. For André, God used St. Joseph as a bearer of healing. But in André's eyes, St. Joseph was still, as he put it to Cousineau, only

† Work by the late London researcher C. Maxwell Cade and associates, using electroencephalographs to monitor brain waves, shows that individuals of very high spiritual attainments can be actively engaged in nonmeditative activities, even intellectual debate on a subject like physics, while maintaining the brain waves associated with a contemplative state. This suggests that in cases in which individuals are cured by seemingly very mundane contact or conversation with a healer-saint, prayer *is* actually involved, because the saint's basic union with God is seldom, if ever, disturbed on the deepest level of his or her being, in spite of the activities on the upper levels of consciousness.

an entrance hall to the mansion. The mansion was Christ, the King of Kings.

If Brother André sensed his petitioners were fallen-away Catholics, the good old man told them the story of the Prodigal Son. To all his visitors, incipient saint and great sinner alike, he recounted in simple words, seasoned with the tenderhearted saint's own sobs, the story of Christ's Crucifixion for love of each of us.

He did this, he told his superior, because it is hard to love God if we don't often think about what he endured for us.

Although he worked thousands of cures, Brother André encouraged many people not to seek "an end to your trials but only grace to bear them well," since "God will have an eternity to console you for any suffering here." To some (not all) priests, nuns, and his fellow brothers, he often flatly refused prayers for healing, declaring their vocation demanded reparatory suffering. Obviously he was not a man who had any ego need to say what people want to hear!

To a number of visitors he groused, "There's absolutely nothing wrong with you!" However taken aback or even insulted, these people found they were cured of the most diverse ailments even as he spoke to them in this way that adroitly forestalled any adulation of himself as their healer.

Men friends who had been cured or converted by one they considered a saint, by turn drove him during evenings around the area (except on Fridays, which he reserved for meditation on the Passion of Christ), so he could call on five or six more sick. "Often," one of these helpers remarks, "Brother André was in worse shape than the people I drove him to see." Still the feeble visitor took no precautions even with virulently infectious diseases. That, to him, would have lacked charity. He was also fearless even on the iciest roads. He loved fast cars, it's recalled, because that way he could call on more sick. Once, a friend remembers, their car was almost turned over by the terrible winds of a winter storm; coming back, ferocious lightning menaced them. The driver was terrified, but Brother André, tranquilly saying his rosary, didn't even seem to notice. He lived what he used to say: "When one puts oneself in God's hands, one gives oneself to whatever He wills."

His friends, like the sick he cheered by these visits, found him good company. Quick with a witticism and gay of heart, according to his insistence that merriment was of God, sadness of the devil, a friend has recalled that with little jokes and the laughter of a child the saint covered his pitiful health and piercing fatigue.

Home anywhere from ten to midnight, the helpers still loved to follow the indefatigable brother to the chapel for his late-night, slow, and prayerful Way of the Cross.

"A good evening: they were so glad to see you," André would say after the hour or so of prayer in farewell, "and one cured someone ill," spoken, the friend testifies, as if *he,* not André, had been the carrier of grace.

His friends gone, André prayed in his tiny cell, according to the sick men he let stay overnight. The little room had an opening so he could see the tabernacle in the chapel. Often he returned there to pray penitentially, the tired old body erect, arms out in the shape of a cross. Exhausted, he would fall asleep, then wake and pray again. Once, when a fellow religious asked solicitously if the old brother couldn't just offer God his well-deserved sleep as a prayer, André said solemnly, "If you knew the state of those who ask my prayers, you wouldn't suggest that."

Sleeping often only a couple of hours, some nights not at all,‡ he was up again before 5 A.M. to pray some more. By preference he liked to serve six or eight masses a morning, but in later years, with his office hours, he could only attend two before he had to grab a quick breakfast and open the door to the first sick.

If his prayers took up most of his spare moments starting

‡ Unreasonable as this seems, experiments with electroencephalographs show that certain states of the brain in prayer can apparently give the benefits of sleep.

long before he joined a religious order (an early employer already remarked this habit), it was not a case of intercessory prayer being part of his healing ministry. His healing apostolate was the overflow of his prayer, the love in deeds of his union with Christ. And those prayers were so efficacious, his friends saw, because of his great, simple, and rocklike faith. That faith left him calm while hurtling through the night on icy roads. It let him remark, "Dying today or tomorrow, what's the difference?" to shaken friends in New England, when his heart almost gave way in his late eighties.

Throughout his life, he did things which in one with less faith would have been superstitious or (recall rubbing the boxes) the act of a madman, but in his holiness were symbolic gestures of childlike confidence in God's goodness and the intercessory claim on God's heart of his saints. Thus to a group of religious just entering the area who asked his prayers for needed vocations, he asked, "How many do you want?" They looked at each other.

"Twenty," one ventured.

"Well, cut out a paper chain with twenty figures and put it around the neck of St. Joseph's statue in your chapel."

They got their postulants. Exactly twenty.

A priest was sweating blood to pay off the mortgage on an orphanage. Brother André asked, "Whose name does the place bear?"

"St. Joseph's."

"Write a paper: 'St. Joseph, pay your bills,' and put it up in front of his statue." With trepidation, the moneyless priest put a much politer note to St. Joseph before the statue. From the most unlikely source he could imagine, money came to pay the mortgage.

To buy the mountain next door to the Holy Cross School so the healing shrine to St. Joseph could be built there, Brother

André and friends "seeded" St. Joseph medals all over the area. Stubborn owners eventually capitulated.

The gestures, of course, did not cause the events; they merely expressed the real mountain mover, André's faith and unceasing prayer. In that faith the tiny religious could say, "If one knew what recompense awaited one in heaven for the least suffering borne well, one would demand on one's knees to suffer." But he was aware that most people are not spiritually mature enough for reparatory suffering, even for their own ills and sins, to say nothing of suffering—as André did—for others'. Filled with the compassion of Christ, "who healed all who came," the old brother gave himself to prayer and to penance for the ill and the sorrowing. He lived in the hope that healing would either open them to God's reality and love or establish them in grace.

Perhaps the definitive source of information, including numerous statistics, on Blessed André and his cures, is the out-of-print, eleven-hundred-page French work *Le Frère André, 1845–1937,* by scholar Canon Étienne Catta. For a typical year of André's ministry, 1926, two of Catta's figures hint at the magnitude of the humble old man's work: 7,334 people go to the effort of writing or coming in person to speak of favors received at the shrine; 1,611 of these are physical cures. Many who are healed never write or return.

Some do not even stop to say a word of thanks, like the man who arrives with legs so lifeless they swing like boughs in a breeze as he maneuvers his crutches. Cured completely, he rushes down the hill and jumps onto a tram. A friend of André's watches from a window at the shrine. No one has even gotten the cured man's name. Around this time, André's mail ran to eighty thousand letters a year. Cures reported included every possible human ill, from alcoholism to gross physical deformity or the last stages of heart disease or cancer. By no means were all healed. Some failures he put down to sin, like the blind man weeping for a cure who refused to give up another man's wife;

many he ascribed simply to destiny, since we all have a time to move into the next life.

It became necessary at times to send the elderly wonder-worker away for a rest. Often this was to the United States, where André had two married sisters, a brother, and cousins. Unfortunately on these trips his presence was usually discovered, like the time a cousin invited him to a dinner at a New England hotel and found that a thousand people had joined them. At the impromptu prayer meeting, a miracle occurred. Such events led more pilgrims to Montreal and made André's life ever more a holocaust to others' healing. Ordered to Pasadena, California, in 1921 for a week's rest, he was asked by the pastor of St. Andrew's Church there to pray for some people. Five hundred showed up and seven known miracles took place, including cures of the blind, the deaf, and someone whose crutches the saint carried back to Montreal to add to the two roomfuls already left as mute witnesses by those cured.

"Brother Andrew cures only by prayer," the Los Angeles papers reported.

"St. Joseph is the intercessor," he corrected. When a man in Montreal blurted out, "St. Joseph's worthless; you're the one who gets graces for us . . . ," the saint became so upset he shook with chills and had to be put to bed.

Sheltered under the glory of St. Joseph, the tiny, seemingly ageless old man never seemed to have any idea he personally had a thing to do with the thousands of pilgrims, the cures, or the erection of the largest church in the world dedicated to St. Joseph.

"Those people are so stupid to think Brother André works miracles," he complained often. "The good Lord works miracles. St. Joseph's prayers obtain them." To avoid such misplaced attention, he made himself scarce on big feasts or processions outside office hours. He liked particularly to hide behind the high altar, where he could pray for hours unseen. When a homilist on one big occasion eulogized "the venerable old man who presides over this sanctuary," André completely misunderstood. "How well he preached about St. Joseph!" he remarked happily.

If he "considered the impossible not at all unfeasible," as someone said, his expectant faith, like his compassion, was rooted in his French-Canadian backwoods heritage and tested in the crucible of personal suffering. In truth Brother André Bessette is one of the most unlikely of healers, as must be evident to anyone familiar with studies of such people. He had neither health nor energy to give. Charming with friends, he was shy and had little personal charisma with strangers. To avoid adulation, he further affected an irascibility that often offended even while he cured. Finally, his whole life from birth was one of such physical weakness, radical poverty, and neediness, that he seems more a candidate for healing than one able to dispense it.

The eighth child of a poor rural family, Alfred, as he was christened, was such a pitiful specimen at birth that he was baptized on the spot. Possibly he was born with some defect in his stomach. He failed to thrive physically in spite of an exceptionally nurturing mother, who, rather than aggravated by his weakness, loved best her puniest offspring. Fatherless at nine, by twelve his mother was also dead, a victim of TB brought on by poverty and grief. The relative who took him in was a robust, hearty man who frowned when Alfred couldn't work as he did. In fact, try as he would, Alfred proved too weak for every job, whether baker's or shoemaker's apprentice in Quebec, factory work in several New England towns or even such easy jobs as horse groomer. People liked him but had to let him go when tasks proved beyond his strength. His big-hearted mother, known for her lovely smile and quick song, had seen her ten living children split among relatives after her husband's tragic death under a falling tree; yet she never became embittered or despaired of God's love. An utter failure at life, Alfred's poverty, too, only drew him deeper into the heart of God, with its mysteries of suffering and healing, poverty and grace.

Almost totally illiterate, he came to the Congregation of the Holy Cross, an order dedicated to education, recommended by his parish priest as no less than a saint. But, again, he could only agree with their evaluation that he had nothing to give. He neither could teach nor was he robust enough for manual chores. He could not even make a claim to sacrifice if they took him. For having succeeded at nothing in the world, he had nothing to give up. Holy Cross turned him down, then relented. After his novitiate, they declared that his health made him too great a liability to be kept. Finally, they accepted him as a sort of charity case when his spiritual director harrumphed that if Alfred, now become André in honor of his old pastor, became too weak to work at all, he certainly could still pray for the rest of them. That he knew how to do.

Assigned to answer the door, the new porter remained the same miserable physical specimen. He was unable to digest much more than flour stirred into boiling water. Yet he found the energy to race all over the boarding school to summon this pupil or that priest. He also delivered the laundry, ran everyone's errands, and washed and waxed miles of floor. He was the last to bed, because he had to lock up at night. Somehow, amid all this, he maintained a prodigious prayer schedule and quietly carried on a vast, discreet apostolate to the sick.

For his humility, one suspects, God would always leave him in the utmost poverty, whether of physical health, learning, of status and ability as the world judges, even of reputation (many would call him "the old nut" and "charlatan"). His very personality showed the deprivations and poverty, of his life. The backwoods semi-illiterate remained marked by shyness and timidity. If his union with God let him remark with assurance to comfort someone, "It isn't necessary to study for fifteen years to love God," the fact remains that he lived with students and teachers and always remained aware of his inadequacies. He was uncomfortable, to a degree, with the learned and the important. He was overly sensitive to slights even though he bore them charitably. He hid unease under brusqueness.*

And to further humble the humblest of men during the last few years of his lifetime (he lived to ninety-two), the nervous and physical strain of standing on his feet listening to his endless stream of petitioners—some of whom would have made anyone impatient, so inane were their requests or remarks†— was sometimes so great that a quick retort escaped him.

"I've made someone cry again," he would sorrow in his "feeble, hoarse, almost extinct voice," often weeping himself in distress and begging his confessor to tell him whether it was "all right" for him to dare receive communion.

"Will you pray for my conversion?" he felt the need to petition on his deathbed. Out of that spiritual poverty, that naked, hungry dependence on God for sustenance and healing, have come so many thousands of miraculous cures, even with a second chapter I can give only a brief sampling of the healings during his lifetime and since his death in 1937.

---

* How much of this was the result of shyness and how much deliberately to stave off those who wanted to idolize him is impossible to separate, but his Holy Cross confreres believe shyness played a role.

† For instance the girls who ask him to prevent their brother's marriage because he supports them and they do not want to go to work; the man who inquires whether it is magic or hypnotism that works the cures; or the woman who claims God owes her a healing at once because she goes to daily mass.

❧ 7 ❧

Wonders in Montreal

I was very sick. According to my doctor I was going to die this same night [this is 1923 or 1924] of peritonitis. Azarias Claude, my boss, brought Brother André to me. At this time, I had been unconscious for three days.

The first knowledge I had of the brother's presence was his shaking my hand three times. He asked, "How are you doing?" I replied with a groan. Shaking my hand again, he repeated, "Things not so good?" Then I replied, "They're really bad." The third time, still holding my hand and squeezing it, he said to me, "It's going to get better."

At this moment, I experienced a sensation of relief, as if a weight broke loose from my brain to slide down my shoulders, along my body and depart through my feet. . . . I asked Brother André, "Am I going to sleep?"

"Yes, you're going to sleep and tomorrow morning you're coming to the Oratory." I asked, "Will I be *capable* of coming to the Oratory?"

"If you're not sick, there's nothing to prevent you."

Then Brother André, accompanied by Mr. Claude, left my bedroom. The nurse returned. She took my temperature, which had become normal. She telephoned the doctor, who told her, "I'll be right over. Prepare his wife, because when the temperature falls that means death will follow quickly."

——◆——

[The doctor arrived and found the "dying man" sleeping peacefully.]

——◆——

. . . I slept the entire night until nine-thirty in the morning, when Mr. Claude woke me up, saying, "Get dressed; we're going to the Oratory."

I felt very well. I dressed. The nurse made no objection to this visit. Mr. Claude drove me in his car to the foot of the mountain. We went up from there to the shrine on foot [note that this is ninety-nine steps] and I was able to climb without any fatigue. In Brother André's office I said simply, "Good morning, Brother."

"Good morning, sir," he replied.

——◆——

The rest of the account tells nothing more dramatic than Brother André's counsel to get a medal of St. Joseph. The man who should be dead goes to the gift shop and buys one. He returns to ask the saint if it's okay to eat, since he's hungry. The saint says, "Sure. Eat whatever you want. You'll come and see me again."

At home, the nurse has orders he should have nothing to eat. He sneaks something anyway while she is taking a nap, but is caught with a bowl of tomato soup. Telephoned by the nurse, the doctor says emphatically, "If he wants to die, let him go ahead and eat." He eats and, by evening, the doctor throws in the towel: "As a physician," he says, "I cure with medicines. But Brother André can work miracles."

Only then, says Moses Roberts in his testimony before the beatification tribunal, does it hit him that the simple, undramatic events of the past twenty-four hours actually add up to a miracle.

"You'll come see me again," Brother André had said. Moses does. An honest man, he confides: "I know you cured me, but I

still have no confidence in you and I don't want to be a hypo-
crite."

Normally any reference to the saint himself doing anything
puts the little brother in a fury, but this time he only says,
"What would I have to do to give you confidence?" and Roberts
says he'd like to see someone's cure with his own eyes.

"If you come more often to the Oratory, you'll have the
chance to see something." André smiles. Then "Next." Moses
drops by daily from then on. And the fourth or fifth day after
his conference with Brother André, the brother calls him into
the little office.

A man about thirty years old arrives, an English-speaking
veteran of World War I. For the past ten years or so he has
borne his war wound, a forearm completely bent back and rigid
against the upper arm. Brother André assumes an irascible air.
"Do you understand French?" he questions.

"Yes."

"Take off your coat." This requires help, and it is Moses who
gives it.

"Arms at your side!" Brother André barks in the manner of a
sergeant at drill. Grabbing the stiff arm with one hand, with the
other he strikes a blow full strength to the elbow joint. Immediately the dead forearm falls to the man's side. Without missing a
beat, the tiny brother continues his commands: "Arms in the
air, arms behind your back, arms straight out. . . ." With complete suppleness the arm, dead these many years, functions perfectly. Then the saint grumps, as much to Roberts as to the war
veteran, "You're not sick: why do you come here making me lose
my time?" Hastily, without any help, the newly healed individual grabs his clothes and clears out. Roberts scurries away too,
but as Brother André has undoubtedly foreseen, he will be back,
three to five nights a week, to put himself at the disposal of the
ministry that saved his life: he has seen with his own eyes and
he believes.

Photographs of the dead André in his coffin will clearly show the walls of the shrine literally "papered" with crutches hung there by those cured through his intercession. A typical case is that of Joseph Jette, twenty-two years old when the scaffolding he is climbing collapses, leaving him with a fractured spinal column: he will be a cripple for life, say physicians. At first his mother keeps the pair going by selling off some property. Soon they are destitute and faith brings them to Brother André. The young workingman must be carried up the steep steps to the shrine. "After praying for several minutes," Joseph recalls, "I went to see Brother André; he ordered me to put down my crutches and walk. I obeyed. I was cured!"

The mother, the son, onlookers all wept. Brother André disappeared without a word.

One of André's many friends was due for an operation: a cancerous ulcer was eating away his thumb. Even a touch caused profuse bleeding. Brother André rubbed the diseased part a moment, and lo, once more a perfect thumb! He joked, "The remedy you've been using relieved the pain for a minute; the doctor relieved you of your money; now St. Joseph has relieved you of everything!"

While his cures of wage earners favored the poor, Blessed André also cured a number of medical men. His own physician, Dr. Lionel Lamy, one of those, was treating a case of fatal diphtheria and caught the deadly disease. Brother André arrived at the doctor's home that evening worn out, holding the banisters with both hands so he could pull himself up the stairs.

"It appears you're sick," he said to his doctor. "I'll give you a rubbing." For about a quarter of an hour he rubbed the sick man's throat.

"His hand," later recalled Dr. Lamy, "was cold and rough."

"Courage! Have confidence in St. Joseph."

The night passes very well for the sick man. In the morning he coughs up a great deal and is saved. Several days later, he discovers Brother André has left a little note that twits him good-humoredly: "What do you think of a doctor who gets himself cured by a charlatan?"

Besides helping men who needed their health for livelihood or good works, Brother André also seems to have favored children in his cures. For instance there is his friend Camille Gravelle's nineteen-month-old child who swallows lye, burning the interior of mouth, throat, and esophagus. Even after six months of medical care, the child's esophagus is so contracted that only a few drops of milk can be taken at one time—and that with the aid of a tube. Brother André declares she will be cured. Soon another doctor is shaking his head and mumbling, "I don't know what the little guy did!"

Alphonse Metivier, one of the boys who will grow up to join the Holy Cross Order and become a missionary in Bengal, witnesses in 1963 that as a young student his vocation was in peril due to his deafness. Sitting under the professor's very nose, he still couldn't hear. "My parents," he testified, "brought me to see Brother André at the College of Notre-Dame. We prayed together for St. Joseph's intercession for about ten minutes while the brother rubbed my ear with a medal. My father heard a little cracking sound in my ear. I heard!"

Then there is the two-and-a-half-year-old whose parents have been told he must have eye surgery. "Will you guarantee this will save his eyes?" the father has asked the doctor.

"No, those eyes are finished," is the heartless reply. The mother, Mrs. Albert Cardinal, later recalls: "I took my poor little one . . . ; I put him in the arms of Brother André and he took him . . . and said that there was nothing wrong. He [the son] has wonderful eyes. . . . He has never had any [more] eye trouble. . . ."

A child paralyzed from polio is carried in. Brother André orders Mrs. Comtois, the mother, to have little Rita walk. The toddler is afraid to try.

"But I've put your boo-boo in my pocket," the saint encourages. Nothing doing! The poor mother leaves discouraged, carrying her two-year-old. But when they reach the sidewalk below the shrine, Rita demands to be put down and immediately begins to walk.

A young Holy Cross scholastic is brought in by a priest.

"What's that on your face?"

"Eczema, and the doctor says he can't do anything more." He is told to rub himself with a medal and drink a bit of the oil from St. Joseph's lamp "to purify the blood." Quackery? Whatever, the young man follows the instructions, and the next morning his skin is perfect and remains so.

From California a mother brings a child of six. The boy is in a plaster corset from which a shaft of iron juts out to grasp his head. He suffers from degeneration of the spinal column. The mother says to the tiny old man, "I have confidence in St. Joseph and in you to help my child."

"He's cured," Brother André replies simply.

The woman of faith immediately begins trying to wrench the child out of his plaster dungeon. Father Clément has himself had his eyesight given back through André's hands, but he protests, "Watch out, Brother André, or you'll be dealing with the police."

"You ought to have more confidence in St. Joseph," retorts André. But Clément worries, What if the boy takes off his support and collapses? Even if the mother forgives André, what about the father? Especially if the child sustains further injury from being without his brace—it can't just be slipped back on—it would be understandable that the out-of-towners ask the police to close the shrine as one of those bogus places where charlatans encourage people, to their injury, to ignore medical help. Trying to deflect the mother from her purpose, the priest urges her to go pray about the matter. She goes into the chapel, followed a moment later by both Father Clément and Brother André. Has she vanished? No, from the sacristy comes plenty of noise. She has put the child on the counter and with whatever comes to hand, she is pounding relentlessly on the plaster, breaking it open. Out of deference to the priest, André is silent. But the child freed, he gives him a hand down, and orders, "Walk!" The child does. Whereupon a new witness intervenes and demands, to prove the cure, that the little boy climb on a chair and *jump* to the ground. Three times the child does; then he runs off to joyfully race up and down the walk by the chapel. Father Clément finds his legs trembling uncontrollably. As for the audacious witness, he says: "Father, I want to go to confession. It's been a long time. . . ."

André prays for some little ones at a distance. For instance the eight-month-old whose pneumonia has gone into meningitis; the right arm and foot are paralyzed; the poor head oscillates continuously on the pillow. The doctor says the baby will not last this night. The nurse counsels relatives to consult André. He sends word to rub the child wherever he has symptoms with a medal of St. Joseph. From the first contacts of the medal, the head stops its movement; the next morning, the limbs work again. Only a fool, of course, will be deflected by the rubbing from considering Brother André's prayers the real cause of the change. The physician is the first to call it "a miracle," according to the mother, Mrs. Armand Grothe.

Mothers were another group who could always count on André's compassion. Rather than a number of capsulized examples, I give one case in some detail because it shows the impossibility of suggestion, and the power of saints to heal at a distance. A very early cure of his ministry, it was done when very few—certainly neither the recipient nor her husband—knew Brother André had the gift of healing. He was known then merely as the good-natured little porter of the Holy Cross boys' school in Montreal.

In that guise he opens the door one day around 1880 (André is then about thirty-five) to a dour man who answers to his "How are you? How are things going at home?" with "What does that matter to you?" There to see two sons, the visitor stalks off. When he passes the brother on his way out after the visit, André confronts him: "You seem in a bad mood?"

"I've good reason for it."

"What's the trouble?"

"I've got two boys in school here that cost me a bundle; my wife has been sick for years, so I have to have a nurse for her; the doctors cost me. . . ." As he spills out these troubles, with the gait of a man in a hurry, he keeps walking toward his carriage. André follows him all the way. He says, "At this very hour, things are better at your home. You'll give me news [about it] the next time you come to see your boys. So long."

The pressured husband drives away, he reports years later, paying no attention to what the Holy Cross porter had said. On his two- or three-hour drive to his home, he has many other things to mull over.

At that home, at the moment the little porter is speaking to her husband, the sick woman, bedridden for several years, suddenly says to her nurse, "Bring me a chair. I want to sit up."

"But you can't get up," the nurse objects. "You aren't capable."

The patient answers, "Yes, I am capable. I feel better." The chair is brought. The wife next says she thinks she would like to take the air on the porch. Would someone bring her chair out there. And the bedridden woman walks out to the porch, seats herself, and waits for her husband to bring her news of her sons.

As he nears home, the husband has no expectation of anything but finding his wife in bed. He has not thought of Brother André's remark at all. But as he pulls into his property, where the house, with a big porch, sits well back from the road, he notices someone on the porch. "Who could that be?" he wonders. The nearer he gets, the more it seems to resemble his wife.

When he sees it *is* his wife, he drops the reins, leaves horse and carriage, and runs to the porch. Only then will he give thought to André.

Years later, as an old man, and his wife still in good health, he will confide the whole story to Azarias Claude, one of André's co-workers. Claude will relate it to Brother André, who admits: yes, it is true.

Another group who seem to have a special place in Brother André's heart are those who have no faith. In fact he will tell a friend that he believes whereas individuals like the man healed on his twenty-second visit to the shrine are often people of great faith who are tested in the fire, so to speak, to increase their virtue even more, many instant healings are given to those with no faith. This is to heal them of their spiritual weakness. Again, I give just one example in some detail to stand for a whole group of healings. I give the testimony of Sister Saint-Jacques of the Order of Sisters of the Holy Family as she gave it in 1958 (my translation from the French):

I was sick at the mother house [at Sherbrooke, Quebec, Canada] since 1925. All the doctors had said my case was incurable. In 1934, driving to the States, Brother André said to the driver, "Let's stop at the Sisters of the Holy Family."

The infirmarian proposed to me to see him. I refused, saying, "I'm going to the infirmary chapel. I don't want to see him because I have no confidence." My spine was interiorly twisted and I didn't want to hear, as I knew Brother André often said, "You've nothing wrong with you," or something of that sort. [Note: In the text there is no final quotation mark; I have arbitrarily placed it at what seems to be the end of her remarks and the beginning of her interior thought.]

But it happened that the infirmarian told him and I couldn't get away. He was there, probably praying, at the statue of the Virgin Mary. "Try to walk," he said to me. I wasn't capable. "Go on, then; sit down," he said, and he began to pray some more. Then he came back toward me. He said to me with a tone of authority, "Get up and walk!" This [tone] produced an enormous change. My knees began to swell, as did my hands and my face. But I started to walk.

"Go thank St. Joseph."

I was so astonished to be walking without crutches! "Would I be able to go to the big chapel?" I asked. It was so long [since] I had been there.

"Go to whatever chapel you want!" he answered. I came back [later] to Brother André. My knees, my hands, my face were not losing their swelling. "Am I going to become paralyzed?"

"No, that's just blood that hasn't started to circulate."

And indeed I got over everything. I don't even believe I thought to thank him.

●━◆━●

Later, she not only thanked him, she worked at the Holy Cross institution where he lived, along with others from her congregation. And in fact, when she broke her arm three years later, in 1937, and he was on his deathbed, she would be the last person Brother André saw in this life for healing.

Her account continues:

●━◆━●

I asked myself, "Why did it happen that I was cured when I had no faith?" Another sister replied, "He came to give you faith."

I am the only sister that he cured in that visit to the infirmary and there were many sick there. The infirmarian told me, "He came expressly for you."

●━◆━●

If one figures a very modest thousand cures per year for the roughly sixty years when his healing ministry was in full swing (and cures were more likely double that or more), Blessed André can confidently be termed one of the greatest healers the Catholic Church has produced among its saints. Yet when his friends wondered aloud what they would do after his death, he assured them, "I'll be able to help you a lot more after my death, because I'll be much closer to God than I am now." In 1937, when Pope Pius XI was in danger of death, ninety-two-year-old André offered God his life for the Pope's.

"But the Oratory still needs you," someone complained.

"When someone does good on earth," the venerable old healer remarked with typical impersonality "it's nothing in comparison with what he'll be able to do when he gets to heaven."

Those words began to come true as soon as the Pope had unexpectedly recovered and Brother André had quietly died. In his lifetime it had been said that perhaps his most extraordinary gift was that of inspiring others with something of his own boundless confidence in God. In the seven days of his funeral services, the more than a million people who filed by his bier showed something very like his fervor. Even a dying man was brought in on a stretcher. Conversion had always been the cure he sought most avidly; and while conversions are healings outside the scope of this book, it must be noted here that the confessionals were full day and night.

But there were physical cures too. An asthmatic on the point of death after six years of sufferings is healed instantly; likewise, a four-year-old child is held up by his father, touches the dead saint, and is instantly able to take his first steps. A young girl in a wheelchair is another who hears the saint's silent command with the ears of faith—and is healed. Eight-year-old Arthur Ducharme, in an accident five months earlier, has had the nerves and muscles of his right arm cut to the bone by shards of glass. The hospital surgeon's recommendation: amputation. That step vetoed by the mother, the arm heals as far as the wound's closing is concerned but remains inert; a sling is necessary to support it. Various treatments have been useless; there is no way to rejoin the severed muscles and nerves in 1937. Young

Arthur touches the saint's body and is instantly able to use his arm. He demonstrates by carrying chairs around the sacristy. There remains a certain flabbiness, but the limb will serve him for all his needs in the years to come, even playing hockey.

The first of several days' triumphal rites for the humble brother is broadcast January 6, the day André dies. Among the listeners is retired policeman François Lecuyer, of Montreal. Lecuyer, in nineteen years as a traffic policeman working near the shrine, has become so crippled by rheumatism in his joints that he has had to retire early as an invalid. No treatments have helped. Periodically his feet swell, causing terrible sufferings. At such times he can walk only with crutches or cane. As the Lecuyer family respond aloud to the radio prayers, the father, who has been praying to Brother André as to a saint, from the moment he heard of his death, feels himself sicken. His coloring becomes like that of impending death and tears run down his face. Painfully the family haul him out of the living room; they fear he is having a heart attack. But as the prayers end, Lecuyer sits up. He reaches for his cane, his crutch, realizes they remain by the radio in the living room, gets up without either and begins to walk. He says later it is only after seven or eight minutes that it hits him that he is cured and that Brother André has obtained this grace from God.

Excitedly he calls to his wife to bring his shoes and the still-shaken woman exclaims, "You know very well you can't put on your shoes! Your foot is too swollen." But Lecuyer's foot slides easily into the shoe. Together he and his wife go to the Oratory, where he squeezes the saint's foot in thanks as they pass, part of the endless line of people who ignore the January cold to pay their respects to the body of a saint. Later Lecuyer remarks that while he was praying along with the radio, "I had never prayed like that. At that moment I had confidence as I had never had it before." Similarly, listening to the same service, a deaf boy who joins in the prayers is instantly healed.

On January 8 a mother rushes to the corpse. Her daughter is

in extreme danger in a hospital from peritonitis. She prays and touches to the body several objects of piety which she will give to her daughter to evoke faith in André's intercession. Arriving once more at the hospital, the word is still, "The child won't live through the night." But, by evening, she is already on the mend.

The end of the funeral ceremonies by no means halts the cures. From January to October that year, letters testify to 6,700 favors, 933 cures. And that is only the beginning. A few years later, 1941 to 1943 for instance, the Oratory receives 10,408 letters giving thanks just for *cures*. Of these, 6,610 specifically cite Brother André as intercessor. A medical bureau along the lines of the stringent one at Lourdes is set up to examine the most extraordinary cures. Eight physicians under direction of Brother André's old doctor, Lionel Lamy, select to investigate 791 impressive cases of claimed healing in the next fourteen years, that is, 1944–58. Of these, forty prove so beyond any possible medical or human explanation that they are set aside to be submitted to Rome, already moving to beatify the man who laughingly called himself "St. Joseph's little dog." Here is one:

Beginning in 1933 a young girl of fourteen, Thérèse Cousineau, suffers more and more from a deviation of her spinal column. From this period her stomach also refuses to keep down food. It is necessary to give up the plaster corset that aims to squeeze her into normal shape. Then the deformity of the shoulder increases and a hump bends her into a hunchback. Beginning in 1937 she suffers convulsions. On January 11, four days after the saint's death, Thérèse is brought to his coffin; but she only gets worse from the effort. Still as March begins, she and her parents begin a novena following precisely the use of St. Joseph's oil as Brother André often used to recommend it, but asking Brother André's intercession specifically. Again she gets worse, and is unconscious nearly three hours. The physician believes it is the end and she receives the last rites. But, beginning the next morning, her stomach starts functioning.

She is hungry, eats, and digests easily. The spinal column, however, is still as before. On March 22 the family begins a second novena, begging daily, "Brother André, obtain her cure!" Her sufferings she offers God as a prayer for his servant's beatification. Four days later, the pain is less. Thérèse sleeps. Waking, she is much better. "Doctor," she challenges, "I bet I'll be cured at the end of this novena."

The month dedicated to St. Joseph ends. So does the novena. The morning of April 1, as her mother rubs her back with the oil beloved of Brother André, suddenly, with loud pops and cracks, the bones of the spinal column simply realign themselves. The hump is gone. Besides the delirious joy of Thérèse and her parents over the complete (and permanent) cure, her cousin Albert, last superior of Brother André, is unspeakably grateful to his old friend for one more favor.

The cures are not all local. One child's inexplicable healing takes place in Africa. And the estimated three million annual visitors to the Oratory come from all over the world. In the early days of his ministry they asked simply for "the porter" or "Brother André." Since 1982 their prayer requests address Blessed André, a bona fide beatified saint of the Church. The man who failed at every livelihood until he gave himself full-time to God's service today is cited as a model of humility, faith, and charity for the whole human family. Credit for Blessed André's cures is still often hard to disentangle from that due to the intercession of St. Joseph. Considering the friendship between the two, that seems somehow appropriate.

❧ 8 ☙

America's First Homegrown Saint

All saints are healers. But their cures may take vastly different forms. In the case of St. Elizabeth Ann Bayley Seton, America's first native-born saint, had she lived today her passionate compassion and activism might well have led her into a ministry of physical healing. But in God's designs, Elizabeth lived her life as a Catholic in the early nineteenth century, an era when ideas of God's giving physical cures were little mentioned.

It would be over a century after Elizabeth's death in 1821 before Bible students began pondering that Jesus healed "all who came to him" (Matthew 12:16) and never spoke of illness as one of the crosses his followers are meant to bear. In Elizabeth's time the Church acknowledged miracles *could* happen without *expecting* they would; the big thing in illness was to pray, not for healing, but for resignation to God's will (which was seen as the cause of the illness—even in cases such as lung cancer in a heavy smoker, which today we would trace to very human factors).

The American spiritual landscape was also sombered with Puritanism as well as the residue of a dour European Catholic heresy, Jansenism. God was stern, much of life's good things were to be feared as traps of Satan, salvation was hard to come by, and the smart thing to do was opt for pie in the sky and live in this "vale of tears" as self-denyingly as possible, accepting all suffering as willed by God.

In such an atmosphere, Elizabeth Seton's sanctity understandably flowed into spiritual healings. And a particular sphere
became spiritual care of the dying. In fact if anything is characteristic of "Eliza" or "Betty" Seton, it is the strength and tender-
ness with which she helped those she loved so passionately die:
from her personally immature, professionally heroic physician
father; her charming, slightly spoiled and irresolute husband; a
number of the friends of her heart, including three young, un-
married sisters-in-law, the youngest of whom she had raised
from the age of ten; and both the oldest and the youngest of her
five children.

Still, neither inborn courage nor precocious spirituality
spared Elizabeth from the normal human progression of
growth. When, in her twenties, she helped her first loved one,
her adored, irreligious father, die, for all her piety she was still
spiritually confused and immature. In her anguish and her fear
of Richard Bayley's possible damnation, she lifted her baby toward the heavens and offered its life to God in exchange for her
father's salvation. Did God laugh at her earnestness? Or weep
that the young Episcopalian believed him so implacable? At any
rate, her father did turn to Christ before dying, the baby, Catherine, became Elizabeth's healthiest daughter (she lived to be
over ninety), and Elizabeth went one step deeper into realiza-
tion that God is *really* love.

Death, for all of us, is potentially the great final healing of our
earthly lives. But, sadly, it isn't always that, due to our lack of
spiritual preparation and/or facilitators for that preparation.
The more Elizabeth advanced, in spite of her confusions and
imperfections, in the knowledge and love of God, the more her
heroic self-giving, sacrifices, and prayers joined to the example
of her own faith to bring this literally vital kind of healing to the
dying.

Even individuals who had not been "religious" died healed,
that is, convinced of God's love and able to turn with hope and
trust to him. In instances in which her influence had been long,

as with her daughters or through drawn-out illness, those tended by Elizabeth Seton died exceptionally holy deaths. Both her daughters, I believe, died saints.

Did the holiness she gradually achieved mean Elizabeth Ann Seton became an otherworldly creature spared any suffering in losing loved ones? Far from it. Even after she had been through many deaths and was considered saintly by many, Elizabeth broke down emotionally when her oldest daughter, Anna Maria, lay dying at age sixteen of tuberculosis spread to the bones. Ten-year-old Rebecca and twelve-year-old Catherine sent their mother to the chapel during their sister's last moments because of Elizabeth's anguish. Although she had been cared for night and day by her mother, Anina, as the family called her, died in her young sisters' arms. For at least three months following, in spite of her intellect's sincere "Thy will be done," the mother felt she might go mad with grief.

Four years later, her youngest child, Rebecca, died at age fourteen after developing a tumor in the thigh following an ice-skating accident.

"How will you live without me, Mother?" warm-hearted Rebecca asked ingenuously just before her death. Only in this last great sorrow did Elizabeth achieve an inner strength so heroic she did not break down but simply soothed the child in her arms: "Don't worry, darling; Mother will soon wear away and follow you."

Five years later, only forty-seven, Elizabeth died peacefully of TB.

Far from being immune to her losses, they had molded her. The theme of St. Elizabeth's life, beginning with the loss of her mother when she was a toddler of two, became the search for God, in whom alone is permanence and freedom from partings, sorrow, and loss. Already at the death of her two-year-old baby sister when she was four, the lonely little girl explained she wasn't crying because "Kitty is in heaven. I wish I could go too [to be] with Mama."

Her life one long deathwatch, Elizabeth Bayley Seton became a saint because even her most agonizing losses spurred this passionate woman to throw herself into God's arms, rather than turn away in bitterness or despair. And instead of contracting in self-centeredness, her heart expanded in grief so that others in need could find a shelter there from life's storms.

Born into the upper crust of old Dutch-English New York City when such a world represented high moral standards as much as social prominence, Elizabeth Bayley was the most admired beauty and charmer of her generation. A brilliant-eyed, petite debutante with masses of dark curly hair and lovely, finely cut features, she flirted, smiled, and laughed through balls and society luncheons. Yet even in the gayest moments of her youth there was absolutely nothing shallow about Betty Seton.

Spurred by the early bereavements, rejection from her stepmother, and long periods of total neglect by the career-absorbed physician father she adored, from early childhood hers was a rich inner life with a strong spiritual bent. The little nominally Protestant girl (actually her only living parent was a humanitarian with no real religion) wore a most un-Protestant crucifix around her neck, bowed her head at the name of Jesus, and wondered why her playmates thought it funny. How could she explain to them she was born with a soul that cried out for God in the same ardent way her oversized heart cried out to give and receive human love?

Her marriage when she was nineteen to handsome William Seton, son of a prominent and much-loved wealthy businessman, was a social "event" as was the ball at which the young newlyweds were among the official hosts greeting General Washington. Gratitude one of her strong traits, a happy marriage and the first true home she had known since her mother's death only turned Elizabeth more toward God. She followed her physician father, who would give his life for epidemic-stricken Irish immigrants, in her deep affinity with the poor.

Those who saw her and "the friend I can tell anything," her sister-in-law Rebecca Seton, going out many mornings with food and medicine for New York's poverty-stricken, dubbed her prophetically "a Protestant Sister of Charity." At the same period, her wonderfully vivid, witty, and charming letters to friends or her father (separated from his second wife) reveal the doting mother who is sure her babies (there were five in seven years) are among the wonders of the world.

Any wife and mother reading these letters and the notes as banal as our own ("My love: I send your toothbrush and comb which I forgot this morning. . . .") can relate absolutely to this woman, so maternal, so earthily in love, so willing to share her troubles with her intimate friends without that false pride which maintains a front of unreal competence and confidence, so grateful for her friends' support, and so willing to give it lavishly in return. From long-ago-penned pages, Elizabeth smiles so warm and witty a friend, so perceptive and intelligent an adviser, so stout-hearted and steady in a crisis like her husband's bankruptcy, even as she openly admits her fears and inadequacies, so gifted with good humor, optimism, and sheer charm that it is impossible not to cry across time and space, "Elizabeth, be my friend!"

At the same time, how one longs to ease her sufferings as one sees her across time. As in a photo album, certain pictures stand out. The lonely motherless child lavishing her love on little half brothers and half sisters. The young wife quarantined under guard in Italy with no way to keep warm or decently fed her dying tubercular husband (who has insisted this trip will restore his health) or their eight-year-old, Anna. Elizabeth laughs to raise the others' spirits and prays like an angel to turn William from thoughts of his bankruptcy to spiritual preparation for his death. When she weeps in the night, she is careful not to make a sound.

In New York a year or so later she lies on her bed in an agony ("My God, show me your truth") over whether the Protestants or Catholics are right in claiming, as both do in that bigoted era, that only they have the key to salvation. It is a day when a WASP turning Catholic dies to family and social status. Although she can be sure a few Protestant women friends will remain loyal, however saddened, the penniless young widow, trying to teach school to support and educate five children, knows she will cut herself off from financial and community support, as well as chance of remarriage; and there will be no place in the New York of her Bayley, Barclay, Charlton, Seton, and Roosevelt kin for her Catholic children, either. But once convinced that Catholicism is the mother church of Christianity, Elizabeth joins the Irish maids and grooms in worship at their dirt-floored church, even though she soon loses her teaching job and finally is driven from the city to refuge in Catholic Maryland.

As her children grow, one sees her enduring heartbreak and humiliation time and again over her sons, both unsteady, irresolute characters. She is always trying to get them settled in life. To her embarrassment, they use her devoted friends and their connections not to achieve but as ne'er-do-wells and drifters who dip freely into the fruits of others' labors. In her lifetime she will never get them turned around.

Along the way of her arduous life it seems almost incidental that Elizabeth Ann Bayley Seton begins the Catholic parochial school system, opens the first Catholic orphanage in the United States, and starts the first American religious community, an American branch of the Sisters of Charity, who will serve the young nation in schools, hospitals, and child care across the land. Perhaps Elizabeth's accomplishments fade next to her relationships, because whether with the poor children she educated, the postulants of her order she guided toward spiritual wholeness, her many lifelong friends, or her own five offspring so dearly loved, Elizabeth Ann Seton is foremostly a maternal woman: one who will always be more attuned to relationships than to projects for their own sake. Out of her greatest love relationship, that with God, she gladly becomes a nun, but only on the unheard-of condition that she can keep her children with her and retain full control of their rearing. In her daughter Rebecca's battle with cancer, Elizabeth will run her religious order and all its undertakings for months from the young girl's bedside so as not to abandon her child for an instant.

In spite of her ardent love, she could save neither Rebecca nor Anna Maria from agonizing deaths that tore her own heart to shreds. And among her dear spiritual daughters (including Harriet and Cecilia, two young Seton sisters-in-law who followed her into the Church in spite of the ostracism of the Seton family, and [Cecilia] into religious life), the death toll was very high due to the poverty of the infant order. But after her own death the great-hearted mother could answer the cries for help of her nuns and of mothers with dying children with even more powerful prayers. And she did.

Her own darling Rebecca had died of a tumor. And cancer is the disease the majority of Americans fear most. It seems doubly fitting, then, that St. Elizabeth Bayley Seton, America's first homegrown saint, should have been beatified after cures of two cancer victims were attributed to her intercession.

Early in 1934 Sister Gertrude (Korzendorfer), the Sister of Charity who ran De Paul Sanatorium, New Orleans' 250-bed psychiatric facility, was nauseous and in terrible pain. Dr. James T. Nix, a doctor in whom she had complete confidence, was consulted and removed her gallbladder on April 14. In the sister's words:

After . . . I felt some relief from pain and nausea, but I never felt entirely well nor physically able to fulfill my duty. I was continually losing weight. In October of the same year my condition grew worse. I had sudden spells of intense pain in the right side of my abdomen, followed by chills and attacks of fever; and my temperature rising to

103. These attacks occurred at intervals of approximately
one week. I became dark yellow.

On December 25, after a more serious spell, [Dr. Nix]
. . . ordered that I should be transferred immediately to
the hospital.

━━◆◆◆━━

Sister Gertrude's fellow Sisters of Charity were very concerned. The nun, who was about sixty years old, was "a treasure
to the community" because "of very fine qualities of mind and
heart." Now the other nuns saw:

━━◆◆◆━━

The hospital treatment was unable to bring about any
improvement in her condition. She continued to fail rapidly. Unable to receive nourishment her weight melted
away daily. Her normal weight up to this illness was about
one hundred and sixty-five pounds. Now she was reduced
to one hundred and eighteen pounds. A consultation of
physicians was called. . . . Three other physicians together with Doctor Nix agreed on the pre-operative diagnosis that Sister had a cancerous condition of the pancreas
[because of her symptoms]. . . . An exploratory surgery
was recommended. . . .

━━◆◆◆━━

Dr. Nix later recalled the operation which took place on January 5, 1935, with gastroenterologist A. L. Levin and surgeon
Marion Souchon observing:

━━◆◆◆━━

The entire abdomen was examined through a median
upper abdominal incision. All structures were normal ex-
cepting the head of the pancreas which was enlarged to
three times its normal size, presenting itself as a firm tumor mass and having all the appearances of carcinoma of
the pancreas. There was no other pathology. . . .

It was impossible to do surgery of any kind because of
the extent of the lesion. Even a cholecystduodenostomy or

a cholecystgastrostomy* was impossible. It was my opinion at the time that if any further surgery were attempted, the patient would have died promptly as a result of it. She was extremely emaciated, anemic, and deeply jaundiced. No corrective surgery was done. The abdomen was closed.

. . . From gross appearance Sister Gertrude had an inoperable carcinoma [cancer] of the pancreas, the mortality of which is 100%.†

Tiny tissue samples had been cut from the tumor mass and were now sent, for purposes of absolutely accurate diagnosis, to three separate pathologists: Dr. Maurice Couret, director of the Hotel Dieu pathology lab, Dr. John A. Lanford of Tulane University of Louisiana and Dr. W. H. Harris of the University of Tulane School of Medicine. All three reports agreed the tissue was a carcinoma, that is, a cancerous tumor.

Both the operation results and the pathologists' reports merely confirmed what the Sisters of Charity, women who ran the Hotel Dieu and other medical facilities in the country, could see from their years of medical experience by just looking at Sister Gertrude: She "was wasting away almost hourly" and medical science could do nothing about it.

These medical workers were also women of prayer, their feet as firmly planted in things unseen as seen. The moment exploratory surgery confirmed fears of Sister Gertrude's terminal condition, they began a novena. For the next nine days they placed their petition for Sister Gertrude's restoration to health in the hands of their dead foundress, Mother Elizabeth Seton. They believed she was a saint. Her prayers must be powerful. Let her ask God for this grace.

Exploratory surgery itself is a trauma to the body and Sister

---

* Operations to bypass the tumor-created blockage of the bile duct.

† Overall five-year survival rates from this killer is still less than 2 percent. Where the tumor is truly localized to the pancreas (less than 20 percent of cases), the five-year survival rate rises to 5 percent.

Gertrude was extremely weak, jaundiced, and anemic. Yet from the very beginning of the novena, that is just the second day following surgery, the dying nun says:

———•◄••►•———

I felt neither pain nor nausea. I was able to eat with relish and retain any nourishment presented to me. My strength returned. I gained weight and I was discharged from the hospital February 1, 1935. However, my Superiors thought it would be better for me to remain there a month longer, which I did. I returned to my duty the 1st of March. Since then I was able to follow the common life and to attend to all the duties of my office as Sister Servant [i.e., Superior] of a 250-bed hospital for the insane.

I have never had any relapse of my former sickness, and I attribute my cure solely to a novena made to Mother Seton in order to obtain it.

———•◄••►•———

Could the pious nun be mistaken? Could the exploratory surgery, cutting into the tumor, have triggered a spontaneous remission? On this point Dr. Nix says, "I do not believe the cure could be in the least attributed to any surgical intervention," and he reminds questioners that in 1935 cancer of the pancreas had a 100 percent mortality. Furthermore, as information on Sister's case notes:

———•◄••►•———

The common experience in surgery is that whenever a cancer is cut and the growth has not been completely removed there follows what surgeons call a metastasis, that is, there is generally a spreading of the cancerous infection throughout the system. In Sister Gertrude's case, the cancer was cut, the growth in its entirety practically speaking, remained in the pancreas but instead of the infection spreading throughout the system, the disease was arrested and a complete cure effected. This contrary to all the expectations of the medical men in attendance. . . .

For seven and a half years, the well-loved nun continued her stressful work as sister superior of the large psychiatric facility. Then, in 1942, while eating a meal at the Villa Saint Louise in Normandy, Missouri, "life left [her] as suddenly as a light goes out when you press the switch," according to a sister with her.

Because of the suddenness of her death and the earlier extraordinary cancer cure, an autopsy was performed at De Paul Hospital in St. Louis, Missouri. Dr. Walter J. Siebert, hospital pathologist, found the immediate cause of death was a massive pulmonary embolism, a condition totally unrelated to either the pancreas or cancer in any form. The biopsy of 1935 had been sent Dr. Siebert from New Orleans. He agreed "there is no question but that the biopsy section removed from the head of the pancreas . . . shows an adeno-carcinoma. . . ." However, seven years later, careful autopsy shows "no evidence, whatever, of this cancer and furthermore does not even show evidence of a scar in the pancreas where this tumor had been."

Understandably the cure of Sister Gertrude was accepted as an authentic miracle in favor of Elizabeth Seton's beatification.

☙ 9 ☙

"Hey, You, You're a Mother!"

Born in Baltimore, Maryland, on October 7, 1947, Anne Theresa O'Neill was a healthy child until early 1952, when she was four years old. Then her parents, William Richard O'Neill and Felixena Phelps O'Neill, discovered with alarm "blood blotches" covering the little girl's neck. They rushed her to the family doctor, E. W. Johnson, M.D., who did a blood test, looked somberly at the results, and sent the child at once to St. Agnes Hospital.

Admitted to St. Agnes on February 17, 1952, Anne "was very sick, extremely pale, lethargic and had enlarged glands in her neck." The following day a bone-marrow test provided the deadly diagnosis "acute lymphatic leukemia." Two weeks of blood transfusions and other treatments proved futile. The parents were given the heartbreaking news that it was only a matter of time before the end.

Unwilling to accept that, Anne's parents looked for new medical advice. They turned to Dr. Milton S. Sacks, of University Hospital (the University of Maryland), a brilliant physician and authority on leukemia.

Dr. Sacks was using a new drug, aminopterin, on leukemia victims. Anne was admitted to University Hospital on February 28. But aminopterin proved no miracle drug.* Her condition only got worse. After three weeks in the hospital her suffering

---

* The National Cancer Institute does not even list it among leukemia chemotherapies in 1987.

was intense, her little face swollen way beyond normal proportions. Her case judged "hopeless," she was sent home on March 27. But Dr. Sacks kept her under his personal care and in a desperate bid to keep the dying child alive, after only three days at home he rushed her back to the hospital for another blood transfusion. After the transfusion he wished to keep Anne at the hospital, but the O'Neills insisted on taking their daughter home. If they could not cure her, at least they could give her the comfort in her last days of care at home.

But even that began to seem impossible. Within a couple of weeks Anne had sores all over her body. She smelled like something decaying. Her fever was high. Nutrition was no help: She was able to take only sips of Coke. In that pitiful condition, the little girl came down with chicken pox. Not even just chicken pox, but, according to Dr. Sacks, one of the worst cases he had ever seen. During Holy Week of 1952, Anne gasped for breath and the end seemed very near.

April 9, she simply could not breathe. This time the parents phoned Dr. Johnson, who rushed her to St. Agnes for oxygen. Once there, however, her breathing eased somewhat. Still Sister Angelica (Inez) Howell, who saw Anne, could later testify that she "thought the child was about to die, so critical was her condition."

Sister Mary Alice Fowler, supervisor of the children's ward, reports:

> Anne Theresa was in a pitiful condition. She was very pale, her face was swollen, she was irritable and was so weak that she could neither sit nor stand. The diagnosis this time was "advanced leukemia . . . [with] chicken pox. . . ."

Although the hospital was run by Sisters of Charity, the O'Neills had never heard of Mother Elizabeth Ann Seton until Easter Sunday. That day, Sister Mary Alice later remembered:

Little Anne's mother was a woman of great faith. When I saw Anne's condition . . . the thought came to me that this case would be a good one for Mother Seton to show her power with God and, if it be God's holy will, . . . [to obtain] the cure of this incurable disease. . . .

I talked to the mother and told her what I wanted to do. I also told her what Mother Seton had done for another patient I had for whom all hope of recovery had been given up and that this patient is living today in wonderful health.

The desperate mother and compassionate nun concocted a plan. Sister Mary Alice would get the Sisters of Charity and the children in the homes and schools run by the order started in a crusade of prayer for Mother Seton's intercession with God. Mrs. O'Neill would get as many people as she could to join in. A novena as well as informal petitions to the saint began from that moment.

Sister Mary Alice testifies:

During the novena Anne seemed to show some improvement. She began to eat and to take notice of things about her. Later she began to sit up and within a few days she was allowed to be up and walking.

By April 27, eighteen days after she had been admitted in critical condition from what was at that time an incurable disease, Anne O'Neill was discharged from the hospital with healthy blood. The doctors diagnosed "a remission."

The family did not drive straight home. Instead they went first to Emmitsburg, where Mother Seton had watched her own daughter die of cancer. At the saint's tomb they prayed with fervor, aware that in 1952 no child with Anne's disease had ever escaped death.†

† Today 80 percent will go into remission, up to 50 percent will have long-term disease-free survival.

Dr. Sacks had the heavy knowledge that the reprieve was certainly temporary. Remissions in acute leukemia did occasionally occur, particularly following a viral infection such as the very severe case of chicken pox Anne had. But the remissions were always brief. In 1952, even when aminopterin worked—and it had not worked on Anne at all—the longest remission had been two and a half years. Typically, spontaneous remissions, which occurred in 1 percent or less of his cases, Dr. Sacks knew, lasted less than one year.

Weeks and then months passed. Anne remained well. Again and again the O'Neill family returned to pray by Elizabeth Seton's tomb or invoked her prayers at home. The year 1952 ended. Then 1953. Blood tests continued normal. In 1956 and 1957 the child went through the painful ordeal of bone-marrow punctures. Results: normal. In 1957 she passed the five-year cancer-free mark. At that time the longest remission in Dr. Sacks's records was about two and a half years.

Ten-year-old Anne, "an intelligent child loved by all because of her genial and pleasant disposition," had made medical history.

Still, for a cure to be an official miracle, there must be no doubt it is permanent. Only after ten years was this designation applied.

Today Anne is alive and well and the mother of several children, one of them named Mary Alice for Sister Mary Alice Fowler, the Daughter of Charity nurse who first introduced the O'Neill family to Mother Seton. Understandably Anne and many of her family feel a special devotion to St. Elizabeth Ann Seton. Even twenty years after the cure of one of her five daughters, Felixina Phelps O'Neill, Anne's mother, praising God for his goodness in an illness of her husband's also credited the saint's prayers, adding, "Mother Seton is very important to this family." A painting of the saint by Anne's sister Celine hung at the entrance to one of the institutions run by the Daughters of Charity, the Seton Home in Richmond, Virginia, while its duplicate held a place of honor in the O'Neill living room, along with the original small statue of Mother Seton given to the anxious parents by Sister Mary Alice during Anne's illness. As someone wisely remarked, "When you love someone, you like to have their pictures around."

Without in any way obscuring recognition that the healing ultimately was God's gift, the O'Neill-Seton friendship begun in his name when a little girl was dying is proving to be a lifelong relationship for this family.

Dr. Sacks's experience with remissions triggered by viral infections was that these were short-lived. Research by other physicians makes it legitimate, I believe, to suggest that the particularly virulent case of chicken pox and accompanying high fever may be very important factors in Anne's cure. I refer to the work of doctors such as Dr. William B. Coley, who practiced at New York's Memorial Hospital until his death in 1936. Dr. Coley found a positive relationship between spontaneous cure of cancer and infection. By deliberately infecting individuals who had inoperable cancer with strong toxins, he achieved some extraordinary cures. In the 1980s the use of Coley's toxins at Beijing Children's Hospital, the largest pediatric hospital in the world, has achieved complete disappearance of extensive inoperable cancers in some children. Research along these lines is also going on at some United States institutions, including a program under physicians Herbert Oettgen and Sanford Kempin at Memorial Sloan-Kettering Cancer Center in New York.

Other researchers, noting that a fever of over 105 seems to be a factor in infection-linked remissions, are pursuing the role of fever. Among their findings: fever stimulates the immune system, restricts the circulation of iron, which cancer cells require, and is deadly to cancer cells, which cannot take heat like normal cells.

To note the possible role of virus and fever factors in Anne's case is not to say either prayer or a saint's intercession were necessarily credited inappropriately with the child's healing. Chicken pox could have been the answer to her mother's faith-filled prayers. And her improvement began on Easter Sunday, the first day prayer was specifically directed for Mother Seton's intercession. I mention all this because one day our medical knowledge may suggest a virus and fever were the means by which God healed Anne. For the present, the medical investigators, following a thorough study of the case, could only conclude with her physician that there is no natural or medical explanation which will account for the survival of this one child alone where all the others in her situation, including those with viral infections or fever, died.

St. Elizabeth Seton has continued to help mothers and their children after her canonization no longer necessitated asking, "Is this cure a miracle?" Here is the detailed testimony of one of those healings, written by the grateful mother, Mary Porter, in June 1977, when the family still lived in Lakewood, Ohio. It was first printed in a now defunct periodical of the Daughters of Charity. While a doctor could undoubtedly cite factors such as the vitality of youth, a family that never stopped pulling for their child, and luck in the cure, to the Porters and many others, this is Mother Seton's work as God's agent.

On Sunday, July 6, 1975, at 11:30 P.M. my twenty-one-year-old son, James, was riding home on his newly purchased motorcycle when a car that had been parked at the curb . . . pulled out in front of him. Jim's bike smashed into the car, sending Jim soaring thirty feet into the air. He landed headfirst onto the street.

The impact forced brain tissue through his skull and out through his right ear, inside the helmet he was wearing.

The neurosurgeon, Dr. David Lehtinen, told us Jim had sustained a massive brain injury, both sides of the brain had hemorrhaged massively, and parts of his skull on both sides of his head had to be removed to allow for the tremendous brain swelling that ensued.

"I was working on a dead man," the surgeon said, "working only for survival."

Thanks to the prayers of over seventy young people and relatives who gathered at Lakewood Hospital emergency room that night, Jim did survive the operation. Minimally. His brain remained swollen, heartbeat and temperature were out of control, breathing needed mechanical aid, and seizures shook his body. He sank into a deep coma and his healthy, uninjured body started wasting away.

The atmosphere at the hospital was *pray for his death.* The staff worked hard to keep Jim alive, but I think it was only because of our deep belief that a miracle could, would happen. As sincerely, as kindly as they could—including the neurosurgeon and other consultants—they insisted that even if Jim could come out of the coma, nothing but existence in a vegetable state was possible for him.

Nothing more medically could be done for our son. He was merely being kept alive. After only three weeks in the Intensive Care Unit he was moved to a regular hospital room and removed from the extraordinary life-sustaining devices of the Intensive Care Unit. There was no discussion about "let him die" at this time, but I knew this was the feeling. Jim continued to hang on to life.

On September 3, 1975, Jim had to be moved to another facility for long-term care, Highland View Hospital, in Warrensville Heights, Ohio, about thirty miles from our home. At this time we were told again by Dr. Lehtinen that in his opinion *our son would never wake up.*

As a family we were devastated. We had already buried a six-year-old daughter, Patsy, twelve years before; and when Jim's tragedy happened we were just recovering from the death of another son, Hal, aged twenty, who was killed

in another automobile accident two and a half years before
Jim was struck down.

Physically, mentally, emotionally, and yes, spiritually, we
were exhausted. We went through the motions of living,
but my husband and I, and Jim's two older sisters especially, were just empty shells traveling those sixty miles
every day to pray over that comatose skeleton. . . .

We ranted and raved, and screamed and cried and
stormed at an unjust God—and relented and repented and
begged His Son, His angels and His saints to have pity on
us and our half-dead, half-alive son. But the pain continued.

On September 8, 1975, I read in our diocesan paper,
The Catholic Universe Bulletin, about some woman, an
American, who'd had five children and was going to be
canonized on September 14. Another saint. I, we, had
prayed already so much, . . . [asking] so many [saints] to
intercede for us, and we were still hurting. Oh God, the
hurt!

But this Elizabeth Seton was the mother of five. Surely
she could feel my feelings if anybody could. She knew the
trials and suffering involved in raising a family. She would
know my agony . . . wouldn't she? Hey, you! Mother Seton! You know I'm dying inside. You know how desperate I
am. Don't you? Please, can't you help me? Please, Elizabeth
Ann Seton! Please help me! Please, please, please, God,
work another miracle through this new saint of Yours. Let
her glory be even more, God. Please give her a miracle for
her canonization day. Come on, God! Come on, Mother
Seton! You can do it! . . . won't you?

My tears soaked that September 8 newspaper. Elizabeth
Ann Seton, first American saint, mother of five children,
help my child. Mother Seton, help my child. M.S. help my
child. Every page of the diary I was keeping about Jim's
ordeal, from September 8 on, has this brief prayer scrib-

bled at the bottom of the page—Mother Seton, help my child.

On September 12 when I arrived once again at Highland View I found our neurologist Dr. Patawaran and an eye specialist buzzing around Jim's bed. Through the brain trauma his right eye had been irreparably damaged. *If* he woke up, ever, from the coma, that eye as the organ of sight would be useless, since the cornea, iris and pupil were plastered together in one layer. Our doctor, another ward doctor and the eye specialist were amazed and mystified. Dr. Alan Moss, the eye doctor, declared that some kind of "spontaneous remission" had taken place: the eye was healed. At the bottom of my diary's September 12 page it reads: M.S. keep working.

September 14, 1975 [diary]: He was aware. Seemed to hear us. Attentive, concentrating. Was he?

September 16: Got relic of Mother Seton from Sister Patricia Newhouse, principal at St. Mel's. This is too much! M.S. is the founder of her community and they're teaching at our school!!

Diary reads: Left relic over his bed after I rubbed it all over Jim's poor head. New strength in neck and spine! Lifted his head and body completely over on his side by himself. A spastic kind of movement, without intent, but his head did not flip-flop like a rag doll as it had done all these months if not supported!

September 22: Staph infection worse. Mother Seton, clear his infection—please.

September 23: High fever, ear draining all night, pus and fluid.

September 27: Brain swelling gone!! Was this the reason for fever and draining? Thank you, St. Elizabeth Seton!

September 30: Mother Seton, bring him sight and hearing.

October 2: Holy God, we praise Thy Name! Staph infection gone, disappeared . . . completely! He is awake!! He is aware of us in the room, seems to be able to see something straight ahead. Mother Seton, intercede. Mother Seton, thank you! . . . Give him comprehension. Please, God. Please.

October 12: Thank you, God. Thank you, Mother Seton. Jimmy very awake . . . a look of knowledge or understanding in his eyes. Or is it recognition? The dull, vacant, robot stare is gone. Holy God, we praise Thy Name!

October 14: Very, very awake! Tongue moving in and out like an infant. Ready to eat food, to talk, God? Thanks, God, Mother Seton and everybody!

October 16: He's trying to communicate! When I talk to him he forces air out the trach [note: she refers to tracheotomy, the opening into the windpipe made through his neck enabling Jim to breathe without use of nose or mouth]. He is truly awake, knows I'm there and is answering me. Mother Seton you are something else. You are a miracle-worker!

Highly skilled doctors believed Jim would never wake up, his staph infection would never yield as long as he lived, and *if* he ever regained consciousness, he would be blind in the destroyed eye. But when this writer spoke to Mary Porter, mother of eight and a free-lance writer herself, twelve years after Jim's accident, he was alive and well, has held various jobs, and is able to share the physical work of the farm where he lives with his family near Erie, Pennsylvania. If his vision is not twenty-twenty, he still has the use of both eyes.

And from the beginning he was able to function mentally, according to Sister Patricia Newhouse, the Sister of Charity of Cincinnati who not only organized prayer for Jim but, says Mary Porter, "brought our devastated family back to life." Sister Patricia still talks of Jim's highly successful volunteer work with children in the school where she was principal in the period when he was retraining himself following the massive brain injury.

"How the kids loved him," she recalled to this writer.

"A case in a thousand," says his original neurosurgeon.

Mary Porter says gratefully of her son, "He is *slightly* slow normal. *We* know he sustained a massive, killing brain injury; strangers cannot tell."

All the medically unexpected improvements which began with the strange "putting back together" of his mashed eye, his mother emphasizes, "took place within the first month of Mother Seton's canonization! And usually as I specifically requested them."

"Why did our prayers go unanswered until I became aware of her existence?" the mother muses in her written account. ". . . Did God pick us to spread her fame? Or was it as I believe she heard the awful anguish in my cry: 'Hey, you, you're a mother!' "

❧ 10 ❧

"Maybe He Wasn't Really Dead"

On a sunny spring day, Father John Bosco was in Lanzo, Italy, paying a visit to one of the schools he had founded. When he arrived, seven boys were in the infirmary, quarantined with smallpox. Sick or not, their faith in one they believed a saint was so great they were sure that if Don Bosco, as they called him— "Don" being Italy's title for priests—would only come up and bless them, they would be healed and not have to miss the fun and entertainments scheduled for his visit. From their sickroom, they sent out an urgent request that the visiting priest come see them.

With his usual total unconcern for his own well-being—he once snapped at a hovering woman, "Madame, I did not become a priest to look after my health"—the saint entered their off-limits quarters.

With cheers and roars, all the boys began to clamor, "Don Bosco, Don Bosco! Bless us and make us well!"

Boys were never too raucous for this saint. He only chuckled at their exuberance. Then he asked if they had faith in Mary's intercession, for like all saints, Bosco never attributed his cures to his own prayer power.

"Yes, yes," they chorused. If Don Bosco was praying, they were full of faith.

"Let's say a Hail Mary together then," he proposed. Perhaps he reminded them that, as at Cana when Jesus worked his first

122

public miracle at her request, when Mary asks her son for a favor, she gets it. At any rate, only *after* the prayer which asked for the cure through Mary's prayers, not Bosco's, did he bless the sick students in the name of the Father, Son, and Holy Spirit, from whom all healing comes.

As their hands completed the answering sign of the cross, the boys began reaching for their clothes.

"We can get up now, right?"

"You really trust Our Lady?"

"Absolutely!"

"Then get up!" He turned and left, and six boys, ignoring the deadly pustules that still covered them head to foot, hopped into their clothes and raced out to the festivities.

The seventh boy, John Baravalle, was a worrier. Might he not get worse if he got up? he stewed. After all, the school doctor had been insistent on bed rest and complete quarantine. Anxiously John decided to see if the school's priest director would second Don Bosco's permission. Although Baravalle was no sicker than the other boys, the director, seeing the pupil's lack of faith, advised he should probably stay in bed. It took him the twenty quarantined days to recover. As for the six impudent, roof-raising rascals who dashed out to the fun and games with complete confidence, their pustules began to disappear as they played. The only near-casualty of the day in May 1869 was the poor conscientious school physician, who almost had a heart attack when he saw the small-pox patients "infecting" the entire school with an often fatal illness. While he was understandably furious, in fact no one caught the disease.

"He likes me best!"

"Liar!" Dark eyes spit fire from one slum child toward the other.

"I can prove it. Look, he gave me this slick new comb and a pile of doughnuts this high and—

"Hah!" the other interrupts, "that's nothin'! Don Bosco's going to get *me* a job as a 'prentice."

"So!" The too-thin face thrusts forward belligerently. "That's only 'cause you're too dumb to get your own—"

A roar and a lunge connect the two undersize bodies in a twisting tangle, each heartily pounding the one who dares question his special status with the young, curly-haired priest who comes running to separate them, his laughter and warmth easing the hunger for love beneath each grimy, brawling exterior.

Many years later, as clean, decently clad, well-mannered adults, long deflected from incipient delinquency into honest workingmen and stalwart Christians, the same pair and hundreds like them, plus many slightly better off boys like those seven at Lanzo, would recall Don Bosco with the same fierce, if less combative, love.

"How he loved us!"

"Remember his fatherly smile."

"And his gentleness. Wasn't he more tender than a mother?"

"He had so little to give us actually: a handful of doughnuts or chestnuts, maybe a cheap comb—but those days with him seem to me like Paradise."

The man whose love healed lives and sometimes bodies as well, canonized as St. John Bosco in 1934, only forty-six years after his death in 1888, was years ahead of his time—and ours. A master psychologist, nurturer, and educator, his boys' clubs and schools—whether academic, technical, or seminary—lovingly educated the whole child, intellect, emotions, soul, and body, with remarkable results.

Bosco founded technical schools to augment or replace the system of apprentice training of the young, midday retreats for workers and students and vacation camps for Christians. Beginner of Italy's Catholic press apostolate, he knew how to turn every available medium of communication or entertainment—from almanacs and magazines to theater and music—to Christian use. One of the most winning personalities among the

Church's saints, he was gifted by God with perhaps more charisms than any nineteenth-century saint, from prophecy and reading of hearts to the working of all sorts of miracles, including healing minds, souls, and bodies.

Fatherless himself at two, already in his ninth year John had been given his life's work in a numinous dream in which Christ and Mary showed the Piedmont farm boy he must turn wayward boys from wolves into lambs. Founder of the Salesians, today the third-largest and one of the Church's most vital orders, Bosco and his spiritual sons and daughters have saved hundreds of thousands of young people living in poor neighborhoods and slums all over the globe from meaningless and/or destructive lives. But before this vast enterprise took off, the peasant boy himself underwent an arduous spiritual conditioning that taught him to hope when all hope seems futile. Not only could his widowed mother not afford to send her youngest child to school and seminary, but the oldest of the three Bosco boys, John's half-brother Anthony, the son of the dead father by his short-lived first wife, flew into rages at the very sight of young John with a book.

"We're peasants. We don't need this kind of foolishness. Get out in the fields, where you belong," and Anthony would throw his youngest half brother's reader as far as he could.

By the time John was fourteen and still out of school, Margaret Bosco had to send him out on his own to escape abuse. Working as a hired field hand, John saw his dream apparently recede farther and farther. But instead of giving up, he went deeper and deeper into prayer, mining toward that golden lode of trust in God and abandonment to Divine Providence which later formed the treasury for all his extraordinary works.

When the boy's remarkable intelligence—for one thing, he was gifted with a photographic memory—and immense charm brought him to the attention of a saintly priest who promised help, the man soon died. No human can help you—trust only in me, John later revealed God seemed to say to him at this time. It would take him many years, sometimes fighting discouragement and certainly not always aware of the character and virtues he was developing as he surmounted obstacles, to make it through school. During those years it is said he mastered thirty-seven trades. Certainly he held every kind of job, from tutoring to janitor at a pool hall, where he slept in a cubbyhole under some stairs.

When he finally completed his training as a diocesan priest and began his apostolate, critics sprang up at once. What was the young, handsome priest doing hanging out in areas known as hotbeds of vice? Why was he seen entering a tavern late at night with a vicious gang and standing these young hoodlums a round of drinks? Had John Bosco no thought for the dignity of the priesthood? Why, most priests, some reminded him, forebore even to *speak* to slum people or any young person in order to maintain the proper awe toward their sacred calling.

When Bosco told his fellow mid-nineteenth-century clergymen that he was going to form a cadre of laymen and priests "in shirt-sleeves" to live in the slums and work with the young spawned there, kids who would otherwise end up dead of drug or alcohol abuse, jailed for violent crime or victims of the gang system, some of his fellow clergymen were horrified. They actually made arrangements to have "poor unbalanced Don Bosco" confined to a mental institution, but the quick-witted Bosco outfoxed them.

Another hardship was the political situation. It was a period of political instability. The small kingdoms of Italy were breaking up interiorly or being invaded by foreign powers. The entire Italian Peninsula was moving toward unity as a new nation.

Church and states, particularly Piedmont's government, were locked in battle over everything, from the Pope's earthly kingdom, the Papal States, to the role of religious orders in the new era. Many anticlericals in government looked with a jaundiced eye at the muscular, athletic young priest, a spell-binding speaker who could lead boys—and men—anywhere he proposed. When he marched through Piedmont's capital city, Turin, with several hundred young slum toughs on their way to the country to hike or picnic, sinister political maneuvers and the building of a personal power base were suspected.

On all sides, criticism or misunderstanding. No substantial help anywhere. His mission seemed doomed before it got off the ground. Finally came the crisis on Palm Sunday 1846, when he was going to have to tell his hundreds of followers they were being evicted from even the bare field he had rented as their meeting place when they had been thrown out of every building in Turin. Only in this last great temptation to despair, when he was asked to trust a God who seemed both deaf and cruel, did Bosco interiorize a faith so heroic that nothing could defeat it and a humility bottomless enough to defeat every impulse to pride in his enormous human and spiritual gifts. That same afternoon he was offered the lease on a dirt-filled shed leaning against a brothel across from a tavern. From this beginning, his mission never looked back. Neither faith nor humility failed him in the years ahead as he built schools, workshops, and training institutes, seminaries, churches, and living quarters all over Italy and in mission lands with no means of support but trust in Divine Providence.

His splendid body—he could pound a nail into the wall with his bare hands and into old age easily outran all comers in the footraces so dear to his boys' hearts—he literally wore out in service to the young, so that a doctor described him at sixty as like a coat become so ragged it is good only to hang in the closet.

"You must give up all work and do nothing but rest," the physician ordered

"That, Doctor, is the one thing I cannot do," the saint answered with his wide grin. And he went on with his killing schedule for another dozen years although nearly blind, suffering emphysema, and weak in almost every organ and system.

To reduce himself to such a state from the superb health that was his from birth, he had been guilty of self-abuse. Very early in his apostolate he wore himself into such a run-down condition that he caught pneumonia, the disease which had killed his strong young father when John was only two. Don Bosco's young toughs prayed, fasted, and wept to no avail until, on the night the doctors said the priest would die, a friend browbeat him into a single prayer that, if it were God's will, he might recover. The next morning he was pronounced out of danger. Medical advice was for many quiet months in the country to recoup his wasted strength. Bosco went to his home village, but aware that without his guidance boys could resume their former deadly habits, he returned to the slum before his body was fully recovered. For this loving folly he paid with bouts of emphysema the rest of his life. His eyes he ruined by overuse, never sleeping more than four or five hours a night, and staying up for years one entire night a week to answer letters and work on his books and articles (as today, youth needed Catholic literature to counter the paganism of the times), and making no allowance until almost blind for the weakness caused by a direct hit from a bolt of lightning.

Yet God assisted him. For instance, if he could not see with his eyes, God gave him other means. Take the testimony of a boy making his confession to the saint. Don Bosco, who had been in the church hearing confessions for hours, informed him in which building on the large property he would find a boy hidden away and smoking an illegal cigarette.

"Don Bosco asked me to go to this fellow and tell him he should think about coming to confession."

When the messenger stepped gingerly into the dark hallway he saw no one but smelled cigarette smoke. He called out the message hurriedly, because he wanted no dealings with the older, bigger youth. Then he dashed outside, hid in the bushes, and a moment later saw the boy named come out the door and head for the church.

Letters that the saint sent to various Salesian institutions throughout Italy and in other countries sometimes gave detailed advice about people and events there while he was far away, noting casually, "I dropped in on you in the spirit." Besides bilocation, Bosco's ailing eyes also got another assist. Consider this testimony:

———•———

[Don Bosco] was writing and I sat down near to him, watching him keenly, studying a certain movement he made while he was writing: he turned his head slowly from left to right, to accompany and follow the movement of the pen across the page. I did not understand why. . . . As soon as he stopped writing . . . I [asked]. . . . "Why did you turn your head to the right to accompany the movement of the pen when you were writing?"

Don Bosco smiled as he answered, "This is the reason why. . . . [I] can no longer see with this eye, whereas the other eye, too, sees only a very little."

". . . Then, how was it that, when I was quite some distance from you the other day in the courtyard, you looked at me very directly and keenly, as clear as a ray of sunlight?"

"Come, come now! All of you imagine things . . . whereas there is really nothing at all. . . ." . . . We began to talk about [another] matter. . . .

But now to return to this topic of his look. I was at recreation in the playground one day. As usual, I was completely absorbed by the game. As I stood still a moment, I heard some boys talking with great animation. I turned around and espied Don Bosco surrounded by a crowd of boys at some distance from me. There were a great many of them, as there always were whenever Don Bosco came down into the playground, and they were all talking loudly, and merrily with him. Absorbed as I was in the game I was playing, I did not feel like joining them. So I stood there hesitantly, and looked toward them again, where Don

Bosco stood. Then all of a sudden I was struck by the brilliance of his eyes, as he looked toward me. I really could not describe it. I stood at least some thirty paces from him, and was not even directly opposite him, but found myself at a lateral angle of his vision. Don Bosco was literally besieged by the boys, and held the hands of several. I recall these things very clearly. . . . I say that his eyes were like a ray of light, like a shining ruby, a diamond, something quite unconceivable, and which could be compared to a flash of lightning. I was quite entranced by what I saw, and quite automatically, without knowing what I did, I approached the group. As I reached him, I felt Don Bosco take my hand, although I had not tried to push my way through to him. . . .

The account, by Peter Fracchia, speaking many years after the fact, in 1937, makes it clear that Don Bosco could use his nearly blind eyes like the most keen-sighted of individuals at times. Spirit dominated flesh, one might say.* Or looking at it another way, like one who is at the same time both infirm and healed, he possessed, as Scripture says, in God's grace a strength made somehow more perfect in his weakness.

Lovable, human Don Bosco exemplifies in still another way that people madly in love with God can still behave as foolishly as the rest of us. Don Bosco not only acted as a priest, a catechist, and a teacher of subjects from music to metrics to his slum kids, he also took many homeless or abused boys to live with him. He cooked for them, cut out and sewed their suits, barbered their hair, made their beds, and in all ways acted as both a mother and a father. Surely this was enough self-giving, but not for the saint. When a boy came to him moaning piteously with a toothache, an earache, or other infection in those pre-antibiotic days, Don Bosco would ask God to heal the kid by

* For a similar case, see the description of cellist Pablo Casals in Norman Cousins' *Anatomy of an Illness.*

giving the pain or the illness to him. God, of course, may answer
our idiotic prayers as well as our sage ones. Finally, when Don
Bosco couldn't function for his hundreds of boys because he
was incapacitated by the terrible toothache he had taken on for
one boy, he came to his senses. He realized that this love that
cries out to physically bear the loved one's pains and troubles,
spiritually speaking, was a youthful excess. From then on, when
led by the Holy Spirit to pray for healing—certainly not always
the case, for he assisted many people in their deaths—Bosco
prayed people well with the assumption God could spare the
cure: it did not have to come, physically anyway, out of Don
Bosco's hide.

Of course he reserved the right to make occasional excep-
tions, like the time he arrived at a Salesian school to find that
the youngster who was to take the lead in the evening's entertainment had lost his voice.

"I'll lend you mine for the evening," the saint said. For the
rest of that night the boy projected his voice beautifully, while
Don Bosco was hoarse as a foghorn.

Because his sanctity was so widely known, in spite of his
efforts to keep himself out of the limelight, Bosco's door often
opened to people in search of healing. How many miracles occurred in the little room where, in his later years, he received
his visitors for three hours a day, or on his many trips, only God
could say. It is suggestive, however that at his death, one hundred thousand turned out for the seventy-two-year-old priest's
funeral, while it took thirty-four thousand pages to record all
the testimonies of those who came forward two years later and
asked to enter into the official record under oath their stories of
Don Bosco's sanctity and what he had done for them and theirs.
Many of these testimonies included healing.

One well-authenticated cure took place the same year the six
boys were healed of smallpox at Lanzo. It occurred about 5 P.M.
on May 16, the evening of Pentecost, in the church of Mary,

Help of Christians, which Don Bosco built† next to his complex of homes and schools for boys in Turin. Maria Stardero, a blind girl of ten or twelve, was led in by her aunt to the church, where dozens of boys were standing about or kneeling in prayer as they waited for Don Bosco to arrive for confessions. Father Francis Dalmazzo, one of the first Salesians, spoke to the woman. In his testimony he later recalled, "I was grieved to see that the young girl's eyes had no corneas and resembled white marbles."

When Don Bosco arrived, he questioned the girl about her condition. She had not been born blind, but as a result of eye disease her sight had been completely lost two years earlier. When he asked about medical treatment, the aunt began to sob that they had tried everything, but doctors could only say the eyes were "beyond hope."

"Can you tell whether things are big or small?" the saint asked.

"I can't see a thing."

He led her to a window. Could she perceive light?

"Not at all."

"Would you like to see?"

"Oh, yes! It's the only thing I want," and she began to sob about how miserable she was.

"Will you use your eyes for the good of your soul and not to offend God?"

"I promise I will, with all my heart!"

"Good. You will regain your sight," the man whose own vision was in need of help assured her. With a few sentences he encouraged the visitors to have faith in the intercession of Mary. With them he recited a "Hail Mary" and another prayer to Mary, the "Hail, Holy Queen." Then urging them to have abso-

† Put up by the penniless priest at a cost of a million lire in only three years, one hundred ten favors—including cures of the caliber of the one I give here—had been recorded in 1875 only seven years after the mother church of Bosco's Salesian order opened its doors.

lute trust in the prayers of the mother of Christ, he blessed the girl. After that he held a medal of Mary, Help of Christians, in front of her and asked, "For the glory of God and the Blessed Virgin, tell me what I'm holding in my hand."

"She can't . . . the elderly aunt began, but Don Bosco paid no heed, while the girl after a few seconds shouted, "I see!" Immediately she described the detailing on the medal. When she stretched out her hand to receive it, however, it rolled into a dim corner.

The aunt moved to retrieve it, but Don Bosco motioned her back.

"Let her pick it up to see if the Blessed Virgin has thoroughly restored her sight," he insisted. Unerringly the girl bent into the shadows and picked up the tiny object. As the many witnesses looked on, awed and profoundly moved, Maria, beside herself with joy, bolted for home, while her aunt thanked Don Bosco profusely with sobs now of joy.

If Maria Stardero was so wild with joy she forgot to even thank the one whose prayer obtained her cure, she returned soon afterward to make her small donation to his work and offer thanks. Forty-six years later, in 1916, when some Salesians checked on her, she still had perfect vision.

The cures he worked for his individual boys were even simpler. For instance, a teenager who lived at the boarding school in Turin suffered a sudden mental breakdown. Far adrift in some interior world, the boy was brought for the saint's blessing before sending him home.

Blessed, the comatose-appearing teen suddenly started as if coming out of a trance.

"Where am I?" he asked, looking around bewildered.

"You're here in my office," Don Bosco smiled. "You weren't feeling well. How are you now?"

"Fine, but I'll bet I'm late for Latin," and the boy dashed off to class.

That was the end of his breakdown.

Many of the saint's cures were worked while he traveled to beg funds for his works, to oversee their development, or while on missions for the Church. In Paris in 1884 he healed the son of the Marquise de Bouille after the child had already received the sacrament of the dying, then called Extreme Unction. Ignoring the doctor's sentence of death and the youngster's condition, Don Bosco gathered the family around the bed, invoked Mary's intercession, prayed with them, and left, assuring the parents the child would soon be convalescent; the next day the boy began to recover. A few days later it was a dying girl of twelve, whom the saint prayed over, who was cured.

Such healings electrified the usually blasé Parisians. The coachman driving Bosco in the city muttered, "I'd rather drive the Devil than drive a saint" on one of the occasions he was unable to budge his vehicle because of the mob attempting to get close enough to touch the priest or scissor off some handy portion of his cassock. As for Bosco, he murmured disgustedly, "These people are nuts."

Born poor himself, Don Bosco dedicated his order to work for the poor; but some of his miracles God gave to the wealthy, who often responded generously to support his undertakings. One such cure took place in Florence. A rich noblewoman there had a very young godson she loved as if he were her own child. While Don Bosco was visiting Florence, it happened that the little boy fell ill. When the doctors said he was dying, this woman went into a frenzy. She sent messengers everywhere searching for "the saint" and she rushed out herself to join the search. By luck, it was she who found Don Bosco. Being given a tour of their boarding school by some priests known as the Somaschi Fathers, he was suddenly confronted in this sedate group of clergymen by a madwoman, her hair undone, her clothes improper for outside the home, shrieking out her grief and pleas.

Understandably, the priests conducting the saint around their institution were not thrilled. But Don Bosco was not repulsed.

He excused himself and went at once with the wailing woman.

At the child's house, they found the little boy had just died. On his tiny bed, the small corpse lay glassy-eyed and still. Almost in a whisper, Don Bosco invited those in the room to beg the intercession of Mary, Help of Christians. Then he blessed the little body. At the last word, the chest began to move. After a few more breaths, the child yawned, then opened his eyes. He smiled at the stupefied faces hovering over him.

In a short time he was perfectly well.

His godmother became such a benefactress to Don Bosco and his Salesians that they referred to her as "our good Mama in Florence."

Years later, Don Bosco was present at her dinner table when she began relating the story to other guests. Head bowed, his eyes never left his plate during her tale. Only when she finished did he speak, murmuring softly, "Perhaps he wasn't really dead."‡

Among the other cures that seemed to be given by God to gain benefactors for the humble priest's work were a number in Rome. For example, when Don Bosco had great trouble there getting approval for his radical new congregation, God used the saint to give healings to several important church officials who opposed approval or to members of their families. For all today's theology about not bargaining with God, God seemed himself to barter the cures for approval of his saint's congregation. Among these cures a key opponent, Monsignor Svegliati, was healed overnight of virulent influenza following the saint's visit; Cardinal Antonelli, in great pain and immobilized by gout, when Don Bosco called on him was well the next day; and the eleven-year-

‡ To Bosco is also attributed a similar miracle in Turin.

old nephew of Cardinal Berardi, dying of typhoid, was inexplicably healed after the saint came to pray over him. To each of these churchmen, before working the cure, Don Bosco made it clear that their vote was expected in return. These changed votes gave the Salesians approval.

Like all the saint's projects, the Church of Mary, Help of Christians, in Turin was paid for by donations, from pennies to large sums, by people who wanted to help Don Bosco save poor and troubled youths; but many gifts to his building fund came from individuals the saint cured or promised protection from illness. For instance, during terrible cholera epidemics, Don Bosco liberally promised freedom from infection, in Mary's name, to his donors. He said he was acting on instructions from the Virgin and, in fact, although hundreds died in some neighborhoods, none of the donors was among them. Even odder, he promised immunity to those of his boys who would join him caring for victims of the disease which was so infectious and so deadly that its sufferers were often abandoned by their own families—as with AIDS today. Though they should have been infected by their close contact, not a boy sickened.

Unbelievers were also among those healed by the saint. I think of the prominent doctor who came to visit Don Bosco. After a few social remarks, he said, "People say you can cure all diseases. Is that so?"

"Certainly not," the saint answered.

"But I've been told—" The well-educated man was suddenly stammering. Fumbling in his pockets, he pulled out a tiny notebook. "See. I've even got the names and what each one was cured of."

Don Bosco shrugged. "Many people come here to ask favors through Mary's intercession. If they obtain what they seek, that's due to the Blessed Virgin, not me."

"Well, let her cure me," the doctor said agitatedly, tapping the notebook on his well-clad knee, "and I'll believe in these miracles too."

"What's your ailment?"

"I'm an epileptic." His seizures, he told Don Bosco, had become so frequent during the past year that he couldn't go out any more. In desperation, he was hoping for help beyond medicine.

"Well, do what the others do who come here," Don Bosco said matter-of-factly. "You want the Blessed Virgin to heal you. So kneel, pray with me, and prepare to purify and strengthen your soul through confession and holy communion."

The physician grimaced. "Suggest something else. I can't do any of that."

"Why not?"

"It would be dishonest. I'm a materialist. I don't believe in God or the Virgin Mary. I don't believe in miracles. I don't even believe in prayer."

For a space the two men sat in silence. Then Don Bosco smiled, as only he could, at his visitor. "You are not entirely without faith—after all, you came here hoping for a cure!"

As the saint smiled at him, something welled up in the doctor. Don Bosco knelt and he knelt too without another word and made the sign of the cross.

Moments later, he began his confession.

Afterward, he declared, he felt a joy he would never have believed possible. Time and again he returned to give thanks for his spiritual healing.

As for the epilepsy, that simply vanished.

After Don Bosco's death, there were many miracles to testify to the sanctity of this great friend of God. Ignoring those involving after-death appearances by the saint* because I treat this subject at length in another book, and ignoring those in which the saint's relics played the predominant role, I offer as examples the cures of two women.

* See p. xx of the Introduction for reference to one case.

Sister Mary Joseph Massimi, of the convent of Santa Lucia in Selci, Italy, was about to die in 1928 of a duodenal ulcer. Her confessor gave this Augustinian nun a relic of Don Bosco, who was not yet beatified, and advised that she make a novena for his intercession. During the novena, instead of improving, her condition got worse. It could be seen that her recuperative powers were simply gone. But the nun's faith was unshaken. She simply began a second novena.

This time, too, she deteriorated further. It appeared her death would occur any moment. Still, on the fifth day of the second novena, May 15, she dreamed Don Bosco said to her, "I've come to tell you you will recover. Just be patient. Suffer just a little longer. On Sunday you'll be granted the grace [of healing]." Sunday was then four days away.

Friday, May 18, she dreamed again. This time Don Bosco carried the black habit that her order's nuns wear on holy days. He repeated the promise of a Sunday cure. But her condition as Saturday faded into Sunday left room for only one conclusion: Sister Mary Joseph had been the dupe of wish dreams with no real numinous content. Sadly on the very day her dreams had promised healing, her confessor was forced to give her the last rites.

But as the sister received the sacrament, her whole body suddenly "shuddered from head to foot, and in that instant she felt as though she was recalled from death to new life."

Occurring as the Church's experts, in the final act before beatification, were weighing two other cures attributed to Don Bosco for supernatural content, Sister Mary Joseph's healing caused a chuckle among those who recalled how God had so many times furthered Don Bosco's projects with healing miracles.

Beatified the next year, 1929, within twelve months there were already two new postbeatification miracles considered able to meet the Church's criteria. As study proceeded, however, a cure from Innsbruck, Austria, was set aside as not completely verifiable. In its place was offered at once the 1931 cure of Mrs. Catherine Lanfranchi Pilenga.

Mrs. Pilenga suffered from serious, chronic arthritic diathesis, particularly in her knees and feet. The organic lesions caused by the disease did not threaten her life but they practically paralyzed her lower limbs. For twenty-eight years, she had battled the condition; not a single treatment since 1903 had given her any relief.

In May 1931, she made her second pilgrimage to Lourdes. It was no more successful than her first. As she prepared to leave the shrine, Catherine prayed, "Well, Blessed Mother, since I haven't been cured here, obtain the grace for me that, because of my devotion to Blessed Don Bosco, he will intercede for my recovery when I'm in Turin."

She arrived in Turin from France in her usual serious condition. It took her sister and a male helper to get her out of their vehicle and into the church of Mary, Help of Christians, where she sat down to pray in front of the urn that contained the mortal remains of Don Bosco.

Deep in prayer for a while, without thinking she found herself kneeling down. After remaining on her knees about twenty minutes, she stood up, walked to the altar of the Blessed Virgin, and knelt there to continue her prayers. It was only at that point that she suddenly realized the things she was doing, and knew she was cured.

People who had seen this woman laboriously assisted into the church because she was unable to move about by herself now watched in amazement as she moved freely not only on level ground, but climbing or descending stairs. Her disease had simply vanished. It was a permanent, instantaneous, total recovery, verified by three doctors as well as a medical commission appointed by the Church, from a condition that nearly thirty years of medical help had failed to cure. Heaping joy upon joy, Mrs. Pilenga's cure was eventually picked from the many healings God has given through Don Bosco to be held before the world at his canonization as an authentic miracle.

❧ 11 ❧

"I'm Not Leaving
Until You Cure Me"

In New Orleans, the October 6, 1986, issue of the *Times-Pica-yune* featured an article and photo of a special mass in the city's St. Mary's Assumption Church. The newspaper notes "a rare sight in inner-city churches these days: a full house, more than 1,000 strong." The occasion: commemoration of the death of Father Francis Xavier Seelos, a Redemptorist born in Bavaria in 1819 who died in New Orleans on October 4, 1867, and is buried by St. Mary's altar.

"The man's still getting a church full of people 119 years after his death in a town where he worked barely a year," the article quotes one of sixteen priests who joined a bishop in the mass. "I don't know what it is but it's something beyond the normal. . . ."

Among those in the crowd, the newspaper concludes, is a woman who credits Seelos's intercession with saving her life.

Both comments echo the judgment of people during Father Seelos's lifetime that his prayers worked healing miracles and there was something beyond the normal—in their opinion, his sanctity—that filled churches wherever he went, whether that was New York, Chicago, Detroit, Pittsburgh, Baltimore, Cincinnati, or any of a myriad of small American towns and villages from Wisconsin to New Jersey.

To understand Xavier, as his large, devoted family called him, one has to accept that, while in general saints are made, not born, it is also true that in the spiritual life, as in music, there are natural geniuses. They also have to grow to their full powers, but it seems easier for them—or at least they grow faster and go farther than the rest of us. By the age of five, under his father's instruction, Mozart was a prodigy. Similarly, under the direction of his mother, frail little Xavier Seelos very early showed the kind of spiritual precocity one would see seventy years later in small Francesco Forgione (Padre Pio).

The sixth child, fourth living, and second son of ten children who would grow to adulthood, Francis Xavier Seelos entered life in the picture-postcard little town of Füssen, sixty miles southwest of Munich in the Bavarian Alps. The family was a happy one. It was also one with a tradition of healing given in answer to prayer.

A pregnant paternal grandmother had lost both her previous babies to miscarriage. In May 1782, when Pope Pius VI passed through the town of fifteen hundred people, the young wife rushed for a papal blessing that this child might live. It did, her only survivor, for she died, with her next baby, in childbirth two years later. The one living child, Mang (after St. Magnus, patron of the town's Benedictine monastery), became Francis Xavier's father.

After Mang married, he became so ill with some virulent disease that his life trembled in the balance. His wife, Frances, fell on her knees and vowed a pilgrimage to the great Einsiedeln shrine in Switzerland, if his life was saved. In Mang's *Hausbuch*, one can read his grateful "Praise God! The prayer of my dear wife was heard."

Their little Xavier, born January 11, 1819, was in bed much of his early childhood with various ailments, convincing his mother, who had already buried twin girls, that he would not live to grow up. Perhaps for this reason, she talked to him a good deal of Heaven's glories and took special pains to share with him her love of prayer. But early training is not the whole story. Mozart's sister got music lessons too. Mrs. Seelos would later remark that she tried to spiritualize all her children, but Xavier took to such things beyond the others, including two girls who became nuns.

Some see a spiritual prodigy as a somber child. This is the exact opposite of reality: Xavier was a merry, giving child—among his family's simple memories is one of the day the tiny boy "borrowed" the coat his father had been married in and paraded down the streets, sleeves flapping, tail dragging, entertaining his friends. He liked to make people happy. When he went away to school, always necessarily on scholarships, he was called by his friends "the banker," for what little he came by, they could always draw on. One of them says that Xavier had the rocklike faith of his mother melded to the quick-to-laugh, urbane geniality of his father. Those who knew him as a university student in Munich picture someone far along the road to spiritual greatness.

It was no great surprise to his fourteen-year-old brother, Adam, to arrive at his brother's quarters for tutoring and be told by an excited Xavier, "We won't be studying today. Our Lady appeared to me last night." In his youthful elation, Xavier shared with Adam that he, Xavier, was not to remain in his homeland, but go far away. A year later, in 1843, he left Bavaria forever.

In an age when many people thought loving God meant you didn't love anyone else, Xavier wrote his next-in-age sibling, Antonia, who had been his natural confidante and playmate: "Love has bound us two together for time and eternity. Here on earth we will remain united in our hearts and in our prayers for each other—and there in heaven we will be eternally united without the least fear of separation. . . ." In that same long farewell letter with its separate warm notes to the family members, he admits writing in tears. Heavy-hearted, he tells Adam in another letter, ". . . if it concerned my own wishes, I'd stay with you always but I can't resist the inner call—I freely follow it."

Like St. John Neumann, whom he worked under as a young priest in Pittsburgh and loved "like a father," Seelos joined the Redemptorists, missionaries who ministered to German-speaking immigrants. In fact Seelos would serve people of every ethnic background, just as Neumann did.

Redemptorists who knew him declared that Seelos was already considered a saint in the order's American novitiate. The American people agreed. Hearing him give one of his first sermons in not-yet-mastered English, an Irish immigrant remarked that, while she couldn't understand him, it did her good just to see that "holy priest" struggling to preach. In Pittsburgh and New Orleans, parents predicted to their children that Father Seelos would be canonized one day. Bishops concurred. Bishop Michael O'Connor of Seelos's first major post, Pittsburgh, wrote to Rome, "This priest is a man of truly remarkable sanctity" and asked that Seelos be named his successor. In Detroit, Bishop Lefevere said of Seelos, who served there for ten months, "One only has to look at him to know he is a saint."

Early in his priestly career the whispers began concerning physical cures. Michael Curley, a Redemptorist biographer,* with access to many first-person, under-oath testimonies, notes:

In asking God to cure people of bodily disease . . . Seelos seemed to have no doubt his prayer would be answered. This was quite apparent on several occasions in Pittsburgh when the people brought their sick children to him. He said a prayer over them before the altar . . . with such calm assurance that the bystanders were struck by it. They were more surprised when those for whom he prayed were cured. . . .

* *The Cheerful Ascetic.*

One of those cured children was a little Protestant boy whose mother sent Father Seelos a gift in thanks. Another was Philomena Roehlinger, whose epileptic seizures, beginning in infancy, had gradually become so severe her mother privately asked Father Seelos to pray her child would die. Instead the saint worked a total cure as described in detail in the pamphlet *Meet Father Seelos,* by Redemptorist Father John Vaughn. Years later the family's second child was instantaneously cured of an eye affliction five years of doctoring had failed to help. God, testified Mrs. Roehlinger, had given Father Seelos "great power."

Another woman testified that when Father Seelos was stationed in Pittsburgh her condition was such that death seemed near. She told the priest she was not afraid to die but she was worried about her young children. Father Seelos, she said later, told her to begin a novena to Jesus in his Eucharistic form and to receive communion with the same confidence in healing displayed by the woman who touched the hem of Christ's garment. Inspired, the sick woman prayed with faith and was healed.

Because of events like these, a crippled man came to see Father Seelos. "Cure me," he pleaded.

"Now, now, I'm no doctor," Father Seelos began. But the visitor was not about to be denied. Picking up his crutches, he heaved them out the rectory window.

"I'm not leaving until you cure me," he said determinedly.

Seelos shook his head but fetched his Bible. He had the man sit and then settled himself. He began to read in the Gospel of St. John. Finally, he stopped, closed the book, and began to pray ardently.

Next he prayerfully recited the Church's blessing for the sick. Only then, when he had done all he could to sidetrack any healing from connection with himself, did he bless the man.

Immediately the petitioner felt a strange feeling pass through his crippled legs. Sobbing with joy, he began to walk as he cried out his thanks to God and to Father Seelos for his cure.

That same rocklike faith in unseen realities that was at the service of the sick gave Father Seelos words for a couple who told him their child had died.

"Your child is not lost to you," he assured them. "Your child is saved for you for all eternity."

Those coming to Father Seelos for healing or consolation often thought him robust, because he accomplished the work of a strong man. Actually he seems to have experienced a kind of ongoing healing, somehow continually recharged by his union with God so that he could serve others in spite of his bodily weakness. In Lent of 1857, however, as if God were signaling the need for a rest, the preacher broke a blood vessel in his throat and hemorrhaged for three days. His death expected, he wrote a "last letter" home. Later his sister said with great emotion to a visitor, "He, who in his whole life hurt no one, asked our pardon. . . ." Soon he was back at work but forbidden to preach for some time.

Christlike goodness like Seelos's heals, but it also triggers attack by those it threatens. Some of these are simple "bad" people like the man who lured the priest out at night on a sick call in order to beat him to near unconsciousness. Others are "good" people who are *forced* by the purest motives, they would tell you, to act against someone. Thus the newspaper that reported with high-minded horror Seelos having gone in the dead of night to a bawdy house. The priest, who had answered the call to a dying prostitute, said simply, "Well, I saved a soul." Much loved in his religious order, he had been made novice master, then prefect of students. His fatherly treatment of his students —things like letting American seminarians with inadequate Latin take their theology exams in English—incensed one Redemptorist, who wanted Americans rigidly held to every European custom. By a secret letter campaign to Rome, this fellow priest discredited Seelos as "too good" to be effectual. Suddenly stripped of his offices *sans* explanation, Seelos took the demotion with the happy assurance of a saint who knows God is doing him a good turn whatever happens.

Without any rancor, he went on being "too good." When another priest gloated, as they preached a mission together, "Boy, I'm going to castigate them today," Seelos objected, "That's entirely out of place." In a day of "hellfire and damnation" sermons, Seelos's talks emphasized God's pity and love as reasons for childlike confidence in our heavenly Father. If any soul was lost, he assured his hearers, it was never from a sin too big, but only from too little trust in God's mercy and forgiveness. And if anyone was afraid his or her sins were too many or too awful to confess, he promised to hear that person with special gentleness. No wonder two-hour waits before his confessional were common, while in some towns mobs of eager penitents almost tore his confessional door off its hinges.

In such an atmosphere, not only conversions but physical cures flourish. For instance in March 1860 two doctors declared that a woman of Cumberland, Maryland, was going to die from diphtheria. This Mrs. Brinker no longer could feel anything in her hands or feet. Given the last sacraments, she lingered some weeks without improvement. By May 2, when someone asked Father Seelos to visit her, she was unconscious. She later told how she came to, to find the priest praying on his knees next to her bed. To her surprise she could feel again. With his kind smile, Father Seelos told her he was going to make a novena for her. He felt sure, he said, that God would restore her health. From then on she improved. By July 4, she was well.

Several years later the same woman's life was endangered again by some illness the main symptom of which was a terrible cough. Passing through Cumberland on one of his preaching tours, Father Seelos seemed to be amused. "What you need," he grinned, "is another powerful blessing." He blessed her and instantaneously the cough disappeared, never to return.

We have no date on the second visit, but it may well have

been in 1865, for he stopped in Cumberland that year according to testimony by the Simon Sell family. Sell, a workingman, fell from a scaffold that June 6. Worse than his broken hip and ribs and the deep wound in his side were the internal injuries. With his crushed kidneys and other internal damage, three doctors told the family, he was beyond medical skill.

On June 10, Father Seelos, visiting the Cumberland Redemptorist house, was called out to give Sell the last rites. The workingman sorrowed to the compassionate priest that he would leave his family destitute, since he had nothing for their support beyond his labor. Father Seelos was moved. In the next few days, he returned several times to see the Sells. Then one day he said to the children, "Let's kneel down and ask God to heal your father."

On his knees he led them in prayer. The family experienced him as approaching God like a child begging a kind father for a special favor. They were all weeping when Father Seelos stood up and said, "Mr. Sell, you're not going to die. To support this home for your children, you're going to get well."

Sell did not die. In three months he was out on crutches. A little later he was back at work.

In September 1866, Father Seelos was on a train to a new post in a trilingual parish in New Orleans. Sister Maria Largusa of the School Sisters of Notre Dame was on the same train. She noticed that the priest did not use the sleeping car but sat up all night. He seemed, she said, immersed in prayer.

"Will you be in New Orleans long, Father?" she asked the next morning.

He smiled. "I'll be there a year. Then I'll die of yellow fever."

Speechless, Sister Maria filed that conversation away as one to remember.†

In New Orleans, too, people were soon talking of this man

† The July 24, 1866, diary entry of a Redemptorist friend notes that Seelos said the same thing to him.

who so affected people's lives and telling each other about inexplicable cures. Among these was the case of the three-year-old daughter of the George Segel family. She was very sick, refusing all nourishment, when the family doctor confessed he could do no more and advised calling in a specialist. Instead the parents wrapped the sick child and carried her to Father Seelos. Rather than an instant cure, when the priest prayed over the child, she seemed to be violently affected. He advised the parents to go home and assemble their workers to pray for the little girl. They followed this odd advice and the child fell into a deep sleep that lasted so long and was so sound, it was feared she was dead. She woke better. Again her parents bundled her up and took her to Father Seelos. He prayed over her a second time and she was further improved. After a third prayer session she was completely well and remained healthy thereafter.

Another testimony collected for the prebeatification investigation and reported in Curley's official biography tells of the Redemptorists' widowed washerwoman, Maria Jost. She was bringing the fathers' laundry back to the rectory, balancing a large basket on her head, when she was hit by a horse-drawn trolley. After two months in bed unable to even move without help, the doctor gave her the good news that in another month she might be able to sit up for brief periods.

"I'd rather die than lie here helpless another month," she exploded when Father Seelos visited and said something about patience. Without further unwanted advice, he prayed and blessed her. The next morning, she was up and well.

In the fall of 1867 the city and the Redemptorists living there were decimated by yellow fever. Two Redemptorists had already died in the house when Seelos was given the news that the doctors judged him past recovery.

"Oh, what pleasant news!" he exclaimed. While the *Daily Picayune* reported each morning on his condition, Xavier weakened slowly. His humor remained. Asked if he needed to make any arrangements with his brothers and sisters about a family inheritance, he answered, "Before I came to America we arranged this in really brotherly fashion. I get nothing and they get nothing."

To a Brother who, sure this was a saint dying, kept badgering him, he admitted, "Yes," the Virgin Mary was appearing to him on his deathbed. Of course the Redemptorists are quick to add, Seelos may have imagined this in delirium.

One thing they do know for a certainty: Father Michael Duffy, the pastor under whom Seelos was working at the time, did not have yellow fever; but he was just about out of commission anyway. As a child of eight or so, he had cut his knee so badly with an ax that several doctors agreed amputation was necessary. Aghast, his mother begged the intercession of a saint and the boy was healed. The leg served him well for years, but under the strain of the epidemic, making constant sick calls—the city death toll was then about eighty a day—and caring for the ill Redemptorists, the knee went out. Suddenly he could not walk and had to beg a passing wagon to drive him home.

Father Seelos, who had been his novice master, was delirious when Duffy came silently into his room. He never knew that the younger priest knelt by his bed on his one good knee and begged God to cure the bad one through the merits of the dying Seelos. Duffy left that room, he later testified, healed completely of the lameness and the pain. And, in spite of backbreaking work during the rest of the epidemic, he had no further trouble.

Father Seelos did know that Brother Louis, the interrogator on his inner life, wanted a cure. The Brother said bluntly, "Now you cure my knee. This running up and down stairs all day is killing me. My left leg's giving out."

"You sure have peculiar ideas!" Seelos grinned. But he said nothing more when Brother Louis grabbed the sick man's hand and put it on the ailing leg. He even smiled and pressed gently on the sore spot. Brother Louis said the pain vanished immediately and did not return until some days after Seelos's death.

After several days of passing nothing but blood, his face bright with joy in the hymn being sung by his friends, Francis Xavier Seelos died at age forty-eight. He had been in New Orleans just a year.

❧ 12 ❧

In New Orleans: "Our Most Amazing Case"

In life Father Francis Xavier Seelos smiled engagingly for his official priestly photograph while his fellow Redemptorists, in nineteenth-century style, assumed expressions ranging from sober to downright grim. In death, too, Seelos's expression people found benign and inviting.*

In spite of the ongoing yellow-fever epidemic and a hurricane that blew through New Orleans that day, immediately following his death on the afternoon of October 4, 1867, hundreds rushed to St. Mary's Assumption Church where his body lay on view.

Redemptorist Brother Louis feared the coffin would be overturned by the eagerness of the crowd pressing to reach the body. He noted that people, including the Redemptorists, were drawn to *touch* Xavier Seelos's corpse, for there was a general conviction that this was no ordinary body, but the physical portion of a saint whose extraordinary relationship to God and the human family channeled healing.

Among those saying openly that a saint had just graced New Orleans with his death was Christine Holle. Christine had been in bed for a month when she heard the bells tolling Father Seelos's death. As she listened something welled up in her and she felt a great desire to get to St. Mary's. Ignoring the excruci-

---

* An undertaker has assured me that corpses have no expression except as set by an undertaker, but testimonies in dozens of cases convince me that the death of saints habitually breaks this rule.

ating pain racking her abdomen and hip, she dragged herself out of bed and into some clothes. What disease she had is unknown to us today, but we have her testimony that it caused ongoing agonizing pain. Somehow she made it to church and through the pressing crowd to fall on her knees by the coffin. Reaching up, she touched the dead priest's hand. At that moment the terrible pain in her abdomen and hip left, never to return.

The next morning, as the body was being moved for burial in front of the altar area, a grandmother with a baby in her arms called out to Father Seelos in prayer. Would he intercede for this child already marked by impending death? From that moment occurred what one who saw it called "a great cure."

While individual Redemptorists like Father Duffy and Brother Louis were certain Father Seelos was a saint, they knew that only after both a stringent examination of a person's life and verified miracles as signs by God will the Church make such a pronouncement. Hoping an official scrutiny would be initiated by the Church, they dared do little to promote it. Any suspicion on Rome's part that a religious order is drumming up the looked-for popular enthusiasm on behalf of a dead member stops a Cause cold. So while Brother Louis, in New Orleans, and other individual Redemptorists such as Seelos's former seminarian Father Bernard Beck, in Detroit, made careful notes on what people said to them of Father Seelos and the healings recipients attributed to him, publicly the Order remained quiet on the dead priest. It was ordinary people who had known Father Seelos who spontaneously turned to the dead priest as a powerful prayer partner in Heaven. They shared the view of the writer for New Orleans' secular newspaper the *Daily Picayune* that Father Seelos's "only human weakness was his overflowing sympathy and charity for poor, erring humanity." In prayer, they put Father Seelos's sympathy and charity to the test and were not disappointed.

In New Orleans the parents of Cecilia Villars asked the dead priest's prayers when their sixteen-year-old daughter became sick on November 17 during a smallpox epidemic that battered the city late in 1869. Cecilia's "impossible" overnight cure from physician-verified smallpox was followed within a month by her equally inexplicable cure from other life-threatening problems, including a lung tumor.

With what we know about the links between mind and body, it would today be possible to theorize that Cecilia's trust in Father Seelos's intercession triggered remarkable and rapid changes in her body without anything supernatural involved at all. If so, this would also be a wondrous thing that many a victim of infectious disease or tumor would like to experience.

But a cure in Pittsburgh in 1872 shows that healings through the intercession of saints often take place in situations in which the mind-body link cannot be cited—and in which, in fact, spiritual explanations seem the most plausible. On that April 11, a twenty-month-old baby, Julius Stephi, was literally pulling his hair out in the agony of meningitis. The child also had pneumonia. Both were complications from a severe attack of measles. Three physicians, Doctors Hoffman, Foligney, and Clark, had fought for the child's life—and lost. The little one was in prolonged death throes when his grandmother, Mary Magdalena Vogel of another Pennsylvania town came into Pittsburgh and stopped by on her way to mass at St. Augustine's Church.

In this pretelephone era, Mrs. Vogel did not know her grandson's condition. She was shocked to see her daughter and son-in-law waiting in torture for the writhing baby's death agony to be over. During the mass, Mary Vogel testified later, the pain-racked little body in the crib was continuously before her eyes. Just as the priest reached the solemn moment of the mass when, Catholics believe, the bread and wine offered are changed into the body and blood of Christ (Mark 14:22–24),† Mrs. Vogel suddenly saw another face in her mind: Father

† See also Luke 22:19 and 20 and Matthew 26:26–28.

Seelos, who had been her confessor years earlier. Redemptorist
John Vaughn relates:

----•--•----

In this particular church they would ring the bell in the
church tower at the moment of the consecration during
the Sunday High Mass. As the bell rang she said: "Father
Seelos, while you were on earth you had the power to
change bread and wine into the body and blood of Christ.
Now that you are in heaven, you are not less powerful.
Please ask God to heal my grandchild." Then she promised
to make a novena in honor of Father Seelos and have a
Mass said if the child would either end his agony by a
quick death or recover.

----•--•----

Mass ended and Mrs. Vogel rushed back to her grandson.
Her daughter met her at the door. "Mother, mother, the most
wonderful thing's just happened. Just after the consecration bell
rang in the tower of St. Augustine's, little Julius stopped writhing. He's asleep as quiet as a lamb. I think he's going to be all
right!"

An hour later the toddler, who had refused all food for two
days, woke up ravenous—and well.

Cures like this led to opening official investigation into
Seelos's sanctity, which observers during his lifetime predicted.
From 1900 to 1903, testimonies were taken under oath in the
places where Father Seelos spent much time: Augsburg in Ger-
many; and Pittsburgh, Baltimore, and New Orleans in the
States. His Cause for official sainthood was then sent to Rome.

A cure from around this time was that of a handicapped
individual, a pious, if perhaps eccentric, old woman known as
"Holy Oil Mary." Mary Bauer got her nickname because this
staunch believer in prayer for healing used to anoint the sick
with oil according to the command of the apostle (James 5:14).
Using her black-enameled crutches, she made her way each

morning into St. Mary's Assumption Church where Father Seelos is buried. There, after mass, she spent most of her day praying. Apparently one day God spoke to her about her own crippled condition. While every day she paid a visit to the tomb of Father Seelos in the church, this day she asked his intercession for her *own* cure, stood up, set her crutches aside and walked off without them. For roughly the next seventeen years —witnesses place the cure about 1905—until her death on March 11, 1923, the prayerful woman in the old-fashioned black dress walked unaided.

Another cure given in Vice-Postulator Father John Vaughn's pamphlet "Meet Father Seelos" was actually told him not by witnesses, but by the individual to whom it occurred. John Ducote, Grand Knight of the Redemptorist Knights of Columbus Council in New Orleans, reports that in June 1938, when he was six and a half years old, he was attacked by polio, or infantile paralysis, the most dread children's disease of that era. When the disease rampaged through the little boy's body, it left him with both legs and both arms completely paralyzed.

The reader will recall the Notre Dame nun who had ridden on the train with Father Seelos when he moved to New Orleans. Her order still held the dead priest in great veneration, and when John's mother reported her son's condition to a Notre Dame nun named Sister Gertrude, Mrs. Ducote was counseled to ask the intercession of Father Seelos. The mother took this advice. She not only frequently asked Father Seelos to pray for John, but she made repeated visits to his tomb with her request.

In the Knights of Columbus's own words:

I remained totally paralyzed until approximately the end of August. Then one Sunday morning I called for my dad to come to me. He did not hear me because he had the radio on. I then got up and walked through two rooms to the side of my dad. These were the first steps I had taken in three months! I have always felt that I am walking today because of my mother's prayers to Father Seelos [for his intercession].

◄━●●●━►

As the 1980s come to a close, over a thousand pieces of mail a month arrive at New Orleans's Seelos Center where, since official acceptance of the Cause by Rome, records of healings and other favors attributed to Father Seelos's intercession are amassed. A monthly bulletin on the saint publishes some of the letters of thanks to encourage readers to also seek the prayer help of the saint. In a June 1986 copy, a grandmother writes her gratitude for Father Seelos's prayers; she has just attended the high school graduation of her granddaughter stricken with leukemia eleven years earlier. The July bulletin includes a thank-you for no further polyps or tumors from an individual one year into recovery from colon cancer. From Erin, Tennessee, the same month, a mother writes:

◄━●●●━►

My son was in a very bad car accident. The doctor said at the time he didn't see how he was alive. He had a crushed pelvis and left leg. . . . At that time he was told he'd never use his left leg and live a normal life because of his crushed pelvis. Well I asked for your prayers and I began to pray to Fr. Seelos [for his]. Today my son lives a normal life and walks fine even without a cane. Fr. Seelos again has helped. God be praised.

◄━●●●━►

Among the cases believed able to meet the Church's stringent criteria for beatification miracles and forwarded to Rome for further study is a young woman's healing which looks like the first recorded cure of sickle-cell anemia, a disease which to date can merely be controlled but never conquered by medical means. Another case is a crippled woman's surgery which strangely accomplished things far beyond what doctors feel possible. A third is the extraordinary cure of Angela Boudreaux from terminal liver cancer. In an interview for this book, Mrs.

Boudreaux revealed that, besides her cure, which may one day be proclaimed an official miracle by the Church, Father Seelos has been God's channel for several healings in her family.

These begin with a "cure" which seems rather minor—unless you've ever cared day after day, night after night, for a baby screaming, scratching, and crying with the pain and itching of severe eczema. That was the case with the Boudreaux's fourth child, John, who about a year after his birth in 1964 developed an allergy his mother says "was so bad that any creases in the body, such as those of elbows, knees, armpits, the back of the neck, etc., would crack and bleed with an odor like a drainage ditch." Because he scratched and bled all night, crying all the while, his mother had to rig up cardboard restraints when she pajamaed him so he would be unable to bend his arm to further gouge his flesh. This nightmare had gone on about a year, starting not long after he was weaned from breast-feeding to canned formula; yet the pediatrician and another specialist assured the mother it had nothing to do with any food allergy.

Angela says she had reached the end of her rope when she found a pamphlet from the Seelos Center in nearby New Orleans. The pamphlet offered a Redemptorist priest from the Center to visit anyone hospitalized and pray over them for a cure through Father Seelos's intercession.

Little John wasn't hospitalized but his distraught mother, she can now kid, felt *she* might soon be. Two days after his second birthday, on Friday, March 4, she carried the miserable child to the Seelos Center. To her dismay, she found the lone priest (not the gracious man there now) little inclined to pray for the baby; if he extended his offer to the nonhospitalized, he explained, he feared he would be overwhelmed. Angela begged and pleaded that he just bless the child with Father Seelos's crucifix in God's name.

"You're looking for a miracle," the priest accused as if this were an offense.

"I'm asking God," corrected the determined mother, "for a doctor who will find out what's wrong with my child so they'll cure what he has or keep it under control."

Only after half an hour's wrangling and Angela's firm promise not to run out and tell other people her nonhospitalized child had been prayed for at the Center did the priest reluctantly bless the scabby-skinned two-year-old.

The next Tuesday, March 8, a nurse working for the specialist who had been ineffectually treating John suddenly took advantage of her boss's absence to recommend that Angela consult another doctor, who, in turn, immediately sent the little patient to dermatologist James Burke.

Dr. Burke sandwiched the toddler into his day's schedule. To Angela's joy and relief, as soon as he looked at him, he said offhandedly, "Oh, we can get that under control." He ordered John off all soap and a number of foods such as the milk formula, orange juice, egg, and chocolate. For temporary relief he gave a shot. Although allergy specialists would not expect food-triggered eczema to clear up until some days after the last offending item was eaten, that night when Angela bathed John with the recommended over-the-counter soap substitute, the eczemic scales simply floated away with the bathwater.

Put to bed without any restraints in his pajama sleeves, the toddler slept peaceably—as did his grateful parents and siblings.

From then on, he neither scratched nor bled. In 1987, for twenty-three-year-old John his childhood eczema is only a story.

Five months later, in the first days of August 1966, unpleasant symptoms of her own sent Angela to nearby New Orleans' Sellers and Sanders Clinic. There Dr. Alfred J. Rufty took her history, palpated her abdomen swollen to proportions of a six-month pregnancy, and found a liver nine times normal size.

Angela had excellent rapport with her doctor and can say, "I trusted him to the fullest," but when he tentatively diagnosed, "My guess is you have cirrhosis of the liver," Angela recalls:

"I sat up and said indignantly, 'Doctor, I don't even drink.'"

The amused doctor countered that there are all kinds of cirrhosis, some quite unrelated to alcohol.

But the truth was to prove worse. A precautionary biopsy under local anesthesia retrieved no liver tissue at all—only malignant cells. A follow-up brought liver tissue but saturated with cancer.

Exploratory surgery was scheduled immediately for August 8 at Southern Baptist Hospital.

"How long will the operation be?" Angela asked.

Because Rufty respected her wish "to know everything," he told her frankly, "It'll be one hour if there's no hope; if it's five hours long (because removal of the cancer appears possible), you'll be flat on your back for at least a year."

"Well, when I come out I'm going to ask what time it is. Then I'll know exactly how I stand," Angela said with characteristic resoluteness.

Both Dr. Rufty and Dr. Freeman, the surgeon, were non-Catholics but the latter, a genial six-foot-six-inch Methodist, was willing to wear a memento of Father Seelos, as a symbol of prayer for his intercession, on his surgeon's cap while operating (Angela was allowed nothing on herself). Asking that intercession, the young mother of four put herself in God's hands.

The operation took one hour.

Dr. Freeman found the liver simply "replaced" by a malignant tumor (90 percent tumor, 10 percent liver, Angela would be told). Its dimensions nine times normal, the organ "contained multiple nodules of tumor," reported Freeman, "in both lobes." To have cut all the diseased organ away would have been to leave the patient liverless. Freeman could only sew her up. His report ends, "Prognosis: poor."

To verify his findings, the Southern Baptist Hospital pathologist, Dr. Frankie M. Slay, sent tissue samples taken during the operation to other pathologists for biopsy, including Dr. Will Steinberg at Tulane and doctors at the Armed Forces Institute of Pathology, in Washington, D.C. All agreed the liver's invader was malignant. Furthermore, because only children usually have liver cancer by itself, the pathologists agreed it would be very surprising if there was not another, primary (that is, parent) tumor in Angela's body of which the liver cancer was merely a deadly offspring.

Experiments have shown that a doctor shaking his head worriedly over a patient can lower that individual's resistance significantly as measured by white cells. Now Dr. Rufty, whom Angela trusted so, told her that she would most likely be dead of total liver failure within two weeks. In fact she would probably never leave the hospital.

"I'm a very positive thinker," Angela has said. Instead of turning to planning her funeral, Angela's mind went to Father Seelos's prayers and how they had obtained just what she sought for John.

She looked the doctor in the eye.

"What will you do for treatment?" she asked.

"Fifteen pathologists from throughout the United States will study the malignancy and recommend what type of chemotherapy we might try as a treatment *if*"—his voice underlined the word— "you're still alive in two weeks."

Not only alive, but with her liver improving rather than failing, Angela was home by her August 26 birthday. On her way, she had stopped at Fr. Seelos's grave, in St. Mary's. There, although she had been told she could not kneel, kneel she did— to give thanks.

Meanwhile the consulting pathologists, probably figuring that the object of their deliberations wouldn't be alive long enough to profit by them, took their time. It was well over a month after exploratory surgery revealed her terminal condition, before the hospital called to say the recommendation had been received.

Proposed was a purely experimental treatment for the liver

tumor (to the physicians' chagrin, in spite of every possible exploration—was this the first part of a miracle?—no other cancer site could be found).

Beginning that fall, a derivative of the deadly World War I chemical warfare poison mustard gas, called Thiotepa, was given Angela once a week through intravenous glucose solution. She was counseled soberly that she must prepare herself for severe side effects including terrible nausea, the loss of her hair, possible loss of teeth from loosening, bleeding gums, and others. She would, Dr. Rufty told her again, be flat on her back for a whole year suffering greatly and unable to do anything. And there was, with all of this, little hope that the experimental treatment would do anything but add to her miseries.

To say Angela surprised her physicians is putting it mildly. She had absolutely no side effects to the derivative of the gas that decimated both German and Allied troops. Further, once recovered from the surgery, she was up and doing. That Thanksgiving—four months after being given two weeks to live —with help she was cooking Thanksgiving dinner for her family of six and guests. Christmas, she had out-of-town guests who stayed on into January so she could show them all the sights of nearby New Orleans.

Literally she has never looked back, except to tell her story to interested people for the glory of God and to honor the prayer power of Francis Xavier Seelos.

Five years later, in October 1971, Angela elected to have surgery for gallstones, predicting that something extraordinary would be found when her liver was once more exposed to a surgeon's view. It was: Dr. David Weilbaecher's report says he found only tiny scars on the liver surface while the liver itself appeared normally tumorless. Both a needle biopsy and a wedge biopsy were again done. Like a liver scan done at the same time, they showed only a normal liver.

A follow-up report sent to the Armed Forces Institute of

Pathology received the noncommittal comment, "the apparent cure following treatment with Thiotepa is remarkable."

Was the chemotherapy the cause of cure? The men who can best judge that, Angela Boudreaux's physicians don't think so. For one thing, she had already lived on in an inexplicable way before chemotherapy ever commenced. Then, according to Dr. Rufty, her liver shrank and returned to normal too rapidly for the chemotherapy to have been the agent of change. The Protestant presented her case to a group of medical colleagues and said, "This case is definitely a miracle." He and other non-Catholic doctors cooperated fully, as did Catholic David Weilbaecher, in submitting her medical history to Rome in favor of Father Seelos's Cause.

In June 1986, Dr. Rufty, presently working in the field of cardiology as associate professor at Wake Forest University's Bowman Gray School of Medicine, in a letter to Angela said he had discussed her case at length with Dr. Weilbaecher at a Louisiana State University medical school reunion. Noting that both doctors had testified before the ecclesiastical board of inquiry, he added they agreed that "yours was the most amazing case we've ever been associated with."

Even Jesus found that only a small percentage of those he healed returned to give thanks. In the case of Angela Boudreaux, her gratitude to God for the cure and thanksgiving to Father Seelos for his prayers led her to become a tireless worker toward the Church's official recognition of the Redemptorist priest's sanctity.

Perhaps this wholehearted gratitude opened her to receive continued blessings from God through his saint. Then again, in life Father Seelos was a genial, compassionate man who never lost interest in those he once helped—whether they were as grateful as Angela Boudreaux or not. At any rate, in 1975 the Louisiana family feels they once again had proof of the power of Father Seelos's intercession. That year, twenty-year-old Angela

Marie, the oldest of the family's four children, was attending the University of New Orleans. Like many students who get very good grades, she was highly stressed. Besides working her way through school playing the organ for weddings and holding down a part-time job, Angela Marie was readjusting to American life after a year as a scholarship student in France. During periods of stress, such as exam times, she had always tended to have a skin allergy that looked something like ringworm.

That allergy was acting up now, and her mom counseled her to go to the family's dermatologist, Nia Terezakis, a Catholic woman physician from India.

The same evening, Dr. Terezakis phoned Angela Marie's mother.

"Mrs. Boudreaux," the physician confided, "I'm worried. Not about the rash. But about the itty-bitty shiny black mole—a little flat thing the size of a straight pin head. I found it on your daughter's back. I cut it out deep—eleven stitches' worth—and it's being biopsied."

Neither doctor nor her family wanted to frighten Angela Marie. But they all prayed, asking the intercession of Father Seelos, that the dermatologist's worst fears not be realized.

At first it seemed they were. Biopsy showed a malignant melanoma, the most deadly type of skin or mole cancer. Without lumps, any sensation or pain, it quietly kills, not by the pin-size head but through the strangling, fast-growing feelers, or "roots."

Dr. Terezakis dug with her scalpel again. This time, after forty-three stitches were required to close her extensive chase after those roots, she could report that she had removed them successfully, along with the pecan-sized malignancy below the surface of the skin. The deadly feelers had almost but not quite —the difference between life and death—penetrated the young woman's lungs.

With every mole on her body removed and strict instructions to avoid the sun, Angela Marie was no worse for wear from a close brush with death.

"Mrs. Boudreaux," Dr. Terezakis said confidentially to her mother, "if your daughter hadn't come in when she did, she would have been dead in a month or two."

Pure luck? Whatever you think, the Boudreaux family, including now married and healthy Angela Marie, credit God and the intercession of Francis Xavier Seelos.

In 1983, the family believes, they received a fourth cure through the one-time missionary, for son Andre, then twenty-five. Working eighteen hours a day in New Orleans's French Quarter, at about 9 P.M. on December 19, Andre left the restaurant where he was maitre d', walking over to his second job on Bourbon Street. Suddenly two thugs cornered him, sat on him, and shot him in the face, while robbing him of the two hundred dollars in his pocket. Somehow Andre got to his feet and ran back to the restaurant, blood streaming from the gunshot wound, which missed his eye by half an inch. Stumbling in the door, in spite of his injured tongue and missing teeth, he managed to gasp to security men, "Call the paramedics."

By the time he was examined in a hospital, his head was swollen three times normal size, and he was in danger of suffocation. Doctors desired to do a tracheotomy, that is to cut into the trachea, or windpipe, through the neck to permit the body air intake that way; but they wanted Andre's parents' permission as next of kin.

His mother took the phone call at the Boudreaux home in Gretna. She recalls she began at once to pray aloud for the intercession of Father Seelos. Immediately, she remembers, a sense of "calm came over me."

Driving toward New Orleans, she shushed her husband, Melvin, who was screaming and swearing in anger at the thieves and grief over his son, so she could focus on praying. In the middle of crossing a particular bridge, she recalls plainly four years later, Father Seelos, as God's messenger, seemed to say, "Tell your son when you go in [to see him], he doesn't need the operation; he'll be fine."

At the hospital the parents found their son's friends gathered, weeping. Angela calmed them with assurances that Andre was not going to die. Her words may have seemed a mother's need to deny reality, for another young man brought in that night who had been shot in the face with the same-type bullet died the next day.

"Andre should have died three times," the mother says she believes. But as far as she was concerned then and now, Father Seelos had given her a word from God—and she believed it.

After prayer and telling her son he didn't need the tracheotomy, Angela went home and peacefully to sleep, to her husband's amazement. More typical of the parent whose child has just been shot, Melvin walked the floor.

Unable to talk or eat—he lost sixteen pounds almost overnight—and such a sight that his sister had nightmares after seeing him, Andre had only reassurance from his mother that, however things seemed, he was going to be fine.

She was right.

Hospitalized the night of December 19, on December 23 he was discharged. Christmas Eve he was in church with the rest of the family—giving God thanks for his life.

Today there is not even a scar to show Andre Boudreaux was once shot in the face at close range.

Not long after the murderous attack on his son, Melvin Boudreaux developed a rare tropical skin disease that can be fatal; after more requests to the "family saint" for his prayers, Dr. Terezakis was able to control it with medication. Perhaps it was at this point God decided this family needed the mother in a particular kind of supportive environment. Perhaps Father Seelos had simply become especially fond of some of his "best clients." All Angela knows is she found herself unhappy in her job because of the racial injustice there. A woman of prayer, she asked God to get her out of such an un-Christian situation, as usual asking Father Seelos's intercession. In answer, the firm decided to discharge two of their three secretaries, Angela among them. Three days later came a call from the Seelos Center wondering if she would take the secretary's job there.

Are ducks drawn to water?

With Angela now able to make her exuberant volunteer efforts vocational as well, it seems only a matter of time before the prayer power of Father Francis Xavier Seelos becomes a household word.

❧ 13 ❧

Padre Pio:
The Wound That Heals?

Just about everyone has heard of Padre Pio, the Italian stigmatic whose death at age eighty-one on September 23, 1968, was even reported by the New York *Times*. The biographies that sell steadily year after year are crammed with accounts from people whose medically inexplicable healings came to them, they believe, through the gloved, bleeding hands of this Capuchin Franciscan priest. This writer has verified with the friars of Our Lady of Grace, the friary where Pio lived, that the account given in several of these books of a construction worker's eyeball, blown to a smear of jelly by dynamite, being replaced by a new eye through the prayer of the living Padre Pio, is absolutely factual. The young laborer, Giovanni Savino, lived many more years in the southern Italian town of San Giovanni Rotondo, where Padre Pio spent half a century as a friar. A photograph of the healed man in the book *Padre Pio* by Father Charles Carty shows not even a scar from the dreadful eye wound doctors regarded as "beyond repair."

According to ordained Lutheran minister C. Bernard Ruffin, Padre Pio's most recent and, to date, most thorough biographer, who worked in close collaboration with the Capuchins, the archives of Our Lady of Grace show that in Pio's lifetime "over a thousand people pronounced hopelessly ill by their doctors, were delivered of such grave maladies as cancer, heart disease, diabetes, tuberculosis, congenital birth defects and paralysis

caused by spinal injuries." So numerous are these—plus all the
many other cures of nonterminal conditions—that the later biographies do not have to simply repeat cures found in the earlier books; they can give the newest cases. I shall do the same,
reporting a previously unpublished cure in detail in the next
chapter as a sample of the more than one thousand cures attributed to Padre Pio in the first twenty years since his death. First
a bit on a subject which only Ruffin's biography adequately ex-
plores, Padre Pio's own long years of intense—and seemingly
unanswered—need for healing.

The father of the boy born Francesco Forgione on May 25,
1887, was one of those Italian peasants locked in profitless labor
on the sterile lands of the lower Italian Peninsula. Heroically,
Papa Forgione became one of those workers who so pulled at
the heartstrings of Francesca Cabrini as they let themselves be
packed like sardines—often seasick and heartsick for the families left behind—in the steerage decks of ships lurching toward
an unknown fate in the United States. The hope of many like
Forgione was not permanent emigration; rather, enduring years
of separation, discrimination, and labor far from the beloved
homeland, they sought better lives for those left behind and a
decent old age for themselves. By Papa Forgione's labors in
places like Mahoningtown, Pennsylvania, and the community of
Jamaica, Long Island, in New York, he achieved his dream:
Francesco was freed from the fields for the education that made
him Pio, a Capuchin friar.

What Papa's sacrifice, the entire family's and fellow Capuchins' worries and prayers, and least of all the medical profes-
sion's efforts could not do after 1908, it appeared, was make the
young Capuchin well enough to actually live in a friary. No
matter to which friary his superiors assigned him—and they
chose those with the most healthful climates—one foot in the
door and Pio's stomach began to cramp and his temperature to
rise (he may have set the human record here, with physician-

verified levels of 120 and 125 degrees at times) so that he was soon at death's door from vomiting, tuberculosis-like symptoms, and other ills, including, at times, atrocious pains in his chest.

For almost a decade this went on. Pio would report to a new monastery after months of recuperation at home, only to begin vomiting the day he arrived. A number of physicians over the years diagnosed tuberculosis. Others disagreed. Some thought the problem chronic bronchitis, but that left the stomach symptom unaccounted for. In 1912 a Naples physician, without giving any name to Pio's condition, simply said his condition was hopeless and terminal. But whenever the stocky, reddish-haired young friar returned to his native village, he began to improve at once.

If his physical condition improved at home, his confusion, fear, and guilt did not. Counseled by letter to try again to return to a friary, he writes back very humanly, "It seems to me that I have the right and duty of not depriving myself of life at the age of twenty-four! It seems to me that God does not want this to happen." Then the young man who is already believed a saint in his hometown immediately adds in his letter to his superior, "Consider that I am more dead than alive and then do as you believe best, for I am disposed to make any sacrifice if it is a case of obedience."

Chided once more, in his next answer Pio eats humble pie. "With reddened eyes and trembling hand I . . . beg your forgiveness. . . ." In effect, as he says in another letter, he is grappling with the temptation to despair. Year after year the prayers for his healing are not answered, in spite of the fact that he wants a cure so he can answer what he is sure is a genuine call from God to follow the friary life of self-denial and prayer on behalf of the wounded members of the human family.

And he can see, as can his spiritual director, a man wise in the ways of mysticism, that the root of all his life-threatening illness is not something like a TB bacillus, but spiritual. In other words the very area that is the site of all his hopes and dreams appears to be the source of their failure. If his superiors all agree that this young friar is a very rare person already capable of loving God and his fellow human beings beyond what most of us achieve in a lifetime, Pio can also be looked at as, if not a downright malingerer—no one believes that—at least as someone who may be sinning against his vocation by resisting it with every ounce of bodily strength. While they love the young mystic and try to encourage him to see God's loving hand in his strange situation, at other times his spiritual advisers become downright annoyed and badger him that it is hardly edifying for "everyone to know that a priest remains at home because of his health," or chide, "It is being said all over . . . that you are being deceived by the devil, who is taking advantage of your affection for your native soil."

Some days the confused Pio wishes to die to be with God, as it seems he is going to do; on other days, he clamors to live. He broods that perhaps his illness is a punishment for his sins. He panics when it seems he may be dismissed from the Capuchin Order. Yet through all the confusion and varying emotions, he remains in love with God, whom he sees as "both the one who smites me and the one who consoles me."

Since devils were at this time appearing to Pio, buffeting and taunting him, he said, his inability to remain in a Capuchin house may be seen as just one more manifestation of their work, the Hinderer knowing the enormous good Pio would do once he could live in a friary. Others will judge Pio as a young man struggling with the purely interior "devils" we all must face, that is, the shadow portion of the psyche. A third possibility is that both an inner struggle and a cosmic one were involved, as is suggested by the content of some of Pio's visions. And finally some will see Pio, as he himself puts it in a letter, as "toyed with by Love," God playing with the mystic, molding him through this "senseless suffering" into one who has hoped against hope, clung to faith in despair, and continued to love God even when he seemed to treat one most unlovingly, and so become ready to be the first priest who is known to have borne the visible marks of the Crucified Christ in his body.*

The war for which all of Pio—body, psyche, and soul—is the battleground goes into a new phase in 1918. Like the wounded St. Paul, who prayed for healing from "a thorn in the flesh," was *not* healed, and eventually found that God willed His servant's strength be made perfect in this weakness, Pio gets well; that is, he is cured of his mystic's fevers, his vomiting, and the other physical ills doctors say doom him sufficiently to take up permanent residence in a friary; but from this time on, the stigmata he has had intermittently, sometimes visibly, sometimes invisibly, are clearly visible and permanent.

Having begged God for years, with permission of his spiritual guides, for the rarest of human vocations, that of the "victim" who participates in a mystical and/or physical way in the Passion of Christ for the salvation of the world, Pio has his answer. Not that Jesus needs anyone. He alone is the Redeemer. But the Lord will do his humble servant a favor and let him suffer redemptively like a St. Paul, who says, "I make up in my body what is lacking in the sufferings of Christ. . . ." For the rest of the Franciscan's life, he will suffer redemptively for other members of the human family. The outer sign of a much more all-encompassing suffering is for Pio what he calls "the terrible humiliation and embarrassment"—because he sees himself as so unworthy—of his burning, bleeding hands and feet and the deep heart wound of the Crucified One.

However we analyze Padre Pio and his stigmata in terms of soul and emotions acting on the body, we are left with mysteries. Why does this "bodily proof of Pio's neurosis," as some detractors would have it, accompany the priest's inexplicable victory over physical disorders which doctors have said will kill him in a short time? And if he is a religiously obsessed neurotic,

* Francis of Assisi was a brother, not a priest; other stigmatized priests, of course, may be known to God, including possibly St. Paul, who writes, "I bear the brand marks of Jesus in my body." (Galatians 6:17)

how come people find him so lovable and his friends stress how much he has made them laugh? Too, there is the fact that because of the daily ongoing blood loss from his stigmata, Pio's condition should be precarious without careful attention to nutrition and rest. In fact his daily intake of 300 to 400 calories and sometimes less (like the time his stomach is bothering him, he says, so he fasts eight days†) and his two to four hours—two more of the time—of rest at night do not provide a physiological rationale for how for fifty years Pio carries on a most demanding all-day, every-day ministry. The whole event of Pio's extraordinary healing when hope was gone, and his ongoing stigmata become explicable only if somewhere in the analysis of body-mind-soul complexity is the phrase "God acts as he wills." With that it becomes possible for me to suggest I have just put before you a bare outline of the first, and certainly the strangest, miracle of God's healings associated with the adult Pio.‡

Faced with this great mystery of healing involving a permanent wounding, the glib ignore the cure in which a dying man will be robust into old age and turn at once to a shallow form of psychology. Their analysis: Pio has meditated with such neurotic intensity on the Passion of Christ or has such a Christ-Victim complex that these psychosomatic wounds are the result. Other, perhaps more religiously inclined, analysts change "meditated neurotically" to "contemplated Christ's sufferings with such compassion and ardent love" that the signs of the Passion have reproduced themselves psychosomatically on his flesh. This group, too, does not deal with the cure. To both groups, Pio, whose sense of humor is robust, and who is much more a feeling than an analytical personality, snorts, "Right,

† Another indication that "neurosis" does not explain Pio is the fact that after eight days of no food, Pio had gained weight.

‡ As an eight-year-old child, his prayers were involved in the instantaneous healing of a "terribly deformed" little boy at the shrine of St. Pellegrino, according to Pio's reminiscences of this pilgrimage with his father, as told to Padre Raffaele, a fellow Capuchin, and reported in a publication of the friary, *Padre Pio: His Early Years*, by Fr. Augustine McGregor, O.C.S.O.

now you go meditate like that on a bull and see if you grow horns!"

Whether one is willing or not to accept that health *in some people* may require the ongoing presence, as John A. Sanford suggests in *Healing and Wholeness,* of a physical or psychic wound, there is evidence that Pio's stigmata, like his preceding mystical illness, is an event of greater mystery than can be adequately plumbed by even the useful and wrongly derided term "psychosomatic." Literally "of the soul" (psyche) "reflecting in the body" (soma), the word suggests even more today, when it is often used to imply that we have here a multidimensional event, something we now know to be true, if not always as important, in every illness from the mildest to the most catastrophic.

Padre Pio's long years of illness and his strange cure remind us that saints are not cardboard figures, but flesh-and-blood people with emotions and troubles like ours. A saint's spiritual journey, like Pio's, may at times, to the saint, be as clouded and frustrating as anyone else's. The inexplicable physiological facts of Pio's stigmata suggest that the body's potential is still uncharted territory, particularly in such details as how much food is needed or how prayer may fulfill many functions of sleep and nutrition. Further, our brother Pio's cure suggests that those seeking healing whose physical problems can depress them further because of their suspected or confirmed origin in psychic factors (which always includes spiritual dimensions, according to Jung and others) should not throw in the towel.

Today the man who knows his ulcer lies in his inability to confront his boss (in a deeper sense, it lies of course in his inability to confront himself and figures in his past) or the woman who gets cancer following her divorce, in our new sensitivity to the intermingling of the emotions, the soul, and the body, may lose heart, feel "bad," "weak," or at the very least somehow terribly "at fault" for this ill health. Pio reminds us that even saints go through similar experiences. For Pio, healing came not from abandoning the area where his particular difficulties lay, the spiritual dimension, but in going deeper into the very source of his illness. Similarly the way out of the cancer for the divorced woman may be (I do not mean to suggest this is the way for all or that any means of healing can ever be for everybody) to go deeper into the pain, anger, and grief of the divorce, mourning consciously so her body need no longer engage in the process for her. The ulcered man, too, is invited by his very physical symptom to turn his attention inward—and perhaps not just to his stomach and nutrition, important as these are—but to feelings and soul values as well.

From Pio and other saints, those called to the depths of inner exploration, may find new courage to believe it is in the very area of woundedness, explored *prayerfully,* humbly, and determinedly, for as long as it takes, that lies the road to a life of health and service to our human family. Whether he was engaged in telling one of the simple jokes that made his friends smile or reliving the Passion in pain and suffering as he said mass before awed onlookers certainly one can say of Padre Pio that his ministry was so rich and fruitful that any psychologist must exclaim, "If this stigmatic was neurotic, would to God the world were full of this type of neurosis!"

In a sense, the previously unpublished healing I present in the next chapter as a sample of the many cures that have come to us through the pliant hands of this Servant of God is an embarrassment to me. As I stated in the Introduction, there are two types of physical healings I have left out of this book. These are the numerous cures involving after-death appearances by saints and the countless healings in which a saint's relic plays a significant role. Each of these topics I reserve for forthcoming books, since each requires explanation lest something of God's mysterious ways be wrongly equated with, in the first instance, ghost stories, or, in the second, the "magic object" of shamanism or witchcraft. And yet the healing of the next chapter involves both. As I suspend my own prudent prohibitions, I can only hope the reader will focus on the remarkable cure and not dwell on these aspects. For those who are left with questions in either area, I hasten to apologize and assure that two forthcoming books will explore these often misunderstood ways God also sends his healing gifts to humankind through his saints.

Because I am indebted to the kindness of Father Joseph Pius Martin, of Our Lady of Grace friary at San Giovanni Rotondo, for the introductions which made the next chapter possible, I wish to add for his sake that his cooperation does not in any way constitute official approval by the Church or any claim by the Capuchins that the cure is an authentic miracle. While Pio's Cause is under way, it is not yet to the point where such declarations are possible. One day, the cure might be so termed; or, since there are many equally extraordinary healings being attributed to the saint, it might end up being set aside in favor of other cures. In no way could either outcome diminish or increase its unspeakable value to the family involved.

🍂 14 🍂

"Mommy, There's an Old Man in My Room"

Like so many Irish, young mother Ann Wilkinson of the village of Clogherhead in County Louth, Ireland, is a natural storyteller. I give the following account only slightly condensed, basically as Ann told it to me, her lilting Irish voice at times rich with the emotions of the Wilkinsons' experience of human suffering and God's grace.

"On the fifth of December, 1976, my second child and second little girl, Kelly, was born by cesarean section in the Mater Hospital in Belfast. She was delivered by cesarean because they discovered, before the birth, that her heart was beating very rapidly and that she was very distressed.

"While I was still under the anesthetic after the birth, I remember a nurse telling me that the little girl I had just given birth to was very ill. They needed her name, because they were going to baptize her. I remember thinking that if I stayed asleep and didn't answer, maybe it was only a bad dream and when I woke up everything would be all right.

"But when I woke up, I'm afraid the reality was very, very bad. Kelly had been born with a congenital heart defect which also caused a grossly enlarged liver. They weren't expecting her to live through the night.

"I lay in bed in the hospital and prayed that this little girl would live. I always had great devotion to Our Lady and I said my rosary that night as if I was sending a message with no room for error: it had to be from my heart and every syllable had to be said distinctly.

"I thought about all the babies that had been aborted or given up for adoption. And I said to Our Lady that I knew about the heart defect and the liver. I knew, too, that at birth the baby had been very blue and didn't breathe for a few moments so that it was suspected she might have brain damage as well. In my prayer for her intercession I told Our Lady that I didn't care whether my little girl was deformed, handicapped mentally or physically, or *whatever*—I wanted her and I'd accept her however the good Lord would give her to me. The only thing I couldn't accept was for him to take her away.

"The next morning, Dr. Muriel Fraser, who was the consultant pediatrician, visited me and told me plainly Kelly wasn't going to live. They had done a catheterization and discovered the heart hadn't developed properly: instead of the normal two ventricles, there was only one. The older Kelly got, the greater strain it would be on the inadequate heart. Inevitably death would come from a massive heart attack. At the moment, Dr. Fraser said, they were trying to get the baby stabilized on a heart stimulant to keep the organ beating at a regular pace. If that happened, Kelly might have a future—but only for a few months. Dr. Fraser said even a heart transplant couldn't help Kelly. We just had to try and accept she wasn't going to be part of our family for very long.

"While Dr. Fraser was with me, my husband Jim had gone to see Kelly in the special pediatric intensive care unit of another hospital. He remembers walking through this unit wearing a mask, boots, and gown and looking at all the little babies in incubators, some of them deformed and some of them who really didn't look as if they had much life left. Then he came to our baby and he told me later this baby looked so perfect in every way that he said to the doctor who was with him how terrible it was for all the other little babies that were in the ward: they looked so ill and as if they weren't going to survive long. The doctor replied that the other children in the ward had between a thirty to fifty percent chance at life but our baby had not even a one percent chance of survival. There was, the doctor said, absolutely nothing anyone could do for her.

"My husband couldn't accept this and continually tried to have the doctors say they had made a mistake or their equipment was faulty. But doctor after doctor told us the same: our baby wasn't going to live.

"Every waking moment I spent with Kelly in the hospital. I'd be there in the morning when she woke up. I fed her, bathed her, dressed her, each time I held her in my arms knowing it was going to be that little bit harder when the time came she'd have to be given back to God. The love I had for her was so strong that I'd hold her and pray, hope and *will* her to have as strong a will to live as I had to keep her.

"About three days before Christmas I was out shopping for my other daughter, Ciara, who was three. At intervals I'd ring the hospital to see how the baby was. This time I was told a doctor wanted to speak to me.

"The blood seemed to drain out of me as I thought, in sheer panic, Kelly had died. But the doctor who came on the phone asked would I like to have Kelly home. I said I would *love* to have her, and he said I could have her Christmas morning. He stressed the importance of her medicine, which had to be given at frequent intervals day and night. She would have to be brought to the hospital every month for a checkup. In between, if something happened, we must call day or night.

"Christmas morning after Santa Claus had been, I went to collect Kelly. The nurses were crying, because they had gotten so attached to her. Although I was taking her home, the doctor told me, 'You know, Mrs. Wilkinson, the outlook hasn't changed. Her condition is still the same.'

"But it didn't seem to matter that much. Having her home was one step and maybe, please God, the good Lord had heard my prayers and somehow. . . . Even if she could stay alive long enough for some cure or miracle to come through, I thought, that was all I needed. It was the best Christmas I'd ever had.

"Christmas night, Kelly woke up at three in the morning. My mother came into the living room with some coffee as I was feeding the baby and we had a talk. She handed me a prayer for the intercession of Padre Pio and said, 'Say that prayer to Padre Pio and leave it all in God's hands.'

"I responded I couldn't 'just leave it in God's hands.' I needed a miracle and I wasn't settling for anything less.

"My mother, who is a very dear good Catholic woman, thought this was terrible. I think she felt I was flying in the face of God. . . .

"When she gave me the leaflet on Padre Pio with its prayer, I was looking at it while she told me in a few words about his life. She said he was such a holy man that he could look into your soul and tell you what sort of a person you are. And instantly I took a dislike to him. I smile thinking about it now but I felt, 'Well, if he looks into *my* soul, there's no way he's going to give me the miracle I need.' Sinner that I knew I was, I decided there and then Padre Pio wasn't for me—I would stick to asking Our Lady's intercession. Hopefully her help as a mother plus her knowing me as a mother and the distress I was in would get her to intercede for me with her Son.

"Well, month after month Kelly was taken back to the hospital for her checkup. In between times we had quite a few harrowing experiences. For at least the first nine months of her life, she couldn't lie back. She had to sit up in a chair or her breathing became quite erratic. Because of her condition, she wasn't like my other little girl had been at the same age. Kelly seemed to sleep all the time, got tired very, very easily, distressed very, very easily, and at the least exertion whatsoever her lips would go blue. Sometimes she became quite black from minor stresses.

"I remember that each day I woke thinking, 'Dear God, don't let this be the day.' And I'd lie there in utter fear listening for her. When I could hear her laughing or moving in her room I'd know then I could get out of bed and continue on.

"During this whole time, all my friends and family were praying very hard that Kelly would be cured. I think mostly everyone was asking Our Lady's intercession. But my mother said a novena prayer every day to Padre Pio. I still couldn't find it in my heart to turn to him. I didn't honestly believe I was a good enough person to get a miracle through him. I felt he had been such a good and holy person in his life that he would accept nothing less from anyone who wanted his intercession. How wrong I was!

"Yet it was just as if Padre Pio was haunting me. I'd find leaflets pertaining to him. But I was always quite quick to put any such thing out of sight or to pass it on to someone else. Still I prayed constantly. I think the most important part of my day was prayer and meditation.

"When Kelly was about two and a half, I got the chance of taking her to Lourdes. At the grotto my prayer was still the same: pleading she not be taken from me. I looked around at so many other poor souls, mothers, fathers, deformed children, adults so very ill, and wondered, 'My God, of all these people how are you ever going to hear my prayer for my child. I'm sure to each and every one of these people their prayers are just as important.'

"It was a risk just to bring Kelly to Lourdes, and I worried about putting her in the baths* in case she'd have an attack of some sort from the icy-cold water. But I put my trust in Our

* The sick may be immersed in water from the spring that was discovered by St. Bernadette in 1858, directed by the Virgin Mary during the apparitions at Lourdes. Immediately cures began to take place, although the water has no inherent curative properties, one of the earliest being a dying two-year-old who was immersed for perhaps fifteen minutes in the icy water. Although he had been extremely frail and given to serious convulsions since birth, Justin Bouhohorts recovered and became a healthy child. At seventy-seven he attended Bernadette's canonization, in Rome, dying only in 1935 at age seventy-nine or eighty.

Lady's intercession, and Kelly went into the water and came out without any problem. I think it took more out of me than out of her.

"As I prayed in Lourdes for my miracle, it came to me to say to Our Lady that if there was any way that she wanted to lead me, I was willing to go that way; but she'd have to show me. To obtain this miracle, I just lay myself at her disposal, pleading with her again as a mother that she intercede that my child not be taken from me.

"We came back from Lourdes and life seemed the same. Kelly went every month for her checkup, and every month we were told the same thing: her condition hadn't changed and we must just take every day as it came.

"Then one morning I received a letter telling me her doctors wanted to admit Kelly into the hospital for another catheterization to see how the heart looked now. While they were quite sure things were the same, they wanted to give her that chance. It was nearing her fourth birthday and she really was very ill—not able to do very much. I think they felt things were becoming crucial.

"I felt so desperate and lonely that I was going to have to make a decision to have this test done when any little trivial operation could kill her. But I had to give her this chance. Perhaps something would show up they could now fix. Or maybe they would see something that medicine could help so she could continue on with her life.

"Kelly was due to be admitted to the hospital the next Tuesday morning, when, on Friday evening, I went into the village where I live. There I encountered a person with whom I'd had a disagreement through a misunderstanding. Because of that, I would have avoided her by preference, but she stopped me and asked about Kelly and I told her Kelly's condition was just the same and she was being admitted into the hospital.

"The woman asked had I ever gotten Kelly blessed with the mitten of Padre Pio? She said there was a lady in Skerries who had a mitten of Padre Pio.† Then she told me about a man who had had kidney problems, was blessed with the mitten, and was now doing quite well.

"Considering my relationship with Padre Pio, I wasn't too sure about this, but I talked it over with my husband and we decided we would go up to Skerries on Sunday and get Kelly blessed.

"When the day came and we drove into Skerries, I realized I had completely forgotten to ask the woman exactly where this lady with the mitten lived. We were seemingly getting nowhere, just going in circles, when my husband said, 'Now look, Ann, I think the best thing to do is stop the car and go and ask someone if they know where this person lives; otherwise we'll be driving around here all day.'

"He stopped the car, and I got out and asked someone where the lady named Thornton who had the mitten of Padre Pio lived.

"'Oh, sure you've stopped right outside the door' was my answer. Later I would believe Our Lady had brought me to this house and to Padre Pio.

"Kay Thornton, as I know her now, answered the door. In the hall there was a suitcase, and she told us that if we'd been five minutes later we'd have missed her, as she was going to San Giovanni Rotondo [where Padre Pio lived and is buried]. We brought the children in and blessed Kelly with the mitten in the name of Father, Son, and Spirit. I also asked Kay to have a mass said for Kelly's cure in San Giovanni and gave her money for an offering. Kay gave me magazines and prayer leaflets on the life of Padre Pio, all of which I rolled up and put in my handbag.

"We left and as it was such a nice day we decided we'd go visit friends who didn't live too far away. We were with them

† Because of his embarrassment over the wounds, Padre Pio was allowed to cover his hands with fingerless soft gloves. His stigmata were hidden this way except when he was saying mass.

the rest of the day, and as we were driving home Kelly fell asleep in the back of the car.

"As she was still sleeping when we reached home, I just picked her up and put her to bed. After a cup of coffee I went to bed myself. And for the first time I said a prayer asking the intercession of Padre Pio.

"Barely had I finished my prayers when Kelly came into the bedroom and said there was an old man in her room.

"I told her she was only dreaming.

" 'No, Mommy, there's an old man in my room. Come quickly so you can see.'

"I took her by the hand and brought her back into her room, where she pointed toward a corner and said, "Mommy, look! There he is!"

"I could see absolutely nothing, so I tried to explain to her that there wasn't anyone there.

" 'Don't be afraid,' I said.

" 'I'm not afraid, Mommy,' she answered, 'but he's there.' 'Look!' she insisted.

"By this time I was getting a bit cross. I said, 'No, Kelly. Come on, you have to go to bed now and go to sleep, because we're going to Belfast in the morning. We're staying with Granny and then, the next morning, you're going to the hospital. So you need a lot of sleep.'

"But as I was tucking her in, she was still insisting, looking over my shoulder to see him, that there was an old man standing in the corner of her room.

"I remember going back to bed and thinking, 'My God, could she be sickening for something, maybe hallucinating?' I lay in bed, but I could hear her laughing and giggling in her room and somehow I fell asleep.

"The next morning, I woke up and went downstairs to make breakfast. It was the usual morning, getting things organized—this time including things for my journey to Belfast—and getting my husband off to work. Kelly was up running around and

I asked her to go into the living room and get something from my handbag—I think perhaps cigarettes, as I smoked at the time. When she got in there she called, 'Mommy, Daddy, come quickly!'

"Well, we ran into the living room and there she was sitting on the couch with my handbag open and a magazine that Kay Thornton had given me which pictured Padre Pio on the front.

"Kelly pointed to the picture and said, 'Mommy, *that's* him. That's the man that was in my room last night!'

"I almost drop dead at the thought of it now but I said, 'No, Kelly, that's Padre Pio.'

" 'But he's the man, Mommy, who was in my room last night,' she insisted. She didn't say, 'That's Padre Pio, who was in my room.' To her it was just an old man. She had said the night before that he was an old man with a black coat. Now as I looked at the picture and saw the dark Capuchin habit, I had to accept the fact that it could have been Padre Pio that was in her room.

" 'If it was Padre Pio, what did he come for?' I asked myself. Was it to take her? Was this it?

"Every day for four years I had wondered, 'My God, will she be here next Christmas? Will she be here for her next birthday?' After four years of waiting for her to outgrow her inadequate heart, as her last day seemed to be coming nearer and nearer I was inwardly going to pieces.

"When we got to Belfast, I told my mother what had happened. She was delighted. Not only did she know a lot more about Padre Pio than I did, but she was fully convinced that Kelly was going to be all right.

"But I wasn't so sure.

"Tuesday Kelly was admitted, and the following day she was taken for her catheterization. I remember sitting worrying and wondering, 'My God, is this it? Are they going to tell me that all my prayers have been in vain? Or are they going to tell me there's something they can do now to help her?' I remember praying for the intercession of Our Lady and Padre Pio. If he had come to take her, I pleaded, let him not take her *just yet*. I wasn't prepared to give her up *just yet*. There were so many things I wanted to do with her and to show her. And again I said *I just couldn't give her up.*

"Eventually they brought her back. She was lying quite still on the bed and I was sitting beside holding her hand when a nurse came and told me that the doctor wanted to speak with me.

"During the time since Kelly's birth, Dr. Muriel Fraser had retired and another doctor in the City Hospital had taken over the case. She was a cardiologist. As I walked toward her office it seemed as if the long passage never seemed to end. The quicker I walked, the more it seemed that the hall lengthened. Finally I was sitting down in front of her thinking, 'What is she going to say about Kelly's future?'

"The cardiologist began, 'Mrs. Wilkinson, I don't know how I'm going to explain this to you but I'll try. For the past almost four years you have been coming here religiously with your daughter and we haven't been able to give you any consolation or hope. And for that I'm very sorry. But I have in front of me Kelly's catheterization done at birth and it clearly shows she has a single ventricle, a congenital heart defect, and a grossly enlarged liver. And then I have here the catheterization done today. It shows absolutely no congenital heart defect. Kelly's heart today is perfectly normal. *The piece that wasn't there is now there.* And the liver has reduced in size.'

" 'Now last night I don't know whether Kelly told you but we were keeping a close eye on her because her heart seemed quite normal for the first time and her liver seemed to have reduced. I was quite baffled, especially when we did the catheterization, because they both look so different. My diagnosis today is that Kelly is a perfectly normal, healthy child. I can't explain it. There is no medical reason for it. Somehow you have obtained a miracle. So take Kelly home, because there's absolutely nothing wrong with her.'

"I burst into tears and babbled that I knew exactly what had happened, that I *had been* given a miracle, and the man through whom it came to me was Padre Pio."

Normally I would end here this account of how God used Padre Pio eight years after the Capuchin's death to make a new piece for a little girl's defective heart. But with the cooperation of Ann Wilkinson, I would like to look briefly at another aspect of healing which I and other writers on the subject usually ignore—and that is to suggest some of the very human emotions and situations that crop up after some healings, especially those as spectacular as Kelly Wilkinson's. Having myself been in a similar, if much less extraordinary, situation with a child of my own, my purpose is identical with Ann's: to help others deal with comparable situations.

After all those years of worry and waiting, as mother and daughter returned home from Belfast, Kelly was the perfectly normal little girl Ann had longed for her to be. Yet odd as it may seem to those who haven't been there, the young mother found coping with the miracle "a bit of a stress in its own right."

For starters, there was a bit of what this writer has heard called "survivor's guilt" and has personally experienced. As Ann says humbly, "I couldn't understand why God had given *me* my miracle. It was something I'd wanted so badly, but why did he give it to *me?*"

She was finding that a healing miracle is also a spiritual and emotional event, and not just for the individual cured, but for those around them as well. Not that it confers instant spiritual —or any other kind of—maturity; but that it forces one to either run from God or deepen one's spiritual life. In Ann's case, it is obvious that her faith was much deeper to begin with than she modestly sketches it in her story. But in the past seven years since Kelly's cure, it has grown so much more that it now seems strange to her to remember that she actually worried that people might find out about the miracle when she and Kelly returned to Clogherhead. In part she was putting herself in the place of other people whose children hadn't been cured or who had even experienced losing a child. Like any sensitive person who can never forget the enormity of his or her own sufferings, she didn't wish to in any way rub salt in someone else's wounds by proclaiming, "*My* child had a miracle."

There was something else, too. A miracle comes to us as a dreamed-of, longed-for deliverance when we stand in such totally naked need, such obvious misery, that a good part of our acquaintances and sometimes even people who are among our "nearest and dearest" may be so uncomfortable with our situation that they avoid us or lecture us like Job's comforters. We ourselves may be embarrassed that we can't "take it." After all, those mythical superheroes "other people" live through their child's death or whatever tragedy is pending and become stronger people, better Christians—or so we are told or tell ourselves—while we, in our weakness, can only tremble and clamor for a miracle.

A cure, then, in spite of one's profound, ecstatic, never to be erased gratitude to God, is surrounded by such raw emotions that it isn't always the easiest thing to talk about. Or as Ann says of her particular case, while she left the cardiologist's office "walking on air and couldn't wait" to tell her mother, her husband, her close friends, at the same time the cure "seemed a very personal thing" and she wasn't comfortable about sharing it with just anybody.

And, she reminisces today, "I was afraid to tell anybody [outside family and friends] in case they didn't believe me."

Ann's fear of being dismissed as dishonest or perhaps a religious nut extended to anxieties for four-year-old Kelly as well. "I suppose it seems so strange" (it doesn't, only human), she says with characteristic honesty, "but I hadn't the faith to keep saying to her, 'Kelly, do you remember about Padre Pio? Do you remember seeing him in your room?

"I was afraid. I didn't want her going out into the street or into the village and saying she was seeing people, seeing *saints*, in her room, because people can be very hard, especially people who don't have the faith to accept something like that. And I'm sorry to say at that time I didn't have the faith to keep her memory [of Pio] going."

Even today, when Kelly is a normal eleven-year-old, Ann can say, "I worry a bit that because she's been cured, a lot of people now think she'll become a nun and lead a religious life. I don't know what her future's going to be. She's absolutely no different from my other girl, Ciara. And now I have a little boy, Tomás—he's four—and they're all the same. They can be good at times and they can be bold, especially Kelly." The candid mother adds, "I'm also afraid of people thinking Kelly's got some kind of power because she's been cured. I don't think she has."

If these are some of the stresses a miracle can leave in its wake in this imperfect world, as one would expect there have been many more blessings. One of these is Ann's changed feelings for the saint she was afraid would be "too demanding" to ever intercede for someone as ordinary as Ann judged herself. Today she claims, "Padre Pio is almost a part of our family." In fact, following the cure, she developed "a sort of hunger" to know the stigmatized priest. From Kay Thornton, she learned much. And she has pilgrimaged to Our Lady of Grace in San Giovanni Rotondo several times, particularly enjoying meeting friars who knew Pio personally.

Ann shared with me one incident at the friary that helped cement her growing friendship with the dead Capuchin. In her words:

"A lot of people obtained perfume‡ when Padre Pio was near

‡ I have written of this mystical phenomenon associated with Padre Pio and other saints in my book *The Sanctified Body*. Known as the odor of sanctity, it may accompany

them or [felt] some form of presence. When he was in Kelly's
room that night, I didn't feel anything. I didn't smell anything.
But when I went to San Giovanni the first time, I was aware
that people did get this perfume, this saintly aroma. I was wondering if maybe he would let me experience it as I went into his
room. But all thought of perfume, of everything, left me as I
looked at the pair of sandals in the middle of the room. I was
overcome with the thought of the suffering he had gone
through with his bleeding feet and his other wounds. I got quite
emotional, and I remember leaving the room feeling so so sad
that this poor man had gone through so much.

"Then as I passed the statue of Our Lady of Fatima that
stands just before you go into the corridor of cells where the
friars sleep, I got this beautiful aroma of roses and I cried uncontrollably.

"There were no flowers about. There was nothing I could
have obtained that perfume from. And to think that he had
come to me! And given me that perfume, maybe welcoming me
to San Giovanni! But I believe I had to get the perfume just
there, at that statue of Our Lady, because I think he was saying
to me, 'You know it wasn't only I that interceded for Kelly. It
was Our Lady that brought us together, that made all this happen.'"

Ann adds, "I really believe that Our Lady was the intercessor
who led me down the road to Padre Pio, that in God's design he
had to be the one that brought healing to Kelly—and I thank
God for it every day."

There is another reason Ann says things like "Oh, Padre Pio's
a great man in our house, a wonderful man." At the time of
Kelly's birth, the distraught mother listened to her own mother
talk of Pio's sanctity and ability on occasion to see into people's
hearts and immediately took a dislike to the Capuchin friar

certain living saints at times and signal their presence as God's messengers of healing or
other graces after their death. In Pio's lifetime, the odor accompanied many of his
bilocations and clung to the blood from his stigmata.

because, by her understanding of sanctity at the time, she saw Pio as, if certainly not someone to confuse with God, still of a "godlike" splendor so that he must look down on his spiritual inferiors, that is, ordinary, sinful men and women. Today Ann's understanding of sanctity is much different. She says of her friend in heaven, "I marvel that God sent someone like him to earth in our time, a person we can relate to, *just an ordinary human being* but one given so many gifts by God." It is not too much to say her relationship with the Italian Capuchin has changed her life.

"Padre Pio suffered so much," she explains. "Sometimes now when I think of the suffering he may have had to undergo or someone may have had to undergo to obtain my miracle and give me back my child, then I think of any little bit of suffering I have or trouble we have in the family or anything at all that crops up and I try to offer it up to God." Her hope, she says, is "that maybe my suffering, my unhappiness at times, can be offered up (as a prayer) to obtain happiness for someone else." Ann says earnestly, "Today I'll accept my trouble gladly so long as there's good that comes out of it somewhere."

Ann also credits Padre Pio that now "no matter what happens, good or bad, in the family, I can always see God's hand there somewhere [and find] a meaning for everything."

The saint God sent to bless her has also opened Ann more to other members of the human family. "I feel now," she says, "that everyone, no matter who they are, whether I like them at that moment or not, is a child of God. Today I want to accept others blemishes and all. After all, I'm not perfect. . . ."

She also says with emotion, "It's only when you've gone through something like that that you realize that when the chips are down, God is the only person there to help you. Material things, you see clearly, don't matter any more. It's your love, your relationship with him, with his saints—in my case Our Lady and Padre Pio—as far as I'm concerned, that counts."

Listening to Ann, one cannot escape seeing how sharply focused this wife and mother's Christian values have become in the decade since her second child's birth with grave cardiac defects. Hearing her, a listener has no sense of either self-advertisement or that someone is mouthing the proper words. As she once resolutely said her rosary every word "distinct and from the heart" when told her newborn was dying, Ann today says intensely if softly, "I try to live a good life to please God. And I try to instill in the children the love for Our Lady that I have because she's been so good to me and my family. I live every day trying to do good and *be* good. I'm only human and I fall sometimes—but I try very hard and I try to teach my children to lead a good life, because at the end of the day that's all that really matters.

⚑ 15 ⚑

"A Witch Doctor Greater Than Any Other"

Jaw thrust forward menacingly, the stocky native in the loin-cloth pointed to his wounded child: "You bullet removing, we you helping. You not saving, we you killing." To punctuate their chief's pidgin Spanish, eighty-odd men made ominous gestures with rifles, blow pipes, or arrows.

Sister Maria Troncatti blanched as all eyes turned to the forty-one-year-old nun, whose medical education had begun and ended with a wartime Red Cross nursing course.

For days she and two young sisters, with a small escort, had sunk deeper and deeper into the steaming green of the densely packed jungle where Ecuador abuts Peru. Climbing and descending, the heels of their shoes long gouged off by stones or sucked away by the ever present slimy mud, they pressed wearily forward under dense trees so laced together by vines that the sky seemed lost forever. In this endless green tunnel of huge cedar, giant bamboo, and tall palm, attacked by clouds of nipping, puncturing insects, the nuns alternately dripped hot rain or suffocated under the heavy, humid air, while their civilized noses gagged in certain places from the stench of rotting fruits, decaying flowers, and leaves blackening in the mud. With the fervent prayer of intense anxiety, the party plunged into a bridgeless, waist-high river, then were entombed again in the jungle, with its unnerving rustlings of poisonous reptiles, cries of unseen wild animals, and the strident squawks and screeches of the birds.

Once Maria had simply fainted.

"Take heart," one of the accompanying party cajoled as she came to.

"Take heart! What kind of heart have *you* to bury three of us alive in this jungle which has no beginning and no end!" she exploded, her sensitive face, swollen with bites, collapsing into sobs.

Normally so soft-spoken and gentle, serving others with a sunny smile and forgetfulness of self, according to those who had been her companions for years, Sister Maria was half hysterical as every step into this fearsome land drew her that much farther from civilization or, it seemed, from life itself, at least as she could conceive it. In this state of terror, anxiety, and exhaustion, she arrived at her destination, where perhaps some twenty whites lived, and confronted her welcoming committee: a fierce warrior band armed to the teeth who would kill her, the two young nuns in her charge, and the traveling party unless she operated successfully on the chief's child.

"But I'm no doctor. And anyway there's nothing to operate with! No instruments!" she babbled. But there was no way out; it was literally do or die.

Caught four days earlier in a crossfire between her Jivaro tribe and another band of Indians, the chief's thirteen- or fourteen-year-old daughter had a bullet lodged in her chest. At sight of those dark, fever-bright eyes and flushed cheeks, Sister Maria felt that compassion which made her such a gifted nurse rising in spite of her own turmoil. She put a gentle hand on the burning forehead.

Then, with a deep sigh and a murmured prayer, she asked someone to fetch water, someone else to start a fire for boiling it, and began digging in the nuns' bags for clean linen. After that, she looked for a tool that could dig out a bullet without introducing infection.

In a short time her scrubbed hands were sterilizing a tiny penknife. After washing the girl's chest, she applied hot towels over the abscessed area. Then to the Indians' wonderment, she painted the flesh with iodine while she said a slow, thoughtful Hail Mary. Finally, she cut into the abscess. Immediately and wonderfully, the bullet popped out. The chief and his band roared approval.

That night, the girl, her wound cleaned out and bandaged, lay next to Sister Maria, who gave her frequent sips of liquid. In spite of the exhausting journey, the nun could not have slept. The warriors were celebrating. Sister Maria shivered at their fierce, throbbing drums. She did not know they were sending a message into the green darkness: "A witch doctor greater than any other witch doctor has come among us. Free passage must be given to her forever and to all those who are with her."

Born into an exceptionally close-knit family of goat herders in the Italian Alps, Maria Troncatti knew only mountain pastures and villages until, at twenty-one, she left her grieving parents, sisters, and brother to enter a new universe of trains, cities, and educated people as a Salesian postulant. The emotional parting from her family so reluctant to let her go (her father collapsed in a faint, unable to say good-bye, while her oldest sister insisted, "But why can't you do good *here?*") and the alien surroundings brought on such depression and fits of weeping that for six months it was touch and go whether to simply send the goat girl home. That overcome, before her permanent vows, ill health threatened her vocation until a last-ditch novena to Don Bosco put a stop to a succession of ailments.

Ten years after joining the Salesians, now stable and happy in her vocation, Maria was swept away by a flash flood that inundated the convent, drowning another nun. She was saved in an inexplicable manner after agreeing to an unspoken voice which urged, "But you have to be a missionary." Even then the family-lover added to the bargain the life of her brother serving in

World War I. At the war's end, the thirty-nine-year-old nun, who had gained invaluable experience nursing victims of the conflict, was accepted with those half her age as a missionary to South America.

To say good-bye to her family, Maria made her first visit home in her seventeen years as a nun. Two of her four sisters were dead. Old, her parents were still as inconsolable. And nuns sent to South America, they knew as well as she, could look forward to no home furloughs in the 1920s. To end her own and their distress, she cut short her week's stay, only begging they would always write her.

Two years learning Spanish while, in effect, practicing medicine in a doctorless little town on the road to Quito, and Maria was sent to the fearsome jungle, where her life had been immediately put on the line.

Thanks to everyone's prayers more than medical skill, she believed, they were alive for the moment. But the new "witch doctor" trembled with terror and wept continually the next few days as she contemplated being "buried alive," as she put it, in this deadly green dungeon with no road for escape and only five households of colonists to furnish protection from natives so fierce their name meant either "savage" (Kivaro/Jivaro) or simply "enemy" (Shuar).

The morning those who had led them in prepared to leave the three nuns, Maria's silent tears erupted into sobs and she fled to a small clearing. There her anguish boiled over in cries and weeping as if her heart would break, recalls the young sister who followed her and stood silently by. This witness also says Maria's "veritable agony" like Jesus in Gethsemane ended in a peaceful whispered "Oh, Jesus, if you're content to remain in loneliness . . . why shouldn't I be?"

Forty-five years later, eighty-six years old and still in the jungle, Mother Maria was killed in a plane crash in 1969 shortly after making a private prayer offering of her life to bring peace between feuding white settlers and the natives. If few remembered her in her native Italy, in the jungle of Ecuador she was a legend. When news of her death hit settlements like Macas and Sucùa, colonists, soldiers, natives, and her fellow Salesians all wept together for their "*abuelita,*" their doctor, consoler, helper, sometimes conscience, and above all their mother. Other nuns' bodies had been flown out for burial: Mother Maria's had to be left in the jungle that had so terrified her on arrival and yet had become for her a beloved homeland, because armed men would have fought to keep her remains.

Humble and unpretentious, lovable in her tender love for God and the whole human family, bubbling with cheer and good humor, Mother Maria's was the sanctity that comes from a timid soul's saying yes to God even when he seemed to ask of her more than she could bear. From that heroic yes, made in agony and tears, Mother Maria's sensitive heart was enlarged and transformed to meld the courageous, protective strength of a patriarch with the tenderest compassion and love of a mother. From such a heart flowed healing.

Many of her cures came from a genius for makeshift medicine. But others are medically inexplicable.

In 1929, for instance, only four years after making peace with the place God had sent her, the nun was making a now almost routine several days' journey on foot. Stopping at another Salesian mission camp, Mother Maria found Augustus Zuñiga, an eighteen- or nineteen-year-old boy who worked on bridge construction for the remote area with one of the Salesian priests. A partially completed span had collapsed. Climbing up to inspect a girder, Augustus slipped and hurtled onto rocks far below. He was very badly hurt: "Six or seven ribs were broken on the left side of the thorax from his chest as far down as his floating ribs. The last two cervical vertebrae of his spinal column were cracked and his intestines hardened in his abdomen." In the

* "Little grandmother."

fifteen or twenty days since the accident, his only treatment had been saline compresses and chicha to drink.

Begged to treat the boy, Sister Maria could only join the pleader's tears with her own. Then she asked to go into the chapel.

"Mary, Help of Christians, will tell me what to do," she explained.

Although she had been on foot in rough terrain all day, the nun took no time for sleep, but remained in the chapel in fervent prayer for hours. Finally another nun insisted she come out and have at least a hot drink. She obeyed but was at early mass the next morning praying again.

"Now, Mother Maria," they asked after the liturgy, "will you please treat Augustus."

"I'll give him a laxative," she said almost offhandedly, a remark and tone which appeared highly inappropriate, even flippant, considering the seriousness of the boy's condition.

She went to him carrying a tray. On it were a glass and a prayer book, while under her arm was a roll of bandage. She shut the door, then turned to the patient.

"Augustus, all I can give you for your stomach is a laxative, so drink it up." She raised him and he drank.

"Now the rest of your treatment," she said, her countenance seeming to Augustus to radiate light. "Take off your shirt."

Painfully, he did.

From the prayer book she drew a picture of Mary, Help of Christians, surrounded by apostles, evangelists, and angels.

"Kiss it, Augustus. This is your medicine," she said serenely. Running her sensitive fingers compassionately over the broken ribs, she placed the picture over them, then firmly bandaged the whole area. As she worked, she prayed aloud the Hail Mary, Augustus joining in.

"Now the medicine for the top of the spinal column," she went on, this time pulling a picture of the newly beatified John Bosco from the prayer book.

"Kiss it," she said again. Then she had Augustus roll over, and bandaged Don Bosco's picture over the cracked cervical vertebrae.

"Now you must not move until I give permission," she told him. For the next four days she waited on him, as he remained immobile. Then, on the fifth day, she ordered, "Try to sit up without help." Effortlessly he raised himself.

"Now try to get out of bed."

Up with the same ease, he walked.

"How do you feel?"

"Fine, Mother Maria."

"Good. Now back to bed." By the sixth day, even his abdominal pains were gone and he felt compelled to get up and run. But permission was refused.

The seventh day, however, she removed his bandages. After he kissed the two pictures once more, she replaced them in her prayer book. She made him walk, raise his arms, bend over. Nothing caused even a twinge. That afternoon he was swimming in the river, diving and cavorting like any other splendid young specimen of manhood.

The next morning Mother Maria resumed her journey.

During Mother Maria's ten years at a mission station at Macas, with only the most primitive medical equipment but armed with the healing love of sanctity, she performed many other extraordinary cures. Fingers almost completely severed by machete were restored, men wounded dreadfully in jungle battles or farm mishaps recovered, a baby whose eye appeared lost in an accident sees perfectly (she recommended that case to the intercession of St. Maria Mazzarello, foundress of her order), and a child swollen like a melon from some jungle disorder was cured with the help of a relic of Don Bosco.

In 1936, while stationed at Guayaquil, she healed a young nun, Angela Forestan, who had been unsuccessfully treated by surgery for a problem in her thighbone. Decalcifying, the bone would no longer support her weight. Moreover, it caused the

200

nun such pain it appeared she would have to give up missionary work and return to Italy. Worse even than the pain was her depression. When the doctors could do no more, Mother Maria asked permission to try. That granted, she procured the long bone from a cow's leg, crushed it, and dried the powder. Adding a few other, unknown ingredients, she made up some pills.

To Sister Angela, she said, "Here! Take two of these every day, and on January 31 [the feast day of their order's cofounder St. John Bosco, canonized in 1934] we'll go to the Salesian sanctuary for a mass of thanksgiving. Meantime keep quiet and trust Don Bosco."

January 31, Sister Angela walked on her "useless" leg to the Salesian sanctuary to give thanks for what she considered a miracle recovery. Mother Maria was with her, sharing the joy and giving every ounce of credit to the prayers of Don Bosco and the Blessed Virgin Mary.

Although still disparaged by some physicians, bonemeal today is found in pharmacies as well as health-food stores and is considered by many to be both a preventative and a cure for calcium loss, so the pills Mother Maria made were not a placebo. Moreover, a doctor I discussed this case with points out that if a young person begins using a weight-bearing decalcifying bone—and it may be decalcifying, he adds, simply for lack of use because of pain—while ingesting an adequate calcium supply, the bone can remineralize, as it will not do in an older person.

Sister Angela was young. I find no evidence that Mother Maria made her walk, but I would not want, fifty years later, to insist she didn't. Let us not claim, then, anything like a miracle occurred; but, on the other hand, it is clearly appropriate to applaud Mother Maria for having, by whatever means, succeeded where professional medical men had failed.

Another testimony is that of a Salesian missionary priest whose continual vomiting doctors, again, had failed to cure. Says Father Lova:

I suffered with severe liver trouble for three years. She looked after me like a mother. No sacrifice was too great. She was ready for anything day or night. I could have died a thousand times had it not been for her. The worst time of all was when I got sunstroke. . . . Sister Maria was sent for but she declared she could do nothing for me. However she said, "Bring him to Sevilla† and I will look after him." They improvised a stretcher and I was carried to Sevilla. Slowly but surely she cured me.

Asked in 1969 what medicines she used, he could recall none. "I don't know how she did it. I can't explain it," he admitted. "But cure me she certainly did."

Another testimony that the holy nun may have had a healing charism is given by Daniel Gonzalez, who was knocked by a mule into a vat full of boiling cane syrup. It was hours before Mother Maria could make her way through the jungle on foot to the horribly swollen and blistered figure, continually writhing and fainting from the pain. The nun could only apply ointment and bind him up like a swaddled babe, saying, "Mary, Help of Christians!" at every turn of the bandage.

In the case of Sister Angela, Mother Maria's use of bonemeal could be considered evidence she got cures where others failed simply because she was medically ahead of her time. Without discrediting her natural medical aptitude, which could even be considered marked by genius, the case of Mr. Gonzalez discredits any general theory of this kind. I have discussed proper treatment of serious burns with medical men and the consensus from plastic surgeons to family physicians is that Mother Maria used exactly the opposite of today's idea of proper treatment. In fact her primitive handling of the case could have killed the patient, and if he had lived, the scars would have been terrible. But Mr. Gonzalez is not only alive, he has not even a scar from

† Another jungle "town."

this hideous experience. He also testifies that Mother Maria treated him another time when, in his estimation, the situation called for the last sacraments. With a tone of assurance, she insisted, "No, Mr. Daniel, God will cure you," and he recovered.

Poisoned by a hostile native in 1949, Father Albino Gomezcoello was carried to Mother Maria more dead than alive. For many days, he recalls, "I was aware of nothing." Yet occasionally he had a lucid moment. At such times, "day or night I saw her at my bedside rosary in hand." Father Albino also recovered against all expectations.

A servant girl in a colonist's family says:

> I had a bad hand and could not use it. The doctor prescribed expensive injections I could not afford so I went to consult Mother Maria. She said to me, "Do not worry, my child. Take this ointment and use it every night. I will pray for you and I am sure you will get better." The hand did heal in spite of the fact that the doctor had told me I should never be able to use it.

A woman named Juana De Lara tells how she arrived with her third son, who was very frail, for one of those consultations. Sadly she told Mother Maria how nothing could be done for the child, who was skin and bones.

"Leave him with me, Juanita," Mother Maria offered. After three months he returned home completely cured.

Similar tales, some detailed, some as brief as Juana De Lara's, stud the first biography of the Italian missionary to Ecuador, *Beloved Jungle,* by Maria Domenica Grassiano—which has been my source for this sampling of cures during Mother Maria's lifetime.

Since her death the elderly missionary's memory has not gradually faded away; instead her old friends and new ones talk of a desire to help that seems as alive as ever and a prayer power undiminished by death. On September 7, 1986, Maria Troncatti's Cause was officially opened in the cathedral of the town of Macas in Ecuador. The healings which since her death people attribute to Maria's prayers are regularly reported in two sources: the Spanish-language *Boletin Informativo,* which supports her Cause, and the Italian publication *Conosci?,* which gives testimonies of graces received through the intercession of six members of her order whose holiness makes them candidates for eventual canonization. Samples from the one copy of each publication I was sent by the Secretary General of the Daughters of Mary, Help of Christians:

In the early nineteen eighties a father in Ecuador has a daughter "who for a long time was gravely ill." The family consults both medical doctors and local healers. Finally the child is hospitalized for a month; still no treatments bring improvement and physicians cannot agree as to whether surgery should be attempted. Brought home no better, for the child, as her father puts it, "death begins to look like the only way out." While the heartsick parents ponder what to do next, the father appeals to Mother Maria's prayers. Unexpectedly, the girl is immediately restored to normal health.

A mother in Florence, Italy, has similar grateful feelings to God and Mother Maria's prayers in the case of her son in July 1984. Two specialists had said surgery was necessary but will pose grave risks to the child. Trying to weigh the two perilous courses, the mother sees a leaflet on Maria Troncatti, is struck by the expression of goodness in the nun's photograph, and implores her intercession that a third specialist she and her husband are going to consult will guide the parents as to God's will for their son. The third doctor's verdict: without any risky surgery, this condition will correct itself in time.

A man from the jungle town of Macas in Ecuador loses the sight in his left eye. He travels to Cuenca for fifty days of treatment, which, he says, "was absolutely useless. After that," he writes, "I was successively at Ambato, Los Sapos, and Guayaquil in search of other medical care, but I found no help and, what's worse, was robbed of my money." Discouraged, he returns home in January 1981 only to hear of a Shuar Indian who also had lost his sight and been treated in Guayaquil to no avail, then recovered his vision after putting on the glasses of Mother Troncatti with a prayer for her intercession.

"What you have done for my brother, do for me," he prays. Expressing his faith in God and in Mother's prayer power, he, his wife, and their children all promise to make a good confession so the cure might encompass his whole person and the family. Suddenly his sight returns, enabling him to work although there is still some disfunction of the eye. When he writes his testimony, in June, however, this is gone, having gradually cleared up, so that the eye has been perfect for two months.

In 1986 a man hit over the head while working in the mountains believes he is dying and is rushed by plane to a hospital. He calls on Mother Maria's prayers and recuperates without incident.

A Salesian nun who works in the Ecuador jungle dislocates her ankle when she falls in 1981. A woman skilled in massage attempts to put the bone back in position but fails. In spite of salve and wrapping it, the swollen ankle causes Sister Lutgarda Nieto intense pain. Awake in the night, she thinks "of Sister Troncatti, who during her life had given me so many proofs of her affection."

To the dead nun, the living one says, "Now you've got to show you wish me well and get God to cure me; I need to stand on this foot and work."

The result: "She heard me at once," Sister Lutgarda reports. The next day, Sunday, April 5, 1981, without either pain or swelling in her ankle, she is racing about hard at work at a church fiesta.

Andrea Pellegrini, an Italian mother, offers her testimony published in 1984:

———•——•———

This past June the doctor diagnosed that my three-year-old daughter had a massive tumor near her right kidney. The pediatric center in Brescia defined it as malignant. A risky surgery was necessary since its position was so close to the nerve bundles that could impair the lower joints.

The night before the operation, while in the play room of the hospital, I casually picked up the leaflet "Conoscio?"* and I read about the people who had benefited from Sister Troncatti's help.

One case struck me, for it was so similar to ours, for it dealt with removing a tumor that had grown on a vein. Then and there I turned with great faith to Sister Troncatti, extending my prayers right through the operation on the next morning. After two hours the doctor came out to reassure me that the massive tumor was removed without any damage to the tissues or the nearby organs. Further tests proved that the tumor was benign. Now, six months later, my child is perfectly well, thanks to the assistance of Sister Maria Troncatti.

———•——•———

A final sample of cures being attributed to Mother Maria since her death is reported by another nun from Guayaquil, Ecuador, dated April 1984. The nun has a married sister who has had rheumatic fever for a long time and has been at this point hospitalized for more than three months with heart complications. Permitted to go home, almost at once she must return to the Pasteur Clinic in Quito because of "grave cardiac insufficiency with obstruction of two heart valves." She has already had heart surgery; now she must have another operation, but just the catheterization tests cause her situation to deterio-

* "Do You Know?"

rate so seriously that the surgery must be postponed for fifteen days.

After the six-and-a-half-hour surgery, the married woman's condition only becomes more critical day by day. "Each morning," the nun writes, "as I arrived to visit her, I found new and painful surprises." When loss of consciousness, at first hoped to be only a transitory effect of the anesthesia, proves persistent, the nun and other Sisters begin a novena to Mother Maria Troncatti, asking her prayers.

But her sister's condition seems only to worsen. She begins to have attacks of a type of epilepsy and then goes completely blind. At this point her sister says: "I put a relic of Sister Maria near the bedside of the patient praying with new insistence, 'I trust you, Sister Maria. You who in this world never spared yourself to do good, pray my sister gets back her vision and is cured.'"

The next morning the sick woman can see light. Gradually her sight returns until it is once more normal, but she is still not out of the woods. Not only is her entire right side paralyzed, but a grave hemorrhage reopens the surgical incision and almost proves fatal. Still the ill woman's sister writes, "Our prayers continued, constant and faith-filled." And finally the failing body begins to stabilize and convalesce.

When she is ultimately discharged, the bill is stupendous after so many days in such critical condition. But a benefactor comes forward and pays everything, to the nun's joy in God's beneficence. She ends her account:

Two years passed and my sister was truly well. A last surprise we attribute to Sister Maria's prayers, a gift of joy for the whole family: my sister had a daughter, healthy and strong. This gift of God is all the more precious because the doctors had forbidden any thought of pregnancy after the last heart surgery and also told my sister later that her anti-coagulant medication must make the prohibition permanent.

———◆———

More testimonies could be given, but these must do. Even more numerous than her many cures in life and death, however, are the memories and testimonies, among those who knew her, of Maria Troncatti's courage in the face of hardship and danger, her resourcefulness at doing good with seemingly nothing at her disposal, and above all her charity, which finds a way to give when there is literally nothing left to give. Typical is friends' memory, recounted in *Beloved Jungle*, of the time when the nuns and their charges were facing starvation at Sevilla and a man led a three-year-old girl up to Mother Maria.

"My wife left and I'm sick," he said. "You take her."

Eagerly Mother Maria reached for the child, exclaiming, "Another blessing from heaven!"

"Another mouth to feed, you mean," snorted another nun behind her.

"Goodness gracious!" Mother Maria turned her pitifully thin frame to the equally gaunt worrier. "Let us have a little more faith, Sister!"

In every need, that was her answer: turn trustingly to God.

Like every saint, she would insist of any cures attributed to her, "They are all the work of His hands."

Calendar of Feast Days

While many saints have feast days in the Church's universal calendar, others are honored more locally. I have not made such distinctions in this list. Some individuals listed as yet have no official feast day because their Causes are still underway in most cases—or, in the case of Caryll Houselander, only beginning to be urged. When no other date is assigned, the date of death, as the date of entry into heaven, is considered the feast day.

1. Bl. Clelia Barbieri (d. July 13, 1870)
2. Bl. André Bessette   January 6
3. St. John Bosco   January 31
4. Bl. Titus Brandsma   July 27
5. St. Frances Xavier Cabrini*   November 13
6. St. Joseph Cafasso   June 23
7. Fr. Solanus Casey (d. July 31, 1957)
8. St. Antonio Claret   October 24
9. The Cure d'Ars (see Vianney)
10. Caryll Houselander (d. October 12, 1954)
11. St. Theresa Martin (St. Thérèse of Lisieux)†   October 1
12. St. John Neumann   January 5
13. Padre Pio (d. September 23, 1968)
14. Venerable Philip Rinaldi (d. December 5, 1931)
15. Fr. Francis Xavier Seelos (d. October 4, 1867)
16. St. Elizabeth Ann Bayley Seton   January 4
17. Bl. Anna Maria Taigi   June 9
18. Bl. Kateri Teakakwitha   July 14
19. St. Jean Marie Vianney (the Cure d'Ars)‡   August 8

* Patroness of immigrants.
† Copatroness of France (with St. Joan of Arc) and copatron of the Missions (with St. Francis Xavier).
‡ Patron of parochial priests.

APPENDIX

For Furthering Friendship
with the Saints of This Book

The organizations listed below are not out to make a profit; usually run by volunteers devoted to the saint, or individuals who have taken lifelong vows of poverty, with as few paid helpers as possible, they exist as little islands of spiritual and psychological support for our human family. Books and other materials they produce, for instance, are usually sold for just what it costs—or even less—to print them. Unfortunately this kind of service to God's children does not exempt them from utility bills, postage fees, printing expenses, and all the other costs of keeping doors open day after day, year after year.

Please keep this in mind when you ask for their prayers and/or services and, if possible, see that the human exchange you are engaged in is not one-sided, but includes your donation and prayer for them as well.

BESSETTE, Bl. André
  Address prayer requests or report cures or favors to the shrine where the saint lived, worked, and is buried:

  St. Joseph's Oratory
  3800 Queen Mary Road
  Montreal, Canada
  H3V 1H6
  phone: 514-733-2811.

  Use the same address to subscribe to the four-page newsletter published quarterly or to request a catalogue and price list for materials on the saint, which include both booklet-length biographies and full paperbacks in English and French. The definitive book, *Le Frere André*, by Étienne Catta, never translated into English, is out of print; but readers who can handle a 1,148-page book in French might find it worth the effort to try to locate it in a Catholic library in an area with a good population of French-Canadians.

For the services available to the sick and the hours of masses, novenas, and other events, call or write ahead.

BOSCO, St. John

Address prayer requests to either the closest Salesian community or to:

Mary, Help of Christians Basilica
Casa Madre Opere Don Bosco
Via Maria Ausiliatrice, 33
Torino, Italy 10152.

Reports of cures and favors may be sent to the publication *Bollettino Salesiano* at the same address.

If you are in a major city such as Boston, New York, or Los Angeles, consult your phone book for address of the closest church, retreat center, youth club, or school run by Salesians. Call there to see about prayer services for the sick which may be held in your area.

Requests for printed novenas can be directed to:

Provincial Office
148 Main Street
New Rochelle, N.Y. 10802
or
Provincial Office
1100 Franklin Street
San Francisco, Calif. 94109

A catalogue of English books, films, videos, and other materials on the saint is available from Don Bosco Multimedia, Box T, at the New Rochelle address. Biographies sold there include the definitive work on Don Bosco's life, the *Memorabilia,* fifteen of its nineteen volumes to date translated into English.

To subscribe to the *Salesian Bulletin* English edition, which does not report cures at this time but serves those who wish to be part of the Salesian family, write the publication at either the New Rochelle or the San Francisco address. A second English publication available for subscription is *Salesian,* which reports on the order's work in primarily third-world countries, solicits donations, and offers to receive prayer petitions. Address *Salesian* at the New Rochelle address.

CABRINI, St. Frances

Address prayer requests or report cures and favors to:

Mother Cabrini League
434 W. Deming Place

Chicago, Ill. 60614.

Also use this address to subscribe to the bimonthly *Mother Cabrini Messenger,* arrange for group pilgrimages to the Chicago shrine, or obtain materials and books on the saint (request a price list of materials if shopping by mail).

The United States has three Cabrini shrines.

In the East: the saint's tomb is at:

Mother Cabrini Shrine
(this chapel is adjacent to
Mother Cabrini High School)
701 Fort Washington Avenue
New York, N.Y. 10040
phone: 212-923-3536.

Write or call with prayer requests or to arrange group pilgrimages. Books and materials are available, including the fast-moving, popularized biography *Too Small a World* by Theodore Maynard; a more thorough work, if old-fashioned in style, is *Mother Frances Xavier Cabrini* by an associate of the saint, Mother Saverio De Maria. (This second book is sold by the League's Chicago office.)

In the Midwest the shrine is in the chapel of Columbus Hospital. It includes the room in which Mother Cabrini died in 1917 and other memorabilia. Just across from Lincoln Park, near Lake Michigan, the address is:

Columbus Hospital Chapel
2520 N. Lakeview Avenue
Chicago, Ill. 60614.

Open 9–5 daily, a novena is held weekly, and a slide show on the saint's life may be seen by arrangement (write ahead). Some materials are available for purchase.

In the West the shrine is situated at a site sold to the saint for a pittance because all effort to find water there proved fruitless. After prayer Cabrini marked a spot, directed, "Dig here," and water was discovered.

Accessible to ordinary vehicles in all seasons:

Cabrini Shrine
Golden, Colo. 80401
phone: 303-526-0758.

(Head west from Denver on Interstate 70 to exit 259, then take Highway 40 west, watching for signs.)

Call for hours and times of services or to arrange for group pilgrimages. Since the beautiful mountain shrine has no cafeteria or nearby restaurants, plan to bring a picnic lunch.

Other sources of prayer support for those seeking the intercession of Mother Cabrini for the Lord's healing are communities of the Missionary Sisters of the Sacred Heart, the order founded by the saint, which is found in eight dioceses in the United States and fourteen countries of the world. Check your diocesan directory or write the League to see if a group of sisters is in your area.

CASEY, Fr. Solanus
Send prayer requests to:

Father Solanus Guild
1718 Mt. Elliott
Detroit, Mich. 48207-3496
phone: 313-579-2100.

To visit Father Solanus's grave, one formerly went to the St. Bonaventure Friary Cemetery; as of July 8, 1987, the holy priest's body is in a vault inside St. Bonaventure's monastery church in the north transept. Call the Guild to see what hours the church is open.

Also use this address to subscribe to the quarterly newsletter or to purchase either of two biographies or other materials (send for price-list catalogue if shopping by mail). The biographies are *The Porter of St. Bonaventure: The Life of Father Solanus Casey, Capuchin* by James Patrick Derum, published by the Capuchins, and *Thank God Ahead of Time: The Life and Spirituality of Solanus Casey* by Michael H. Crosby, O.F.M. Cap. This book is also available from the publisher, Franciscan Herald Press, 1434 West Fifty-first Street, Chicago, Ill. 60609. Books on Father Solanus will also be found in some bookstores.

For information on enrollment in the Capuchin Mission Association (formerly known as the Seraphic Mass Assn.), address this association at the Mt. Elliott address.

For special services and events in honor of Fr. Solanus or of especial interest to the sick, contact the Guild.

FORGIONE, Padre Pio
In the United States and Canada, the Capuchins have authorized a center for reporting cures and requesting prayers, which are then forwarded to Padre Pio's Italian friary.

National Centre for Padre Pio, Inc.
R.D. 1, Box 134
Barto, Pa. 19504.
phone: 215-845-3000.

Devoted to Padre Pio, the Centre workers also pray there for the petitioners whose requests they are forwarding to Italy.

Write the Centre to subscribe to *The Voice of Padre Pio* magazine, which is put out in several languages and mailed direct to readers from the Italian friary. Because of the postal costs, the monthly is $12 a year in 1987.

The National Centre can also advise you of the nearest Padre Pio prayer group, if you are interested in joining others in praying for the beatification of the Capuchin and in seeking his intercession.

The Centre also arranges pilgrimages and has information on special events relating to Padre Pio.

Request catalogue and price list if you wish to purchase by mail either books or other materials on Padre Pio. Biographies will also be found readily in any Catholic bookstore, the best book as of 1987 being Lutheran minister C. Bernard Ruffin's *Padre Pio: The True Story*. If you live in an area without access to a Catholic bookstore, this book is also available by mail from Our Sunday Visitor, 200 Noll Plaza, Huntington, Ind. 46750 (write for current price) or the Centre.

Individuals may also send prayer requests or report cures directly to the Italian friary where Padre Pio lived. If you are reporting a cure, address your letter to the postulator of Padre Pio's Cause. The address:

Our Lady of Grace Friary
San Giovanni Rotondo, *FG*
71013 Italy.

Individual pilgrims are welcome at Our Lady of Grace, but the friary cannot house you. However, there are accommodations for rent within walking distance. For information on group pilgrimages, watch the Catholic press, consult a travel agency specializing in Catholic tours, or contact the Centre in Pennsylvania. Do not write the friary as they do not organize pilgrimages.

NEUMANN, St. John
The saint's shrine and burial place is situated a mile north of Independence Hall. For all purposes address:

National Shrine of St. John Neumann
St. Peter's Church
1019 North Fifth Street
Philadelphia, Pa. 19123.
phones: 215-627-3080
        215-627-2386

Call or write for times of the masses held there daily (Spanish as well on Sunday), the twice-weekly novena, and the special blessing of the sick.

A museum offers slide shows of the saint's life, and a gift shop carries many materials including biographies and novena leaflets. Among biographies, Father James Galvin's *Saint John Neumann* is lively, Father Michael J. Curley's *Bishop John Neumann C.SS.P.* is for the reader wanting more details on the saint. To purchase by mail, address gift shop requesting their one-page catalogue price list.

Prayer requests by mail should address The St. John Neumann Guild. Send details of special favors or cures in care of the Reverend Father Director.

To join the Guild and/or subscribe to its quarterly publication, call or write.

The Shrine will assist group pilgrimages with many special events, from prayer services and benediction to sermons and veneration of the saint's relics.

For a daily recorded spiritual message, phone 215-627-6110.

PADRE PIO (see Forgione).

FATHER SOLANUS (see Casey).

SEELOS, Fr. Francis Xavier
Send prayer requests or reports of cures or favors to:

Father Seelos Center
2030 Constance Street
New Orleans, La. 70130.
phone: 504-525-2495

Use the same address to subscribe to the monthly bulletin, to request free booklets on the Redemptorist priest's life or, to purchase other mate rials, including a film or cassette for VCR (VHS only).

The Center has a prayer service and mass each Sunday and will also assist pilgrimages to Father Seelos's tomb.

The sick able to come to the New Orleans area who wish to be blessed with Father Seelos's mission crucifix may contact Miss Addie Buhler at 504-895-6176 or the Center (number above).

For a recorded spiritual message from the Seelos Center, dial 504-586-1803.

SETON, St. Elizabeth

The saint's shrine is situated on the property where she lived with her daughters, sisters-in-law, and spiritual daughters while founding America's first religious society. In the nearby cemetery, two of her three daughters and her two young sisters-in-law are buried. A marker shows the original burial place of Mother Seton. Her remains now rest beneath the altar dedicated to her in the shrine chapel. For all purposes, including prayer requests, or to report graces received, contact:

National Shrine of St. Elizabeth Ann Seton
333 S. Seton Avenue
Emmitsburg, Maryland 21717.
phone: 301-447-6606

For dates and details of special services such as masses, novenas, and events in honor of Mother Seton; for tour information and a slide show on the saint; or to arrange group pilgrimages, the shrine should be contacted, as it is closed at certain times of the year.

Besides the museum in the Information Center, at the nearby "White House" where the saint lived, visitors may see a replica of the classrooms and the saint's restored bedroom, where she died. The chapel there contains the original shrine and altar rail used by Mother Seton, her Sisters and students as early as 1810.

Shrine gift-shop materials on the saint include biographies, *Mrs. Seton* by Father Joseph I. Dirvin, and *Elizabeth Bayley Seton* by Dr. Annabelle Melville. To purchase by mail, address the gift shop, requesting a catalogue price list.

Other sources of prayer support for those seeking Mother Seton's intercession with God may be found in the houses of the eight orders of nuns who trace their spiritual ancestry to Elizabeth and are affiliated in a Federation of Mother Seton's Daughters. Variously titled Daughters of Charity or Sisters of Charity, these orders are found in many parts of the United States and Canada.

TRONCATTI, Mother Maria

To request prayer support or report cures or favors received through the intercession of this member of the Daughters of Mary, Help of Christians branch of the Salesian family, write in English or Italian:

Postulator of Sister Maria Troncatti's Cause
Figlie di Maria Ausiliatrice
Via Dell'Ateneo Salesiano, 81
00129 ROMA, Italy

The one English-language biography available to date may be pur-chased from this address which may also be used to subscribe to periodi-cals featuring reports of favors through Maria's intercession.

Spanish-fluent readers may also report cures or request prayer support from:

Boletin Informativo
Rvdo. P. Alfredo Germani
Vice-Postulador de la Causa
Immaculata Concezione
Mendez, Ecuador

BIBLIOGRAPHICAL AND OTHER SOURCES

Bessette, Bl. André

The most important of the materials supplied by Vice-Postulator Bernard Lafrenière, C.S.C., are:

Le Frère André (1845–1937) et l'Oratoire Saint-Joseph du Mont Royal by Étienne Catta, (Montréal et Paris: Fides, 1965); the out-of-print French work includes testimonies from the beatification process and other official data pertaining to the saint's Cause and life);

Brother André, C.S.C.: The Wonder Man of Mount Royal (rev. ed.) by Henri-Paul Bergeron, D.S.C., transl. from the French by Réal Boudreau, C.S.C., (Montreal: Fides, 1958);

three recollections by the saint's former Superior, Albert Cousineau, C.S.C.: "Man of Faith Undaunted," "Brother Andre, as I knew Him," and "Brother Andre and the Power of Prayer," all St. Joseph's Oratory, 1960;

and a discussion of the problems cures often run into with the medical establishment and others: "La Guérison de Martin Hannon" in *Annales de Saint Joseph,* 13ième année, No 3, mars 1924.

Works not supplied by the Vice-Postulator which were consulted are:

The Miracle of the Mountain by Alden Hatch (New York: Hawthorn Books, Inc., 1959);

Brother Andre of Saint Joseph's Oratory by William H. Gregory (New York: William J. Hirten Co., Inc., 1925);

and *Brother Andre of Mount Royal* by Katherine Burton (Notre Dame, Ind.: Ave Maria Press, 1943).

Bosco, St. John

All material on the beatification and canonization miracles was supplied by Editor-in-Chief Diego Borgatello, S.D.B., from both testimonies and the official materials of the Cause being quoted in unedited portions of Volume XIX of the twenty-volume *Biographical Memoirs* in process of translation from the original Italian.

Other healings and biographical information are from published volumes of the American edition of *The Biographical Memoirs of Saint John Bosco* by Giovanni Battista Lemoyne, S.D.B., Eugenio Ceria, S.D.B., or Angelo Amadei, S.D.B., (New Rochelle, N.Y.: Salesiana Publishers, Inc., various years; *Don Bosco: A Spiritual Portrait* by Edna Beyer Phelan (Garden City, N.Y.: Doubleday & Company, Inc., 1963; *Saint John Bosco* by A. [sic] Auffray, S.D.B., (Blaisdon, Longhope, Gloucestershire, England: Salesian Publications, 1930); *Father Alfonso* by Peter M. Rinaldi, S.D.B., (New Rochelle, N.Y.: Salesiana Publishers, Inc., n.d.); and the author's own work in progress on this saint based on the above and other materials.

Cabrini, St. Frances Xavier

Beatification process and other testimonies by doctors, nurses, and others involved in the healing miracles were supplied by Sister Ursula, M.S.C., the archivist of the Missionary Sisters of the Sacred Heart, from materials kept at Cabrini College, Radnor, Pa.

Biographical information is taken primarily from the account of the saint's associate Mother Saverio De Maria, M.S.C., *Mother Frances Xavier Cabrini,* English version ed. and transl. Rose Basile Green, Ph.D., (Chicago: Missionary Sisters of the Sacred Heart, 1984).

Other materials were supplied by Sister Consolata, M.S.C., of Mother Cabrini (formerly Columbus) Hospital, Seattle; Christine Conrath of the Cabrini League, Chicago; Mother Annunciata, M.S.C., of Golden, Colorado; and Sister Alberta Surico, M.S.C., of New York City.

Casey, Fr. Solanus

Materials furnished by Vice-Postulator Brother Leo Wollenweber, O.F.M. Cap., include: first-person accounts of cures in bulletins and other publications of the Father Solanus Guild; portions of the saint's log book entries and other first-person testimonies of cures reported in the earliest sanctioned biography, *The Porter of St. Bonaventure's* by James Patrick Derum (Detroit: The Fidelity Press, 1968); and *Thank God Ahead of Time: The Life and Spirituality of Solanus Casey* by Michael H. Crosby, O.F.M., Cap. (Chicago: Franciscan Herald Press, 1985).

Writings of the saint consulted are primarily letters and the attestation (in the original German and English translation) the saint signed in 1901.

Neumann, St. John

Materials furnished by the Redemptorists staffing Neumann's shrine include facsimiles of portions of the log of cures kept by Charles Fehrenbach, C.SS.R.; accounts of early cures compiled by Postulator Joseph Wissell, C.SS.R., late in the nineteenth century under the title *Sex miracula exponuntur intercessione Venerabilis Episcopi obtenta.*; and accounts of cures in various publications of the shrine, including the quarterly bulletins.

Biographical information is taken primarily from *Bishop John Neumann C.SS.R.: Fourth Bishop of Philadelphia* by Michael J. Curley, C.SS.R. (Philadelphia: Bishop Neumann Center, 1952); and *Saint John Neumann: Bishop of Philadelphia* by James J. Galvin, C.SS.R. (Baltimore: Helicon Press, Inc., 1964).

Padre Pio

Information on several of the major cures attributed to Padre Pio since his death and verification of cures such as that of Giovanni Savino which occurred during Padre Pio's lifetime comes from American Joseph Pius Martin, O.F.M. Cap., of Our Lady of Grace Friary, San Giovanni Rotondo.

Tape and letter exchanges between Ann Wilkinson and the author are the source for the healing of Kelly Wilkinson.

The first cure associated with Padre Pio during his lifetime I report from *Pio of Pietrelcina: Infancy and Adolescence* by Alessandro Da Ripabottoni, O.F.M. Cap. (San Giovanni Rotondo, Italy: Edizioni Padre Pio da Pietrelcina, 1969); and *Padre Pio: His Early Years* by Augustine McGregor, O.C.S.O., same publisher, 1985.

Major sources on Pio's health and stigmata include (of eight biographies and several booklets consulted): *Padre Pio: The Stigmatist* by Rev. Charles Mortimer Carty (Rockford, Ill.: Tan Books and Publishers, Inc., 1971); *A City on a Mountain: Padre Pio of Pietrelcina, O.F.M. Cap.,* by Rev. Pascal P. Parente (Washington, N.J.: Ave Maria Institute, n.d.); *Padre Pio: The True Story* by C. Bernard Ruffin (Huntington, Ind.: Our Sunday Visitor, Inc., 1982); and "The Stigmata and Modern Science," by Carty (Rockford, Ill.: Tan Books and Publishers, Inc., 1971).

Due to their lack of access to many important materials, Fr. Martin warns that most books on Padre Pio (he makes an exception for Ruffin's work completed after the saint's death) contain errors and should not be quoted without further verification.

Fr. Francis Xavier Seelos

Information on the Boudreaux family cures was obtained by the author's interviews via phone and letter with Angela Boudreaux.

Mrs. Boudreaux and Seelos Center Director Joseph Elworthy, C.SS.R., supplied written materials on cures and Father Seelos's life: "Father Francis X. Seelos, C.SS.R.," by Thomas Artz, C.SS.R., and "Meet Father Seelos" by former Vice-Postulator John Vaughn, C.SS.R., the Seelos Center, 1979 and undated, respectively; *The Cheerful Ascetic* by Michael J. Curley, C.SS.R. (New Orleans: The Redemptorist Fathers, 1969); *Times-Picayune* article dated Oct. 6, 1986; and various issues of "Father Seelos and Sanctity," published monthly by the Redemptorists.

St. Elizabeth Ann Bayley Seton

Testimonies and medical attestations by those involved in the Sister Gertrude Korzendorfer and Anne O'Neill cures were originally supplied by the late Sylvester A. Taggart, C.M., director of the now defunct Mother Seton Guild; additional details came from Daughters of Charity archivist Sister Aloysia of St. Joseph's Provincial House, Emmitsburg, Maryland; pertinent to the O'Neill cure, see also "Dr. Coley's Toxins" in *Science,* April 1984, pp. 68–73; details of the James Porter cure, obtained through the Seton Causeway, were elaborated on by Sister Patricia Newhouse, C.M., and Mrs. Mary T. Porter through phone interviews and letters; Sister Anne Courtney, archivist at Mount St. Vincent, Bronx, New York, supplied other important material.

Principal biographical sources are *Mrs. Seton: Foundress of the American Sisters of Charity* by Joseph I. Dirvin, C.M. (New York: Farrar, Straus and Giroux, Inc., 1962); *Mother Seton: Mother of Many Daughters* by Rev. Charles I. White, rev. and ed. The Sisters of Charity of Mount St. Vincent-on-Hudson, New York (Garden City, N.Y.: Doubleday & Company, Inc., 1949); and *Elizabeth Bayley Seton* by Dr. Annabelle Melville (New York: a Jove book published by The Berkley Publishing Group, Inc., 1985).

Mother Maria Troncatti

All biographical material and cures that occurred during Maria Troncatti's lifetime are from *Beloved Jungle: Sister Maria Troncatti, Daughter of Mary Help of Christians, the Kivaros Sister Missionary* by Maria Domenica Grassiano (Rome: Daughters of Mary Help of Christians, 1971).

After-death cures attributed to her intercession, supplied by Sister Emilia Anzani, F.M.A., Secretary General of the Order's headquarters in Rome, are from Boletin Informativo, published in Spanish in Macas, Ecuador, under direction of the Vice-Postulator of Troncatti's Cause, Alfredo Germani, S.D.B., or from the Italian-language bulletin *Conosci?*

Additional publications referred to

BOSCO, ST. JOHN. *The Life of St. Joseph Cafasso: A Brief Account of the Life of St. Joseph Cafasso Given by St. John Bosco in His Two Panegyrics on the Saint Preached on the 10th of July and the 30th of August, 1860.* Former title: *A Saint Speaks for Another Saint.* Translated from the Italian by Rev. Patrick O'Connell, B.D., (Rockford, Ill.: Tan, 1983).

CADE, C. MAXWELL and NONA COXHEAD. *The Awakened Mind: Biofeedback and the Development of Higher States of Awareness* (New York: Delacorte Press/Eleanor Friede, 1979).

CLARET, ST. ANTONIO MARIA. *Autobiography,* edited by Jose Maria Vinas, C.M.F. (Chicago: Claretian Publications, 1976).

COUSINS, NORMAN. *Anatomy of an Illness* and *The Healing Heart* (New York: W. W. Norton, 1979 and 1983 respectively).

GROENEVELD, FR. ALBERT, O.CARM. *A Heart on Fire: An Outline of the Saintly Life and Heroic Death of Father Titus Brandsma, Carmelite* (Faversham, Kent, England: no publisher named, 1954).

KELSEY, MORTON T. *Healing and Christianity in Ancient Thought and Modern Times* (New York: Harper & Row, 1973).

KOLBE, ST. MAXIMILIAN. *Gli Scritti di Massimiliano Kolbe eroe di Oswiecim e Beato della Chiesa,* transl. from the original Polish by Cristoforo Zambelli (3 vols.) (Firenze: Edizioni Città di Vita, 1975).

KRIEGER, DOLORES. *Therapeutic Touch* (Englewood Cliffs, N.J.: Prentice-Hall, 1979).

MACNUTT, FRANCIS. *Healing* and *The Power to Heal* (Notre Dame, Ind.: Ave Maria Press, 1974 and 1977 respectively).

MARTIN, ST. THÉRÈSE (OF LISIEUX). *Autobiography,* translated by John Beevers (Garden City, N.Y.: Doubleday & Co., 1957).

SANFORD, JOHN A. *Healing and Wholeness* (Garden City, N.Y.: Doubleday, 1966; Ramsey, N.J.: Paulist Press, 1977).

SZTYK, BROTHER FELICISSIMUS, O.F.M. CONV., "Misakae No Sono," *Immaculata,* Nov. 1977.

TREECE, PATRICIA. "Even Disabled, the Christian Is Never Useless," (Pecos, N.M. 87552: Dove Publications, n.d.).

ACKNOWLEDGMENTS

My hope that this book will be useful to our human family lies above all in the fact that it has received so much prayer; for that vital content I particularly thank Alice Williams, Eva Engholm, Judith Hodgins, and my daughter Katherine.

Too much research is involved in a book of this type to name all those who assisted me. I can only wholeheartedly thank each of you who shared with me your experience of God's healing through his saints and each of you who assisted me over the past decade with materials and information: archivists, librarians, medical men, researchers on healing and related matters, biographers, vice-postulators, administrators of religious orders, and the staffs of the numerous organizations and publications where lives intertwine with the saints of this book.

I acknowledge my special debt to the following, upon whom I made unusually heavy demands: Sister Ursula, M.S.C., of Cabrini College, Radnor, Pennsylvania; Rev. Bernard Lafrenière, CSC, of St. Joseph's Oratory, Montreal; Mary Maloney and the late Fr. Ralph Lavigne S.S.S. of the Eymard League, New York City; Fr. Maurice Prefontaine, S.S.S., of Salt Lake City; Brother Leo Wollenweber, O.F.M. Cap., of Detroit; Fr. Charles Fehrenbach, C.SS.R., of Philadelphia; Sister Patricia Newhouse, S.C., of Lansing, Michigan; Conventual Franciscans Brother Charles Madden and Brother Francis Mary Kalvelage, of Marytown Friary, Libertyville, Illinois; Sister Emilia Anzani, F.M.A., of Rome; Fr. Diego Borgatello, SDB, of New Rochelle, New York; Mrs. Angela Boudreaux and Fr. Joseph Elworthy, C.SS.R., of the Seelos Center, New Orleans; the late Fr. Sylvester A. Taggart, C.M., of Emmitsburg, Maryland; Fr. James McCurry, O.F.M. Conv., of Granby, Massachusetts; Fr. Valerian Czywil, O.F.M. Conv., of Peabody, Massachusetts; and Fr. Joseph Pius Martin, O.F.M. Cap., of San Giovanni Rotondo, Italy.

For sharing both published and unpublished research, letting me sit in on various projects, and long hours of conversation on healers, healing, and various physiological aspects of spirituality—all of which helped me better understand the healing charisms of sanctity—I thank Geoffrey Blundell, Isabel Cade, and the late C. Maxwell Cade and associates of the Institute for Psychobiological Research, and Elizabeth St. John, all of London, and Edgar Chase of Derby.

For their information on cure rates, treatments, and publications on the various cancers mentioned in this book, my gratitude to the National Cancer Institute, of Bethesda, Maryland, for instituting the national toll-free phone number 1-800-4CANCER and for the Institute's Cancer Information Service in the Jonsson Comprehensive Cancer Center at UCLA.

My thanks to Michael Herbst, M.D. of Malibu, for his help in turning medical terminology into intelligible English.

Finally my gratitude to my friend Franca Aschenbrenner for writing my Italian research letters and checking many of my translations from that language.

I have tried to leave no stone unturned, no clue unfollowed over the past decade to ensure an accurate and neither overblown nor inappropriately minimized sampling of God's dealings in our midst through his saints. For errors, however, including any in my translations of materials otherwise unavailable in English, mine must be the sole responsibility.

More Modern Miracles

Want to know more about modern-day saints and miraculous healings? Three books to encourage, uplift and inspire you.

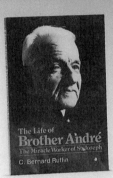  

Padre Pio: The True Story
A man of intense spirituality and miraculous capabilities. Learn of his life from those who knew him personally. By C. Bernard Ruffin, No. 673, paper, $10.95, 460 pp.

The Life of Brother Andre: Miracle Worker of St. Joseph
Pope John Paul II has declared him Blessed. Meet this remarkable man and his miraculous deeds. By C. Bernard Ruffin, No. 492, paper, $6.95, 228 pp.

Father Solanus: The Story of Solanus Casey, O.F.M., Cap.
He's regarded by many as a saint for our century. His Faith cured thousands. By Catherine M. Odell, No. 486, paper, $7.95, 228 pp.

Price and availability subject to change without notice. Available at religious bookstores. Credit card holders may order by calling toll-free **1-800-348-2440** or by sending payment plus $3.95 shipping/handling to:

Our Sunday Visitor
200 Noll Plaza, Huntington, IN 46750

BEST SELLING BOOKS

- [ ] **Catholic Dictionary**.. 507-4 ....$26.95
  Edited by Reverend Peter M.J. Stravinskas
- [ ] **The Teaching of Christ**, 3rd Edition.................................. 850-2 ....$12.95
  Edited by Bishop Donald W. Wuerl, Ronald Lawler, O.F.M., Cap., and
  Thomas Comerford Lawler
- [ ] **One Year Bible**, Catholic Edition NRSV (kivar)................. 232-6 ....$18.95
  (cloth)................. 231-8 ....$24.95
- [ ] **Catholic Encyclopedia** (cloth) .... 457-4 ....$34.95
  Edited by Reverend Peter (kivar)... 475-2 ......$21.95
  M.J. Stravinskas
- [ ] **1994 Catholic Almanac** (kivar)... 271-7 ....$18.95
  Edited by Felician A. Foy, O.F.M., (cloth)........................... 272-5 ....$21.95
  and Rose M. Avato
- [ ] **Catholic Family-Time Bible Stories In Pictures**............... 882-0 ....$14.95
  By Kenneth N. Taylor
- [ ] **Today's Destructive Cults & Movements**......................... 498-1 ....$11.95
  Rev. Lawrence J. Gesy
- [ ] **Making Things Right**.. 351-9 ....$ 3.95
  By Jeannine Timko Leichner
- [ ] **The Catholic One Year Bible**.. 215-6 ....$16.95
- [ ] **The Way**... 831-6 ....$16.95
- [ ] **The Catholic Living Bible** White Gift Edition .... 219-9 ....$17.95
  Black Gift Edition.................. 220-2 ....$17.95
  Red Gift Edition..................... 221-0 ....$17.95
- [ ] **My First Bible Stories In Pictures**....................................... 246-6 ....$10.95
  By Kenneth N. Taylor (with handle) .... 245-8 ....$14.95
- [ ] **You Better Believe It**.. 750-6 ....$ 6.95
  By Father Kenneth J. Roberts

Available at your local religious bookstore or use this page for ordering:

OUR SUNDAY VISITOR • 200 NOLL PLAZA • HUNTINGTON, IN 46750.

Please send me the above title(s). I am enclosing $3.95 per order to cover
shipping/handling. Or, Mastercard/VISA customers can order by phone
☎ **1-800-348-2440.**

Name _____

Address_____

City/State _____ Zip _____

Telephone ( ) _____

Prices and availability subject to change without notice.